Starting a Business on eBay.co.uk For Dummies

D0864789

General tips for sellers

- Answer all e-mail questions from prospective bidders and buyers within 24 hours, and check your e-mail hourly before the close of your auctions. (It can pay off in higher last-minute bidding.) Good customer service goes a long way in promoting and building your eBay business.

- When listing a new item, research it and be sure that you know its current value and the going price.

- Before listing, weigh your item and estimate the shipping cost. Be sure to list shipping (and handling) costs in your ad whether you use a flat rate or the shipping calculator for heavier packages.

- Always see how many other sellers are selling your item and try not to have your auction close within a few hours of another.

- To encourage bidding, set the lowest possible starting bid for your item.

- Check the eBay guidelines to be sure that your item is permitted and that your listing doesn't violate any listing policies.

- Get to know the listing patterns of sellers who sell similar merchandise to yours, and try to close your auctions at different times or days.

When taking auction photos

- Be sure that the item is clean, unwrinkled, and lint-free.

- Take the photo against a solid, undecorated background.

- Make sure the picture is in focus.

- Check that you have enough lighting to show the details of your item.

- Take second and third images to show specific details, such as a signature or a detail that better identifies your item.

- It's unnecessary to use an image that's more than 72 ppi for online purposes. Don't worry about megapixels.

- Try to keep the total size of *all* your pictures less than 50K for a smooth and swift download.

When purchasing merchandise to sell

- Try to pay the lowest possible price for your item – buy at wholesale or less whenever possible.

- If you're the handy fix-it type, find items in need of minor repair and put them up for sale "like new."

- Search for unique items that may be common in your geographic area but hard to find in other places across the country.

- Attend estate sales – many a salable gem is hiding in someone's home.

- Visit closeout stores, liquidators, and auctions regularly.

Starting a Business on eBay.co.uk For Dummies®

Techie terms you might bump into

The industry that surrounds eBay.co.uk (and being an eBay business) is fraught with confusing words, phrases, and references. This list sheds light on some of the more commonly used – but no less confusing – terms you may encounter.

ADSL: This acronym stands for asymmetric digital subscriber line, but of course you knew that already! In lay terms, ADSL means 'always on' connections and ultra-fast download speeds. An ADSL connection is a must if you want to build an eBay.co.uk empire.

CMS: Or content management system, is a platform for managing what goes on your Web site. If you build your own Web site, then you have to use a CMS.

Cookie: Files that are downloaded onto your PC from Web sites and provide info about who you are and what interests you on the Web. Nowadays companies should ask permission before placing a cookie onto your hard drive. Although often harmless or just annoying, cookies can be useful for remembering passwords on your behalf.

Domain name: A unique name that identifies your business on the Web. All Web sites have domain names; in the UK, eBay's is www.ebay.co.uk – as well you know.

E-commerce: This term refers to the act of buying and selling over the Internet – just what you're planning to do!

Hacker: A nasty person. Someone who tries to access information on other people's computers remotely by bypassing security systems. This activity is highly illegal and many hackers get prison sentences.

Host: A server that holds all the information necessary for running your Web site. If you're planning to set up an e-commerce shop separate to your eBay.co.uk shop, then you need to get hold of a host.

JPEG: Compressed image files ideal for sending and downloading on the Internet.

Phishing: Refers to the act of sending out bogus e-mails to try and get people to hand over private and sensitive details – like bank account information. eBay- and PayPal-related phishing scams abound, so check unsolicited e-mails thoroughly before giving out any information.

Spam: E-mails that appear in your inbox without your requesting them, often sent by bogus companies that are trying to scam you. Tread carefully and remember: If a company's promises sound too good to be true, they usually are!

Virus: Malicious computer code that can damage your computer and files contained within it. Make sure your computer is protected from viruses by installing security software and by avoiding disreputable Web sites.

For Dummies: Bestselling Book Series for Beginners

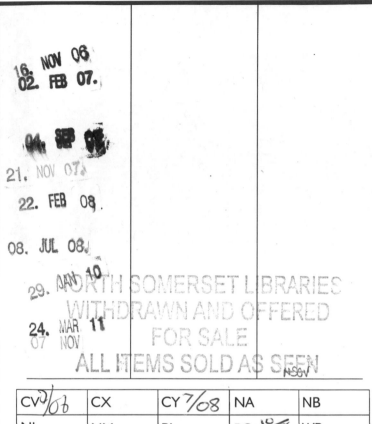

Starting a Business on eBay.co.uk

FOR DUMMIES®

by Dan Matthews and Marsha Collier

WILEY

John Wiley & Sons, Ltd

Starting a Business on eBay.co.uk For Dummies®

Published by

John Wiley & Sons, Ltd
The Atrium
Southern Gate
Chichester
West Sussex
PO19 8SQ
England

E-mail (for orders and customer service enquires): cs-books@wiley.co.uk

Visit our Home Page on www.wileyeurope.com

Wiley also publishes its books in a variety of electronic formats. Some content that appears in print may not be available in electronic books.

British Library Cataloguing in Publication Data: A catalogue record for this book is available from the British Library.

ISBN-10: 0-470-02666-9 (PB)

ISBN-13: 978-0-470-02666-3 (PB)

Printed and bound in Great Britain by Bell and Bain Ltd, Glasgow

10 9 8 7 6 5 4 3 2 1

WILEY

About the Authors

Dan Matthews is online editor of Crimson Business Publishing, which specialises in magazines and websites supporting entrepreneurs and small businesses in the UK. Publications include `startups.co.uk` and `mybusiness.co.uk` as well as Growing Business Magazine, of which Dan is contributing editor. Dan is also founder of `InfoZoo.co.uk`, a website dedicated to helping small businesses and regional organisations spread their message.

Marsha Collier spends most of her time on eBay. She loves buying and selling – she's a PowerSeller – as well as meeting eBay users from around the world. As a columnist, and author of four best-selling books on eBay, a television and radio expert, and a lecturer, she shares her knowledge of eBay with millions of online shoppers. Thousands of eBay fans also read her monthly newsletter, *Cool eBay Tools*, to keep up with changes on the site.

Out of college, Marsha worked in fashion advertising for the *Miami Herald* and then as special projects manager for the *Los Angeles Daily News*. She also founded a home-based advertising and marketing business. Her successful business, the Collier Company, Inc., was featured in *Entrepreneur* magazine in 1985, and in 1990, Marsha's company received the Small Business of the Year award from her California State Assemblyman and the Northridge Chamber of Commerce.

More than anything, Marsha loves a great deal. That's what drew her to eBay in 1996, and that's what keeps her busy on the site now. She buys everything from light bulbs to parts for her vintage Corvette to designer dresses. Marsha knows how to apply her business acumen to eBay, and in this book, she shares that knowledge with you. In *Starting a Business on eBay.co.uk For Dummies*, Marsha and Dan combine their knowledge of business, marketing, and eBay savvy to help you make a smooth and quick transition from part-time seller to full-time moneymaker.

Author's Acknowledgements

I would like to thank everyone at John Wiley & Sons, Ltd, especially Martin Tribe and Sam Clapp, for their help and guidance; David Lester at Crimson Business for being supportive and Gemma Foy for her patience.

Publisher's Acknowledgements

We're proud of this book; please send us your comments through our Dummies online registration form located at www.dummies.com/register/.

Some of the people who helped bring this book to market include the following:

Acquisitions, Editorial, and Media Development

Executive Project Editor: Martin Tribe

Content Editor: Simon Bell

Commissioning Editor: Samantha Clapp

Development Editor: Brian Kramer

Copy Editor: Kate O'Leary

Proofreader: Kim Vern

Technical Editor: Edmund Butler – aerofish.com

Executive Editor: Jason Dunne

Cover Photo: Jupiter Images/IT Stock Free

Cartoons: Ed McLachlan

Composition Services

Project Coordinator: Jennifer Theriot

Layout and Graphics: Carl Byers, Andrea Dahl, Barbara Moore, Lynsey Osborn, Stephanie D. Jumper

Proofreaders: David Faust, Susan Moritz, Brian Walls

Indexer: Techbooks

Publishing and Editorial for Consumer Dummies

    Diane Graves Steele, Vice President and Publisher, Consumer Dummies

    Joyce Pepple, Acquisitions Director, Consumer Dummies

    Kristin A. Cocks, Product Development Director, Consumer Dummies

    Michael Spring, Vice President and Publisher, Travel

    Kelly Regan, Editorial Director, Travel

Publishing for Technology Dummies

    Andy Cummings, Vice President and Publisher, Dummies Technology/General User

Composition Services

    Gerry Fahey, Vice President of Production Services

    Debbie Stailey, Director of Composition Services

Contents at a Glance

Table of Contents

Part III: Serious Business! 163

Introduction

● ●

*T*hank you for taking a look at *Starting a Business on eBay.co.uk For Dummies.* We've written this book to serve as a manual to get you organised and get your eBay.co.uk business off the ground. From handling your selling time on eBay.co.uk more efficiently to stocking your shop to the *real* way to set up your books and daily operations, we give you all the details about running a successful eBay business. From our own years of experience and numerous interactions with hundreds of eBay sellers, we offer countless time-saving and money-saving tips and secret eBay.co.uk hints along the way.

One thing that we can't guarantee is how much money you can earn selling on eBay. We've discovered – perhaps the hard way – that running a business from home takes a good deal of discipline. Time and devotion dedicated to your business will boost your success.

About This Book

Success awaits you! If you've read *eBay.co.uk For Dummies,* you know just how profitable eBay can be. You've probably picked up this book because you've heard lots of stories about people making big money online, and you're interested in getting your slice of the action. If you have a retail business, establishing an eBay.co.uk shop can be a profitable extension of it.

Is selling on eBay.co.uk something that you'd like to do more of? Do you have a full-time job, but you'd like to sell on eBay part time? eBay can easily supplement your income for the better things in life – such as holidays or even private school for the kids. Perhaps you're looking to make a career change, and jumping into an eBay.co.uk business with both feet is just what you have in mind – if so, *Starting a Business on eBay.co.uk For Dummies* is the book for you.

We've watched eBay change from a homey community of friendly collectors to a behemoth Web site with tens of thousands of categories of items and more than 100 million registered users. We bet you've been buying and selling with positive results, and you can see the benefits of taking this a bit more seriously. What are you waiting for? Get started on your new career right now. Thousands of people across the world are setting up businesses online, and now is your time to take the leap of faith to begin a profitable enterprise. eBay.co.uk gives you the tools, the customers, and the venue to market your wares – all you need is a bit of direction.

Starting a Business on eBay.co.uk For Dummies includes tips to give you the opportunity to improve your eBay money-making ability and just might turn you from an eBay novice into a professional running a booming eBay business. We also show the experienced user the prudent way to turn haphazard sales into an organised business. This book has all the information you need! We combine the fine points of eBay.co.uk with real business and marketing tools to help you complete the journey from part-time seller to online entrepreneur.

In this book, you can find the answers to some important questions as I take you through the following points:

✔ Reviewing what you know and introducing some of the finer points of eBay.co.uk auctions

✔ Sprucing up your auctions to attract more bidders

✔ Dealing with customers

✔ Setting up your business in a professional manner

✔ Deciding how to handle inventory (and where to find it)

✔ Looking at what you need to be in an eBay business . . . for ***real***

What You're Not to Read

If you use *Starting a Business on eBay.co.uk For Dummies* like a cookery book, jumping around from recipe to recipe (or chapter to chapter), you can find the answers to your particular questions all at once. Or you can read the book from beginning to end and keep it handy to look up future questions as they come to you. You don't have to memorise a thing; the information you need is at arm's length.

Foolish Assumptions

Because you're reading this, we assume you're serious about selling on eBay. co.uk and want to find out the fine points of just how to do that. Or perhaps you want to know how much is involved in an eBay business so that you can make the decision whether to give it a go.

If we've worked you out and you've decided that it's time to get serious, here are some other foolish assumptions we've made about you:

✔ You have a computer and an Internet connection.

✔ You've bought and sold on eBay and are fairly familiar with how it works.

✔ You have an existing small business or you'd like to start one.

✔ You like the idea of not having to work set hours.

✔ You feel that working from home in jeans and a t-shirt is a great idea.

If you can say yes to my foolish assumptions, you're off and running! Take a few moments to read the following section to get a feel for how we've put together this book.

How This Book Is Organised

This book has five parts. The parts stand on their own, which means that you can read Chapter 12 after reading Chapter 8 and maybe skip Chapter 13 altogether (but we know you won't because that's where we discuss the money!).

Part 1: Getting Serious About eBay.co.uk

Reviewing what you know is always a great place to start. Considering the way eBay constantly changes, you'll probably find a little review worthwhile. So in this part, we delve into the finer points of eBay.co.uk. Perhaps you'll discover a thing or two you didn't know – or had forgotten.

Setting up your eBay shop is important, and in this part we show you step by step the best way to do it – and give you tips to work out when the timing is right for you to open your shop.

Part 11: Setting Up Shop

You need to decide what type of business you plan to run and what type of inventory you'll sell. In this part, we discuss how to find merchandise and the best way to sell it. We also give you the low-down on eBay Motors UK, property, and some of the unusual areas where you can sell.

In this part, you'll also find out how to research items – before you buy them to sell – so you'll know for how much (or whether) they'll sell on eBay.co.uk.

We also discuss the importance of your own Web site for online shopping and how to set one up quickly and economically.

Part III: Serious Business!

In Part III, we discuss exactly how to use available online and offline tools, implement auction management software, jazz up your auctions, and handle shipping efficiently and effectively. Because working with customers and collecting payments is important too, you can find that information here as well.

Most importantly, you also find out how to obtain free shipping material for your business delivered to your door, get your postal carrier to pick up your boxes at no charge, and insure your packages without standing in line at the post office.

Part IV: Your eBay.co.uk Admin

Setting up your business as a real business entity involves some nasty paperwork and red tape. We try to fill in the blanks here, as well as show you how to set up your bookkeeping. In this part you'll find a checklist of the items you need to run your online business.

You also need to know how to set up your home business space and how to store your stuff and we cover that here.

Part V: The Part of Tens

You can't write a *For Dummies* book without including the traditional Part of Tens. So here are ten real-life stories of successful (and happy) people selling on eBay.co.uk. We also include ten strategies that might help you sell your stuff.

We include a random collection of terms in Appendix A. You're probably already familiar with many of these words, but others will be new to you. Refer to this appendix often as you peruse other parts of the book. In Appendix B, we briefly discuss home networking, a perk you'll want to have when your eBay business grows.

Icons Used in This Book

If there's something I need to interject – okay, something we're jumping up and down to tell you but it doesn't fit directly into the text – we indicate it by placing this tip icon in front of the paragraph. You'll know the tip to follow will be right on target!

Do you really know people who tie string around their fingers to remember something? Me neither; but this icon gives me the opportunity to give you a brief reminder to note.

We like this picture of a petard – the round bomb device that Wile E. Coyote slam-dunks in the cartoons. If you don't heed the warning indicated by this icon, you may be 'hoisted by your own petard', or made a victim of your own foolishness.

Here we share some of the interesting thoughts we've picked up from eBay sellers over the years. Because we believe that knowledge is enhanced through making your own choices based on understanding the successes and mistakes of others, we include these little auction factoids so you can gain some insight from them. If someone else has learned from a unique trick, you can benefit by taking heed.

Where to Go from Here

Time to hunker down and delve into the book. If you have time, just turn the page and start from the beginning. If you're anxious and already have some questions you want answered, check out the handy index at the end of the book and research your query.

Take the information offered in this book and study it. Being a success on eBay.co.uk awaits you.

Our goal is to help you reach your goals. Feel free to contact Marsha through her Web site and sign up for the free newsletter. That way you can stay up to date:

```
www.coolebaytools.com
```

Please e-mail with any suggestions, additions, and comments. We want to hear from you and hope to update this book with your words of wisdom. (Humorous stories are also gratefully accepted!)

Part I
Getting Serious About eBay.co.uk

"theworldwillgrovelatmyfeet.co.uk sounds a lovely domain name for your eBay business, Harold."

In this part . . .

Because eBay.co.uk continually makes improvements, some of its features are like hidden gold nuggets. In this first part, we delve into the finer points of eBay.co.uk with you. Perhaps you'll discover a thing or two you didn't know or had forgotten.

Chapter 1

Using eBay.co.uk to Launch Your Business

You've decided to get serious about your sales on eBay.co.uk, so now you have to decide how much time you have to devote to your eBay business. We talk about all kinds of eBay businesses in this book. Even though you're not quitting your day job and selling on eBay full time (yet!), we still think you're serious. A large portion of sellers, even eBay PowerSellers (those who gross more than £750 a month in sales), work on eBay only part time.

eBay sellers come from all walks of life. A good number of stay-at-home mums are out there selling on eBay. And so many retirees are finding eBay a great place to supplement their income that we wouldn't be surprised if the Pensions Service creates a special eBay arm for them. If you're pulled out of your normal work routine and faced with a new lifestyle, you can easily make the transition to selling on eBay.

In this chapter, we talk about planning just how much time you can devote to your eBay business – and how to budget that time. We also talk here about working out what to sell. eBay businesses don't grow overnight, but with dedication and persistence, you may just form your own online empire.

Getting Down to Business

Before launching any business, including an eBay.co.uk business, you need to set your priorities. And to be successful at that business, you must apply some clear level of discipline.

We won't bore you with the now-legendary story of how Pierre Omidyar started eBay to help fulfil his girlfriend's Pez dispenser habit, blah, blah, blah. We *will* tell you that he started AuctionWeb with a laptop, a regular Internet Service Provider (ISP), and an old school desk. Omidyar and his friend Jeff Skoll (a Stanford MBA) ran the 24-hours-a-day, 7-days-a-week AuctionWeb all by themselves. When we began using the service, we had a lot of questions and we always got prompt, friendly answers to our e-mails. When the site started attracting more traffic, Pierre's ISP began to complain about all the traffic and raised his monthly fees. To cover the higher costs, Pierre and Jeff began charging 25 cents to list an auction. Pierre was so busy running the site that the envelopes full of cheques began to pile up – he didn't even have time to open the post.

When Pierre and Jeff incorporated eBay AuctionWeb in 1996, they were each drawing a salary of $25,000. Their first office consisted of one room, and they had one part-time employee to handle the payments. Pierre and Jeff started small and grew.

Choosing eBay.co.uk as a part-time money maker

A part-time eBay.co.uk business can be very profitable. We stress repeatedly in this book that the more time and energy you spend on your eBay business, the more money you can make, but for now we move on to the lowest possible level of time that you should devote to your business.

Maybe you enjoy finding miscellaneous items to sell on eBay. You can find these items somehow in your day-to-day life. Suppose that you can spend at least a few hours (maybe three) a day on eBay. Now you must include the time you take to write up your auctions. If you're not selling only one type of item, allow about 15 minutes to write your auction, take your picture or scan your image, and, of course, upload it to eBay.co.uk or a photo-hosting site.

How much time it takes to perform these tasks varies from person to person and improves according to your level of expertise. Every task in your eBay auction business takes time, however, and you must budget for that time. See the sidebar 'Some handy eBay.co.uk time-saving tips' for pointers.

Only you can decide how much time you want to spend researching going rates for items on eBay.co.uk and deciding which day or time your item will sell for the highest price. You can take great photos and write brilliant descriptions, but cashmere cardigans don't sell for as much in the heat of summer as they do in winter. Doing your research can take up a good deal of time when you're selling a varied group of items.

Some handy eBay.co.uk time-saving tips

Stuck for time? Following are some features that you're sure to find useful and handy:

✔ **HTML templates:** In Chapter 11, I give you some tips on finding basic HTML format templates for attractive auctions. These templates cut your auction design time to a few minutes. Most experienced eBay sellers use preset templates to speed up the task of listing auctions, and this should be your goal.

✔ **Turbo Lister program:** When you want to list a lot of auctions at once, use the eBay Turbo Lister program– it enables you to put together and upload ten auctions in just 15 minutes. Chapter 9 tells you how to use this very cool tool.

✔ **Re-listing (or Sell Similar) feature:** When you sell the same item time after time, you can use Turbo Lister (it archives your old listings so you can repeat them) or the handy eBay re-listing or Sell Similar features. When your auction ends on eBay, links pop up offering to re-list your listing or to Sell Similar. If you want to run a different auction with a similar HTML format to the one that just ended, simply select the Sell Similar option and cut and paste the new title and description into the Sell Your Item page of your new listing.

✔ **Auction management software:** See the 'Software you can use' section in this chapter and see also Chapter 9, which details various programs to integrate into your eBay business.

Consider also how much time shopping for your merchandise takes. You may have to travel to dealers, go to auctions, or spend time online discovering new ways to find your auction merchandise. Many sellers set aside a full day each week for this undertaking. Your merchandise is what makes you money, so don't skimp on the time you spend identifying products. The time you spend on resourcing your products comes back to you in higher profits.

Here's a list of various activities that you must perform when doing business on eBay.co.uk:

✔ Photograph the item.

✔ Clean up and resize the images in a photo editor (if necessary).

✔ Upload the images to eBay Picture Services when you list or before listing to your ISP or third-party hosting service.

✔ Weigh the item and determine the shipping cost.

✔ Choose an auction title with keywords.

✔ Write a concise and creative description.

✔ List the auction on eBay.co.uk.

✔ Answer bidder questions.

✔ Send end-of-auction e-mails.

✔ Carry out banking.

✔ Perform bookkeeping.

✔ Pack the item safely and securely.

✔ Address the label and affix postage.

✔ Go to the post office.

Time yourself to see how long you take to accomplish each of these tasks. The time varies when you list multiple items, so think of the figures that you come up with as your *baseline,* a minimum amount of time that you must set aside for these tasks. Use this information to help you decide how many hours per month you need to devote to running your part-time eBay business.

Jumping in with both feet: Making eBay.co.uk a full-time job

The tasks required for your eBay business can be time consuming. But careful planning and scheduling can turn your business into a money-spinning empire.

The best way to go full time on eBay is to first run your business part time for a while to iron out the wrinkles. After you become comfortable with eBay.co.uk as a business, you're ready to make the transition to full-time seller. The minimum gross monthly sales for a Bronze-level PowerSeller is £750. If you plan your time efficiently, you can easily attain this goal. Head to Chapter 3 for more information on the PowerSeller programme.

Running a full-time business on eBay is the perfect option for working parents who prefer staying at home with their children, retirees looking for something to do, or those who'd just rather do something else than work for their boss. Read some real-life profiles of happy full-time sellers in Chapter 18.

See Figure 1-1 for an example of the eBay.co.uk home page, the first stop for most buyers on eBay.co.uk. Note how eBay makes an effort to reflect some sort of promotion to better market the items you put up for sale.

Figure 1-1:
The eBay.co.uk home page, where it all starts!

Deciding What to Sell

What should I sell? That is *the* million-dollar question! In your quest for merchandise, you're bound to hear about soft goods and hard goods. *Soft*, or non-durable, goods are generally textile products, such as clothing, fabrics, and bedding. *Hard* goods are computer equipment, homewares, and anything else that's basically non-disposable.

Following are just a few points to consider when you're deciding what to sell:

- **Shipping costs:** Some differences exist between shipping hard and soft goods. Soft goods can fold up and be packed in standard box sizes or (better yet) in bubble wrap or jiffy bags for much lower shipping costs. Most hard goods come in their own boxes, which may or may not be individually shippable. You also need to use Styrofoam peanuts or bubble cushioning or double package items in oddly sized boxes. See Chapter 17 for the low-down on shipping and packing.

- **Other shipping considerations:** Do you want to handle large boxes and deal with the hassles of shipping them?

- **Possible storage problems:** Do you have the room to store enough merchandise to keep you going? Soft goods can take up considerably less space than hard goods.

You don't always have to buy your items in bulk to make money on eBay. The first things you sell may be items you find in your garage or loft. To find out about some other fun ways to acquire goods to sell, check out the next section.

Turning your hobby into a business

Admit it, you've got a hobby; everyone does! Did you collect stamps or coins as a kid? Play with Barbie dolls? Maybe your hobby is cars? Did you inherit a load of antiques? Been collecting figurines for a few years? eBay.co.uk has a market for almost anything.

You can't possibly be an expert on everything. You need to keep up-to-date on the market for your items, and following more than four or five basic item groups may divert your attention from selling.

Selling within a particular category or two can be a good idea for repeat business. Should you decide to major in miscellany and sell anything and everything, you may not realise the highest possible prices for your items. If you have a source that permits you to buy items at dirt-cheap pricing, however, you may not mind selling at a lower price.

Collectibles: Big business on eBay

The story goes that Pierre Omidyar started eBay with the idea to trade collectible Pez dispensers (actually, the first item ever sold on eBay was a broken laser pointer). eBay.co.uk now lists countless categories of collectibles (see Figure 1-2), and those categories are divided into many times more categories, sub-categories, and sub-sub-categories. Almost anything that you'd want to collect is here, from advertising memorabilia to Girl Scout badges to Zippo lighters!

If you have a collection of your own, eBay.co.uk is a great way to find rare items. Because your collection is something dear to your heart and you've studied it on and off for years, you can probably call yourself an expert. Bingo – you're an expert at something! Hone your skills to find things in your area of expertise at discount prices (you're liking this more and more, aren't you?) and then sell them on eBay for a profit. Start small and start with something you know.

If there's one thing you know, it's fashion!

Are you one of those people who just knows how to put together a great outfit? Do you find bargains at charity shops but people think you've spent hundreds on your garb? Do you know where to get hold of end-of-line designer gear? Looks like you've found your market (see Figure 1-3).

Figure 1-2:
The
eBay.co.uk
Collectibles
hub with
links to
categories.

Buy as many of those stylish designer dresses as you can, and set them up on the mannequin you've bought to model your fashions for eBay photos. (For more on setting up fashion photos on eBay, check out Chapter 11.) Within a week, you just may be doubling your money – 'cause sweetie-darling, who knows fashion better than you?

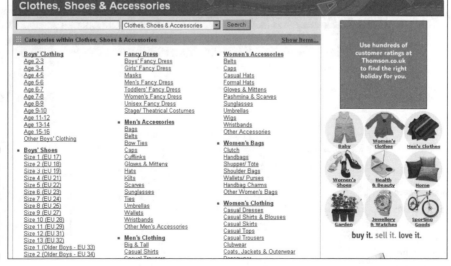

Figure 1-3:
eBay.co.uk
area for
clothing,
shoes, and
accessories.

If a ball, a wheel, or competition is involved – it's for you

Many men like to watch sport, play sport, and look good while they're doing it – opening up venues for a profitable empire on eBay.co.uk. We don't want to leave out all the women out there who excel and participate in many sports. Women may have even more discriminating needs for their sporting endeavours! Your golf game may stink – but you do make a point to at least look good when you go out there, with respectable equipment and a fabulous outfit.

eBay.co.uk has an amazing market for football, rugby and tennis equipment – and that's the tip of the iceberg. The last time we looked, golf items totalled almost 20,000 listings! What a bonanza! New stuff, used stuff – it's all selling on eBay (see Figure 1-4). All this selling is enough to put your local pro shop out of business – or perhaps put *you* in business.

Including the whole family in the business

Sometimes just the idea of a part-time business can throw you into a tizzy. Don't you have enough to do already? School, work, football practice, kids glued to the TV – you may sometimes feel as if you've no time for family time. However, the importance of family time is what brought us to eBay in the first place. We were working long hours in our own businesses, and at the end of the day, when the kids wanted to go shopping, perhaps for some Hello Kitty toys or a Barbie doll, we were often just too tired.

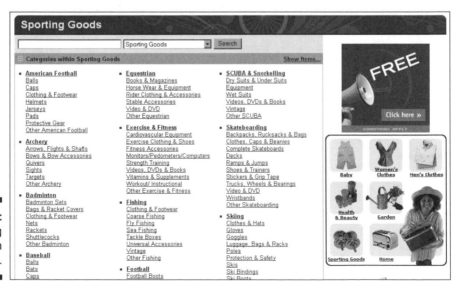

Figure 1-4: Sporting goods on eBay.co.uk.

One of us, Marsha, has a great story:

I'd heard about AuctionWeb from a friend and had bought some things online for my own collections. (Okay, you got me; I collected Star Trek stuff– call me geek with a capital _G_.) I'd also browsed around the site and found some popular toys selling for reasonable prices. So one evening I introduced my daughter to eBay, and life has never been the same. We'd go to toy shops together immediately they opened on Saturday morning, so we'd get first dibs on shipments of the hottest, newest toys. My daughter headed for dolls, and I'd go to the action figures. After buying several items, we'd go home, and post them for sale on eBay. We made money, yes, but the best part was our toy runs – they will always remain a special memory.

My daughter has since graduated from university (she majored in business and marketing – must have been inspired by our eBay enterprise) but she still phones home when she finds a hot CD or a closing-down sale. My daughter and I still purchase and list items together. The family that eBays together . . . always does.

This short trip down memory lane has a point: A family business can succeed, and everyone can enjoy it. An adult can be in charge of the financing and the packing while a youngster can look up postcodes on the Internet and put pins in a 4' x 5' map showing every town that we bought or sold from. Children can learn some excellent lessons in marketing, advertising, and geography, all in one go.

Toys, books, and music

Having children in your home brings you closer to the latest trends than you can ever imagine. We remember sitting in a café a couple of years ago watching some dads and their sons pouring over notebooks full of Pokémon cards. (Actually, the kids were off playing somewhere, and the dads were coveting the cards.)

And what about Star Wars? Star Trek? Men in Black? Can you say action figures? (If boys have them, they're not dolls – they're action figures.) If you have access to the latest and greatest toys, buy them up and sell them to those who can't find them in their neck of the woods.

Is your home one of those where books pile up all over the place? If your children have outgrown educational books (even university textbooks), they can be turned into a profit. Remember that not every book is a classic that needs to be part of your library forever. Let another family get the pleasure of sharing children's tales!

If anything piles up faster than books, it's CDs, videos, and DVDs. Somehow the old lambada or macarena music doesn't hold the magic it once did and those pre-school videos drive you insane. You can get rid of your own items and find plenty of stock at car boot sales – buy them cheap and make a couple of quid.

Selling children's clothes

Last time we looked there were more than 42,000 baby clothes auctions in progress – and the bidding was hot and heavy. For stay-at-home parents, selling baby and children's clothing is a great way to pick up extra income.

If you've had a baby, you know all too well that friends and relatives shower new mums with lots of cute outfits. If you're lucky, your baby gets to wear one or two of these outfits (maybe only for a special picture) before outgrowing them. These adorable clothes can earn you a profit on eBay.co.uk. Many parents, with children a few steps behind yours, are looking for bargain clothing on eBay – a profitable hand-me-down community. As your children grow up (and out of their old clothes), earn some money while helping out another parent.

Bringing your business to eBay.co.uk

Do you already have a business? eBay.co.uk isn't only a marketplace where you're able to unload slow or out-of-season merchandise. You can also set up your shop on eBay (see Figure 1-5). An eBay shop allows you to list a fixed-price item at a reduced fee and keep the item online until it sells. When you run your regular auctions for special items, they have a link to your shop, thereby drawing in new shoppers to see your merchandise.

Figure 1-5:
eBay.co.uk shops central.

Here are a few ways you can expand your current business with eBay.co.uk:

- ✔ **Opening a second shop on eBay.co.uk:** How many people run shops that sell every item, every time? If you're a retailer, you've probably made a buying mistake. Maybe the item that *isn't* selling in your shop *is* selling like hotcakes in similar shops elsewhere in the country. eBay gives you the tools to sell those extra items to make room for more of what sells at your home base.

  Perhaps you just need to raise some cash quickly. eBay has tens of thousands of categories in which you can sell regular stock or speciality items. For a caveat on items you're forbidden to sell, check out Chapter 4.

- ✔ **Selling by mail order:** If you've been selling by mail order, what's been holding you back from selling on eBay? Listing your item on eBay is much cheaper than running an ad in any publication. Plus, on eBay, you get built-in buyers from every walk of life. If your item sells through mail order, it will sell through eBay.

- ✔ **Licensed estate agents:** Plenty of land, houses, and flats are selling on eBay.co.uk right now. List your properties online so that you can draw from a nationwide audience and get more action. You can read more about selling property on eBay in Chapter 2.

You won't find a cheaper landlord than eBay. Jump over to Chapter 5 if you really can't wait for more information about how to set up your eBay shop.

Getting Ready to Sell

We've heard many sellers-to-be say they want to start a business on eBay so that they can relax. Since when is running any business a way to relax? Granted, you don't need a whole lot of money to get started on eBay.co.uk and you don't have a boss breathing down your neck. But to run a successful eBay business, you need drive, determination, and your conscience to guide you, as well as a few solid tools, such as a computer and an Internet connection. In this section, we give you the low-down on these things and more.

Computer hardware

First, you need a computer. In our basic assumptions about you (see this book's Introduction), we think that you have one and know how to use it. Your computer doesn't have to be the latest, fastest, and best available –

but it does help if it has a good deal of memory to process your Web browsing and image touch-ups. One of our eBay selling computers is an antique Pentium 3, an absolute dinosaur next to my new 4.3GHz model. But combined with a speedy Internet connection, my little machine enables me to run many eBay auctions easily.

Hard drives are getting cheaper by the minute and the bigger your hard drive, the more space you have to store images for your auctions. (Individual pictures shouldn't take up much space because each should max at 50K.) A warning: The bigger your hard drive, the more chance for making a mess of it by losing files. When you get started, set up a sensible filing system by using folders and sub-directories.

Check out Chapter 11 for details of the other stuff you may need, such as a scanner and a digital camera.

Connecting to the Internet

If you've been on eBay for any length of time, you know that your Internet connection turns into an appendage of your body. If your connection is down or you can't log on due to a power cut, you can't function and instead flounder around, babbling to yourself. I understand because I've been there. If you're selling in earnest, pull the plug on your dial-up connection unless you have no choice.

Before investing in any broadband connection, visit www.broadband checker.co.uk (see Figure 1-6) and check out details of ISPs in your area. Alternatively, www.broadband.co.uk allows you to compare and contrast the connections available. You can also find a broadband beginners' guide at http://www.broadband.co.uk/guide.jsp, in case you're not sure about the ins and outs of high-speed Internet connections.

Dial-up connections

If you must use a dial-up connection, avail yourself of the many free trials that different Internet Service Providers (ISPs) offer to see which one gives your computer the fastest connection. After you find the fastest, be sure that the connection is reliable and has at least a 99 per cent uptime rate – otherwise you could be in for frustrating delays.

Most of the UK still logs on to the Internet with a dial-up connection, so what can be so wrong? Yet, this type of connection is painfully slow. An auction with lots of images can take minutes to load. The average eBay user wants to browse many auctions and doesn't wait while your images load; he or she just goes to the next auction.

Figure 1-6:
The search
page on
www.
broadband
checker.
co.uk

To make the best use of your time when running your auctions and conducting research, you need to blast through the Internet – answering e-mails, loading images, and conducting your business without waiting around for snail-pace connections. Common quibbles from dial-up users are that transfer speeds are too slow and that their telephone lines are tied up during a session, so they can't even use the phone! Although a modem is supposed to link up at 56K, the highest connection I've ever experienced on a dial-up was 44K – much too slow!

DSL

A confusing number of Digital Subscriber Line (DSL) flavours (ASDL, IDSL, SDSL, and more) are available nowadays, ranging from reasonably priced to out of sight. DSL, when it works as advertised, is fast and reliable. A DSL line depends on the reliability of your telephone service: Crackling or unreliable phone lines can be a barrier to using it.

The main problem with a DSL connection is that your home or office needs to be within a certain distance from your local exchange. This distance is usually several thousand feet and shouldn't be a problem for most people, but it might be worth checking with your chosen ISP if you live in a more remote area. The service runs from about £10 a month, but it usually costs more, especially if you get DSL through a *booster* that boosts the signal to a location farther away than the minimum 18,000-foot border.

If you can get it, true DSL service can give you a connection as fast as 1.5MB per second download. (IDSL is only 144K.)

We had DSL for about a year and was initially blown away by the speed. Unfortunately, every time it rained our service went out. We had to call time after time to get a service call. Sadly, this is a well-known drawback of DSL. Your local telephone company (Telco in DSL-speak) owns your home or office phone lines. Because DSL goes over POTS (plain old telephone service), your DSL provider has to negotiate connection problems with the people at your telephone company. As you can guess, one company often blames the other for your problems.

A friend of ours tried to get around this issue by getting DSL from the local phone company, which sounded great to us. Unfortunately, this arrangement turned out to be not so great because local phone companies tend to form companies to handle high-speed connections. So even though the two companies are technically the same, the two still argue about who's responsible for your problems. Broadband with this much difficulty can be too much trouble.

Digital cable

Eureka, we think we've found the mother lode of connections: cable. If you can get cable television, you can probably get a blazingly fast cable Internet connection. Your cable company is probably replacing old cable lines with newfangled digital fibre optic lines. These new lines carry a crisp digital TV signal and an Internet connection as well. (These fancy new lines have plenty of room to carry even more stuff, and hot new services are being introduced all the time.)

Digital cable Internet connections are generally fast and reliable – you can download data at 1844 kilobauds per second. Compare that speed to the old-fashioned baud rate of dial-up (remember the old 300 baud modems?). And, the service is usually very reliable. Digital cable usually comes as a package with Internet, a phone line, and multi-channel digital TV, so prices vary and it's worth browsing for deals that suit your particular needs.

As far as the myth about more users on the line degrading the speed, a cable connection is more than capable of a 10Mbps transfer – that's already about 10 times faster than DSL. A lot of degrading would be necessary to noticeably slow down your connection. (Your computer still has to load the browser.)

Choosing your eBay.co.uk user ID

'What's in a name?' On eBay, there's a whole lot in your name! When you choose your eBay user ID, it becomes your name – your identity – to all those who transact with you online. These people don't know who you are; they know you only by the name they read in the seller's or bidder's spot.

The low-down on user IDs

When choosing your user ID, keep the following points in mind:

✔ Your ID must contain at least two characters.

✔ eBay displays your ID in all lowercase letters.

✔ You may use letters, numbers, and any symbol except @ and &.

✔ You can't use URLs as your ID.

✔ You can't use the word *eBay* in your user ID; that privilege is reserved for eBay employees.

✔ You can change your ID every 30 days if you want to. When you do, you get a special icon next to your name, signifying that you've changed to a new ID. Your feedback profile (permanent record) follows you to your new ID.

✔ Spaces aren't allowed; if you want to use two words, you can separate them by using the underscore key (press Shift+hyphen to type the underscore key). You may not use consecutive underscores.

✔ Don't use a name that's hateful or obscene; eBay (and the community) just doesn't permit it.

Ever wonder why you don't see many banks named Joe and Fred's Savings and Investments? Even if Joe is the president and Fred is the chairman of the board, the casual attitude portrayed by their given names doesn't instil much confidence in the stability of the bank. Joe and Fred might be a better name for a plumbing supply company – or a great name for blokes who sell plumbing tools on eBay! Joe and Fred strike us as the kind of friendly, trustworthy fellas who might know something about plumbing.

Does your retail business have a name? If you don't have your own business (yet), have you always known what you'd call it if you did? Your opportunity to set up your business can start with a good, solid respectable sounding business name. If you don't like respectable (it's too staid for you), go for trendy. Who knew what a Napster was? Or a Kelkoo? Or a Bubblefast, which is a popular shipping supplier among eBay users in the US.

Are you selling flamingo-themed items? How about pink flamingos for your selling identity? Be creative; *you* know what name best describes your product.

Stay away from negative sounding names. If you really can't think up a good user ID, using your own name is fine.

eBay.co.uk protects and does not reveal your e-mail address. If another user wants to contact you, he or she can do so by clicking your user ID. The e-mail is sent to you through eBay's e-mail system.

If you decide to change your user ID, don't do it too often. Customers recognise you by name, and you may miss some repeat sales by changing it. Besides, eBay places a special icon next to your user ID on the site to show others that you've changed your ID. This icon sticks with you for 30 days.

Finding your eBay.co.uk feedback

The number that eBay lists next to your name is your feedback rating; see Figure 1-7 for a sample rating. Anyone on the Internet has only to click this number to know how you do business on eBay – and what other eBay users think of you. At the top of every user's feedback page is an excellent snapshot of all your eBay transactions for the past six months. For the low-down on feedback, go to Chapter 3.

Figure 1-7: Sample eBay feedback rating.

Member Profile: marsha_c (2743 ★) PowerSeller me		

Feedback Score:	**2743**	Recent Ratings:			
Positive Feedback:	**100%**		Past Month	Past 6 Months	Past 12 Months
Members who left a positive:	2743	⊕ positive	48	384	723
Members who left a negative:	0	⊖ neutral	0	0	0
All positive feedback received:	3265	⊖ negative	0	0	0
Learn about what these numbers mean.		Bid Retractions (Past 6 months): 0			

If you're really serious about this business thing, and your feedback rating isn't as high as you'd like it to be, go online and buy some stuff. Even though eBay.co.uk now distinguishes between Buyer and Seller feedback, the numbers still grow. Feedback should always be posted for both buyers and sellers. Every positive feedback increases your rating by +1; a negative decreases it by –1. To get a high rating, rack up those positives.

Making Your Auctions Run More Smoothly

In this section, we discuss a few more niceties you need to round out your eBay.co.uk home base. The following tools are important, but you must decide which ones you'll use. Some people prefer a totally automated office while others like to do things the old-fashioned way. One of our favourite eBay PowerSellers works with file folders, a hand-written ledger book, and hand-written labels. If pen and paper make you happy, do it your way. I'm going to suggest a few options that ease the pain of paperwork.

Software you can use

Software is now available to accomplish just about anything. An all-encompassing software package exists that can help you with your auction, right? Well, maybe. Whether you use it depends on how much you want your software to do and how much of your business you want to fully control. In this section, we describe some software examples that you may find useful.

Auction management

Auction management software can be a very good thing. This software can automate tasks and make your record keeping easy. You can keep track of inventory, launch auctions, and print labels using one program. Unfortunately, most of these programs can be daunting when you first look at them (and even when you take a second look).

You have choices to make regarding the software: How much are you willing to spend, and do you want to keep your inventory and information online? Maintaining your listing information online enables you to run your business from anywhere; you just log on and see your inventory. Online management software is tempting and professional, and may be worth your time and money.

A good many sellers prefer to keep their auction information on their own computers. This method is convenient and allows sellers to add a closer, more personal touch to their auctions and correspondence. Some people say that keeping information local, on their own computer, is more suited to the small-time seller, but we think it's a matter of preference.

In Chapter 9, we discuss the wide selection of management software available, including AuctionWorks.com, Auction Wizard 2000, and the eBay-owned Selling Manager.

HTML software

You may want to try some basic HTML software to practise your ad layouts. We tell you where to find some templates in Chapter 11, but you'll want to preview your auctions before you launch them.

You can use a full-blown Web page software package, such as FrontPage, to check out how your auction will look, or you may want to keep things simple. We use software called CuteHTML because it's about as simple as it gets. Go to the following to download a 30-day free trial:

```
www.globalscape.com/cutehtml
```

If you like this software package, you can buy it for around £15.

Spreadsheets and bookkeeping

Many sellers keep their information in a simple spreadsheet program such as Excel. The program has all the functionality you need to handle inventory management and sales info.

For bookkeeping, we use QuickBooks. This program is straightforward, but only if you have a basic knowledge of accounting. QuickBooks also integrates with spreadsheets. In Chapter 16, we discuss accounting software such as QuickBooks and Microsoft Money in some detail.

Collecting the cash

Credit cards are the way to go for the bulk of your auctions. Often, credit cards make the difference between a sale and no sale. People are getting savvy (and more comfortable) about using their credit cards online because they're becoming better informed about the security of online transactions and certain guarantees against fraud. So although you may truly love money orders, you need to take credit cards as well. In this section, we discuss another decision you need to make: Do you want your own private merchant account or would you rather run your credit card sales through an online payment service? For more about these options, read on.

Online payment services

Until you hit the big time, you may want to go with the services of an online payment service such as the eBay-owned PayPal. PayPal offers excellent services, and their rates are on a sliding scale, according to your monthly cash volume. Online payment services accept credit cards for you; they charge you a small fee and process the transaction with the credit card company. The auction payment is deposited in an account for you. Unless your sales go into tens of thousands of pounds a month, an online payment service can be more economical than your own merchant account. For more about these services and accounts, see Chapter 13.

Your own merchant account

As you may or may not know (depending on the amount of spam in your e-mail), thousands of merchant credit card brokers guarantee that they can set you up so that you can take credit cards yourself. These people are merely middlemen. You have to pay for the brokers' services and it is wise to keep in mind that some of these brokers are dependable businesses while others are nothing more than hustlers. If you have decent credit, you don't need these people: Go straight to your bank!

Your bank knows your financial standing and credit worthiness better than anybody. Your bank is, therefore, the best place to start to get your own *merchant account* – an account in which your business accepts credit cards directly from your buyers. You pay a small percentage to the bank, but it's considerably less than you pay to an online payment service. Some banks don't offer merchant accounts for Internet transactions because ultimately the bank is responsible for the merchandise related to the account if you fail to deliver the goods. Remember that your credit history and time with the bank play a part in whether or not you can get a merchant account.

The costs involved in opening a merchant account can vary, but you need at least £200 to get started.

Nine banks currently offer Internet merchant accounts. You need to set up an Internet merchant account even if you already have an account for face-to-face transactions. On top of the £200-ish sign-up fee, expect to pay additional day-to-day charges based on either a fixed fee or a percentage of your sales. For example, credit card payments often attract a commission fee, while fixed fees often apply to debit card transactions.

Setting up a merchant account is quite an investment in time and effort. In Chapter 13, we get into the details of a merchant account and explain exactly where all these costs go.

Home base: Your Web site

eBay.co.uk offers you a free page – the About Me page – that's the most important link to your business on eBay (see Chapter 3 for more information). The About Me page is part of your eBay.co.uk shop if you have one. You can insert a link on your About Me page that takes bidders to your auctions. You can link also to your own Web site from the About Me page!

If you don't have your own Web site, I recommend that you get one, especially if you're serious about running an eBay business. Check out Chapter 8, where I provide some tips on finding a Web host and a simple way to put up your own Web site.

You can keep your complete inventory of items on your Web site and list them as auctions or in your eBay.co.uk shop as their selling season comes around. No listing or final value fee is due when you have repeat customers on your Web site.

Setting up your shop

Office and storage space are a must if you plan to get big. Many a business was started at the kitchen table (that's how Pierre started eBay), but to be serious with a business, you must draw definite lines between your home life and your online ventures. Concentrating when you have a lot of noise in the background is difficult, so when I say draw a line, I mean a physical line as well as an environmental one.

Your dedicated office

You must first separate the family from the hub of your business. Many eBay sellers use a spare bedroom As time progresses and your business grows, you may have to move, maybe into your garage. Remember, you'll need electricity and phone lines, lighting and furniture. And don't forget storage space for your saleable items.

One PowerSeller that we know moved all the junk out of his cellar and set up shop there. He now has three computers and employs his wife and a part-time *lister* (who put his auctions up on eBay) to run the show. This guy's cellar office is networked and is as professional as any office.

Your eBay room

If you're able to set up an office, your storage space should be ensured for a while. For a real business, a cupboard just won't do. Seclude your stuff from your pets and family by moving it into another room and get shelving to organise your merchandise and admin properly. We talk more about organising your business in Chapter 17.

Chapter 2

eBay.co.uk Business Basics

*A*t first glance, eBay.co.uk is this behemoth Web site that seems way too large for any novice to possibly master. In a superficial way, that image is correct. eBay is always growing and undergoing facelifts. Under all the cosmetic changes, however, you find the basics. eBay.co.uk is still the same old trading site: a community of buyers and sellers who follow the same rules and policies, making it a safe place to trade.

As anything gets larger, it must become compartmentalised to be manageable. The people at eBay have done this most handily. The original basic eight categories now number in the thousands. The category breakdown is clearer and more concise. When a trend begins, the eBay tech gurus evaluate the sales and, when necessary, add new categories.

All this growth has forced eBay to expand. Aside from the traditional auctions, you'll now find Dutch, private, restricted, and more – it can get confusing! In this chapter, we explain the new eBay features by reviewing how the site does business. Armed with this knowledge, you can effectively do your business.

Choosing Where to Position Your Stuff

The Internet is crowded with auctions, with many major portals including auctions as part of their site. Yet most bidders and sellers go to eBay. Why? On eBay.co.uk, more computers and electronics are sold than at Excite UK;

more used cars are sold than at Autotrader; and probably more toys are sold on eBay than at HamleysToys. Whether you're selling car parts, toys, fine art, or property, you need to find your niche on eBay. Deciding where to put your stuff for sale is pretty straightforward, isn't it? Not necessarily. The task is complicated by the inclusion of thousands of categories on the eBay Category Overview page, shown in Figure 2-1.

Consider the example of a Harry Potter toy. Harry Potter toys are becoming increasingly popular with the continuing saga in both the books and the films. The easy choice is to list the item under Toys & Hobbies: TV, Film Character Toys: Harry Potter. But what about the category Collectibles: Fantasy, Mythical & Magic: Harry Potter? This is the point where you must decide whether you want to list in two categories and pay more (see the review of extra charges in Chapter 10) or count on the fact that your beautifully written Auction Title will drive those using the eBay.co.uk search engine directly to your item.

eBay.co.uk supplies you with a great tool: *Find a Main Category* in the Sell Your Item pages. Type a few keywords for your item, and you're presented with a list of categories where items similar to yours are listed, as in Figure 2-2.

So you aren't selling Harry Potter toys? Suppose you're selling a DVD of the film *The Red Violin*. Would listing it in DVD & Films: DVD be the right choice? Or would you reach the proper audience of category browsers in Music: Musical Instruments: String: Violin?

Figure 2-1:
The eBay.co.uk Category Overview page; numbers next to categories reflect active auctions.

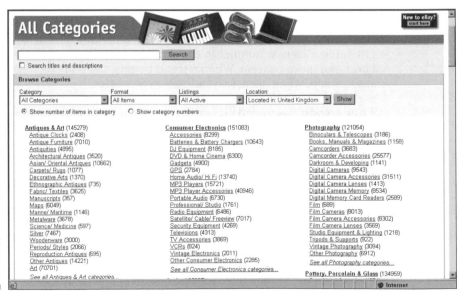

Find a Main Category

8 categories found for **baccarat vase**

You can select a suggested main category below and click **Sell In This Category**, or use different keywords to refine your search.

Enter item keywords to find a category

| baccarat vase | Find | Tips |

For example, "gold bracelet" not "jewelry"

Category

⦿ Pottery & Glass : Glass : Art Glass : French : Baccarat	(81%)
○ Home & Garden : Home Decor : Other	(3%)
○ Home & Garden : Home Decor : Vases : Other	(3%)
○ Pottery & Glass : Glass : Art Glass : North American : Other Makers	(3%)
○ Pottery & Glass : Glass : Art Glass : Other Countries	(3%)
○ Pottery & Glass : Glass : Glassware : Contemporary Glass : Crystal	(3%)
○ Pottery & Glass : Glass : Glassware : Elegant : Other Makers	(3%)
○ Pottery & Glass : Glass : Glassware : Waterford	(3%)

Figure 2-2:
eBay.co.uk's category finder feature.

Should a book on 1960s' fashion be placed in Books: Antiquarian and Collectible? Or would sellers have better luck going directly to the fans of 1960s' fashion in the category Clothing Shoes & Accessories: Vintage: Women's Clothing: 1965–76 (Mod, Hippie, Disco): Dresses.

The popularity of categories varies from time to time. News stories, the time of year, hot trends, or whether Jamie Oliver makes a comment about something all can change a particular category's popularity. How can you possibly know the best category for your item? Research your items regularly using our favourite tool: the marvellous eBay search engine. (Visit Chapter 7 for more about using the search engine.) After you find the right category for the item you're listing, give the search engine a try. However, be sure to occasionally try alternative categories as well.

Even when you've been selling a particular item for a while – and doing well with it – selling your item in a different but related category can boost your sales. A little research now and then into where people are buying can go a long way to increasing your eBay sales.

Selling a car? Go eBay Motors UK

Anything and everything to do with cars can go in the eBay Motors UK category (see Figure 2-3). Following are just a few of the car-related items that fit in this category.

Car parts

Got used car parts? eBay.co.uk has an enormous market in used car parts. One seller I know goes to scrap yards and buys wrecks — just to save some valuable parts that he can resell on eBay.

New car parts are in demand, too. If you catch a sale at your local auto parts shop when it's blasting out door handles for a 1967 Corvette (a vehicle for which it's hard to find parts), picking up a few wouldn't hurt. Sooner or later, someone's bound to search eBay looking for them. If you're lucky enough to catch the trend, you can make a healthy profit.

Cars

Yes, you can sell cars on eBay. In fact, used car sales have skyrocketed online thanks to all the people who find eBay to be a trusted place to buy and sell used vehicles. Check out Figure 2-4 for an example of a used car auction. Selling vehicles on eBay is a natural business for you if you have access to good used cars, work as a mechanic, or have a contact at a dealership that lets you sell cars on eBay for a commission or on a consignment basis. (For the ins and outs of consignment selling, check out Chapter 6.)

eBay Motors UK offers useful tools to complete your sale, including one-click access to vehicle status reports, vehicle listing templates, vehicle inspection and escrow services, and vehicle shipping quotes from dependable sources. Access eBay Motors UK and its services from the eBay.co.uk home page or go directly to `motors.ebay.co.uk`.

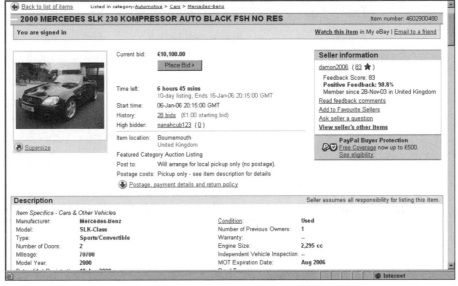

Figure 2-4:
An eBay
Motors UK
auction for a
previously
owned car.

Here are just a few things to keep in mind if you plan to sell cars on eBay:

- ✔ Selling a car on eBay Motors is a bit different from selling on regular eBay, mainly in the fees area. Take a look at Tables 2-1 and 2-2 for significant differences. Chapter 10 includes a table of all basic eBay fees for listings, options, and final values.

- ✔ To sell a vehicle on eBay Motors, you must enter the Vehicle Identification Number (VIN) on the Sell Your Item page. This way, prospective buyers can always access a Carfax report to get an idea of the history of the car.

- ✔ Shipping a vehicle is a reasonably priced alternative to trekking across the UK in order to pick up the vehicle of your dreams. You can make arrangements to transport a car quickly and simply. Expect to spend between £100 and £500 on delivery charges depending on vehicle size (a bike costs a lot less than a van, for example) and how far away the destination is.

- ✔ If your reserve price isn't met in an eBay Motors UK auction, you may still offer the vehicle to the highest bidder through the Second Chance option. More information on reserve price auctions is provided later in this chapter. You may also reduce your reserve during the auction if you feel that you set your target price too high.

Table 2-1	eBay.co.uk Motor Vehicle-Specific Insertion Fees	
Format	*Single Item Listing*	*Multiple Item Listing*
Auction Style	£6.00	£6.00 multiplied by the number of vehicles listed.
Buy It Now Only	£6.00	£6.00 multiplied by the number of vehicles listed.

Note: The reserve price fee for listings in the Cars, Commercial Vehicles, Motorcycles, and Caravans categories is £3.00 regardless of the reserve price level set.

Table 2-2	eBay.co.uk Motors Final Value Fees
Closing Price	*Final Value Fee*
£0.01–£1,999.99	£15.00
£2,000.00–£3,999.99	0.75%
£4,000.00 and above	£30.00

An item that you list on eBay Motors UK appears in any search, whether a potential buyer conducts a regular eBay search or executes a search in eBay Motors.

Properties: Not quite an auction

eBay.co.uk Properties isn't quite an auction. Because of the wide variety of laws governing the sale of property, eBay auctions of houses or land, for example, aren't legally binding offers to buy and sell. Putting your property up on eBay is an excellent way to advertise and attract potential buyers. When the auction ends, however, neither party is obligated (as they are in other eBay auctions) to complete the transaction. The buyer and seller must get together to consummate the deal.

Nonetheless, eBay property sales are becoming more popular and while sales are small in number, they are growing steadily. You don't have to be a professional estate agent to use this category, although closing the deal may be easier if you are. For about the cost of a newspaper ad – the insertion fee is fixed at £35 for property – you can sell your house, flat, land, or even timeshare on eBay (see Figure 2-5) in the auction format.

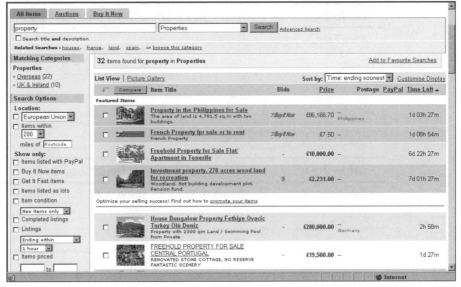

Figure 2-5:
Properties
listed for
sale on
eBay.co.uk.

Fixed-Price Sales on eBay.co.uk

To compete with fellow online giants such as Amazon and Yahoo!, eBay.co.uk now includes *fixed-price sales* on its site. Fixed-price sales are an extension of the eBay Buy It Now feature. You put an item up for sale at a fixed price, and buyers pay the price that you're asking. The process is as simple as that. You can also find fixed-price sales at the new eBay Shops. Each eBay shop is run by an eBay auction seller. eBay Shops has its own space on eBay, which is accessible in the following ways:

- Through the navigation bar by clicking Browse and then Shops
- By clicking the eBay Shops link on the eBay.co.uk home page
- By going straight to stores.ebay.co.uk from the Web

Potential buyers can access your items from anywhere on the eBay.co.uk site. The cost of eBay Shops (see Tables 2-3 and 2-4) compares favourably with any of the Web's mega site shops.

Table 2-3	eBay Shop Subscription Fees
Shop Format	**Fee**
Basic	£6.00 / month
Featured	£30.00 / month
Anchor	£300.00 / month

Table 2-4	eBay Shop Insertion Fees		
Duration	**Insertion Fee**	**Surcharge**	**Total**
30 days	£0.05	N/A	£0.05
90 days	£0.05	£0.10	£0.15
Good 'Til Cancelled*	£0.05 / 30 days	N/A	£0.05 / 30 days

Subscription fees begin after 30 days of trading.

Types of eBay Auctions

An auction is an auction is an auction, right? Wrong! eBay.co.uk has four types of auctions for your selling pleasure. Most of the time you run traditional auctions, but other auctions have their place, too. When you have sold on eBay.co.uk for a while, you may find that one of the other types of auctions better suits your needs. In this section, we review these auctions so that you fully understand what they are and when to use them.

Traditional auctions

Traditional auctions are the bread and butter of eBay.co.uk. You can run a traditional auction for 1, 3, 5, 7, or 10 days, and when the auction closes, the highest bidder wins. We're sure you've bid on several auctions and at least won a few. We bet you've also made money running some auctions of your own.

You begin the auction with an opening bid, and bidders (we hope) bid up your opening price into a healthy profit for you.

Dutch auctions

When you purchase a job lot of 500 kitchen knife sets or manage (legally, of course) to get your hands on a lorry-load of televisions that you want to sell as expeditiously as possible, the Dutch (multiple item) auction is the option you choose. In the *Dutch auction* (see Figure 2-6 for an example), which can run for 1, 3, 5, 7, or 10 days, you list as many items as you like, and bidders can bid on as many items as they like. The final item price is set by the lowest successful bid at the time the auction closes.

For example, suppose you want to sell five dolls on eBay.co.uk in a Dutch auction. Your starting bid is £5 each. If five bidders each bid £5 for one doll, they each get a doll for £5. But, if the final bidding reveals that three people bid £5, one person bid £7.50, and another bid £8, all five bidders win the doll for the lowest final bid of £5.

In the following list, we highlight the details of the Dutch auction:

- ✔ The listing fee is based on your opening bid price (just like in a traditional auction), but it's multiplied by the number of items in your auction to a maximum listing fee of £2.

- ✔ The final auction value fees are on the same scale as in a traditional auction, but they're based on the total cash amount of your completed auctions.

Figure 2-6:
A Dutch auction for a Royal Doulton plate.

✔ When bidders bid in your Dutch auction, they can bid on one or more items at one bid price. (The bid is multiplied by the number of items.)

✔ If the bidding gets hot and heavy, re-bids must be of a higher total cash amount than the total of that bidder's past bids.

✔ Bidders may reduce the quantity of the items for which they're bidding in your auction, but the cash amount of the total bid price must be higher.

✔ All winning bidders pay the same price for their items, no matter how much they bid.

✔ The lowest successful bid when the auction closes is the price for which your items in that auction are sold.

✔ If your item gets more bids than you have items, the lowest bidders are knocked out one by one, with the earliest bidders remaining on board the longest in the case of tie bids.

✔ The earliest (by date and time) successful high bidders when the auction closes win their items.

✔ Higher bidders get the quantities they've asked for, and bidders can refuse partial quantities of the number of items in their bids.

For a large quantity of a particular item, your Dutch auction may benefit from some of the eBay featured auction options detailed in Chapter 10.

Reserve price auctions

In a *reserve price auction*, you're able to set an undisclosed minimum price for which your item will sell, thereby giving yourself a safety net. Figure 2-7 shows an auction in which the reserve has not yet been met. Using a reserve price auction protects the investment you have in an item. If, at the end of the auction, no bidder has met your undisclosed reserve price, you aren't obligated to sell the item and the highest bidder isn't required to purchase the item.

For example, if you have a rare coin to auction, you can start the bidding at a low price to attract bidders to click your auction and read your infomercial-like description. If you start your bidding at too high a price, you may dissuade prospective bidders from even looking at your auction, and you won't tempt them to bid. These prospective buyers may feel that the final selling price will be too high for their budgets.

Everyone on eBay is looking for a bargain or a truly rare item. If you can combine the mystical force of both of these needs in one auction, you have something special. The reserve price auction enables you to attempt – and perhaps achieve – this feat.

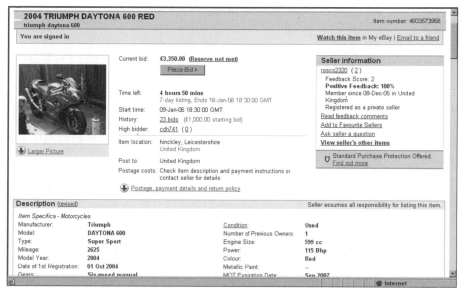

Figure 2-7:
Note that a
reserve has
been set for
this auction.

The fees for a reserve price auction are the same as those for a traditional auction with one exception. eBay.co.uk charges between £2.00 and £100.00 for the privilege of running a reserve price auction. When your item sells, you get that money back. Table 2-5 shows fees for reserve auctions.

Table 2-5	Reserve Auction Fees
Reserve Price	**Fee (Refunded If Item Sells)**
£0.01–£49.99	N/A
£50.00–£4,999.99	2% of the reserve price
£5,000.00 and up	£100.00

Sellers who wish to use a reserve price must set the reserve price to be equal to or greater than £50. You are not allowed to set a reserve price level to be less than this value.

The reserve price auction is a safety net for the seller but often an uncomfortable guessing game for the prospective bidder. To alleviate buyer anxiety, many sellers put reserve prices in the item description, allowing bidders to decide whether the item fits into their bidding budgets.

You can't use the reserve price option in a Dutch auction.

Private auctions

Bidders' names are often kept private when dealing in the expensive fine art world. Likewise, to protect the innocent, eBay *private auctions* don't place bidders' names on the auction listing. No one needs to know just how much you choose to pay for something, especially if the item is rare and you really want it.

As a seller, you have the option (at no extra charge) of listing your auction as a private auction.

The eBay.co.uk search page features an area where you can conduct a bidder search. You – and everyone else – can find the items that you bid on. If you're buying a present for a loved one, a private auction keeps your shopping a secret.

The private auction is a useful tool for sellers who are selling bulk lots to other sellers. A private auction maintains the privacy of the bidders, and customers can't do a bidder search to find out what sellers are paying for the loot they then plan to re-sell on eBay.

A great option for sales of items that are a bit racy or perhaps for purchases of items that may reveal something about the bidder, the private auction can save you the potential embarrassment associated with buying a girdle or buying the tie that flips over to reveal a half-nude female on the back.

Although the private auction is a useful tool, it may intimidate the novice user. If your customer base comes from experienced eBay.co.uk users and you're selling an item that may benefit by being auctioned in secret, you might want to try this option.

Restricted items

eBay.co.uk does not permit the listing of erotica or sexually-orientated materials. If you can't imagine for yourself what this means, you can find more information on what's allowed and what's not in the eBay.co.uk help centre: `http://pages.ebay.co.uk/help/index.html`. Hazardous and perishable items are also restricted to varying degrees. For more information on what you can and can't sell on eBay, visit Chapter 4.

Running Your Auction

The basic plan for running an auction is the same for everyone, except for decisions regarding the timing of the auction and the starting price. If you speak to 20 different eBay sellers, you'll probably get 20 different answers about effective starting bids and when to end your auction. Until you develop your own philosophy, here we give you the tools to make a sound decision.

You can also successfully promote your auctions online and offline, and now you can legally offer your item to the next highest bidder if the auction winner doesn't come through with payment. We discuss a few of these ideas in this section.

Influencing the bidding

The most generally accepted theory about starting bids is that setting the bidding too high scares away new bids. Also, as in the case of the reserve price auction, if the bidding begins too high, novices may be afraid that the bidding will go too high and they'll never win the auction.

Some sellers begin the bidding at the price they paid for the item, thereby protecting their investment. Starting at this price is a good tactic, especially if you bought the item at a price far below the current going rate on eBay.

To determine the current going value for your item, we recommend using the Completed Auctions search, which we explain in Chapter 7. If you know that the item is selling on eBay for a certain price and that there is a demand for it, starting the bidding at a reasonably low level can be a great way to increase bidding and attract prospective bidders to read your auction.

Years of advertising experience can't be wrong. If your item is in demand and people are actively buying, start the bidding low. Shops have done this for years with ads that feature prices starting at £9.99 or £14.99. Even television commercials advertising cars quote a low starting price. To get the car as shown in the ad, you may end up paying twice the quoted price.

When sellers know that they have an item that will sell, they begin their bidding as low as a pound or even a penny. Because of the eBay *proxy bidding system* (which maintains the seller's highest bid as secret, increasing it incrementally when you're bid against), it takes more bids (due to the smaller bidding increments) to bring the item up to the final selling price.

The downside of bidding low is that new bidders unfamiliar with the system may bid only the minimum required increment each time they bid. New bidders may become frustrated and stop bidding because it might take them several bids to top the current bid placed by someone who's familiar with the proxy bid system.

Table 2-6 details the proxy bidding increments.

Table 2-6	Proxy Bidding Increments
Current Price	*Bid Increment*
£0.01–£1.00	£0.05
£1.01–£5.00	£0.20
£5.01–£15.00	£0.50
£15.01–£60.00	£1.00
£60.01–£150.00	£2.00
£150.01–£300.00	£5.00
£300.01–£600.00	£10.00
£600.01–£1,500.00	£20.00
£1,500.01–£3,000.00	£50.00
£3,000.01 and up	£100.00

Auction timing

Auction timing is a debatable philosophy – how long to run auctions and the best day to end an auction. You have to evaluate your item and decide the best plan:

✔ **One-day auction:** This format can be very successful if you have an item that's the hot ticket for the moment on eBay.co.uk. We used this format when we sold some *Friends* TV show memorabilia. The 24-hour auction opened mid-day before the final show and ended the next day – at a very healthy profit!

One-day auctions also give you the benefit of pushing your auction to the top of the heap in the listings. Because eBay defaults to show the items ending first at the top of the page (just below featured auctions), a one-day listing posts higher!

- ✔ **Three-day auction:** If, as in the heyday of Beanie Babies, the item's price will shoot up immediately after you post it, a three-day auction works just fine. And three-day auctions are great for those last-minute holiday shoppers looking for hard-to-find items.

  The eBay.co.uk Buy It Now feature also gives your customers the chance to snap up late bargains. When you list your item for sale, set a price at which you will sell the item; this is your target price. This price can be any amount, and if someone is willing to pay, it sells.

- ✔ **Five-day auction:** Five days gives you two days more than three and two days less than seven – that's about the size of it. If you just want an extended weekend auction, or if your item is a hot one, use a five-day auction. These auctions are useful during holiday rushes, when present buying is the main reason for bidding.

- ✔ **Seven-day auction:** Tried-and-tested advertising theory says that the longer you advertise your item, the more people see it. On eBay, this theory means that you have more opportunity for people to bid for your item. The seven-day auction is a staple for the bulk of eBay vendors. Seven days is long enough to cover weekend browsers and short enough to keep the auction interesting.

- ✔ **Ten-day auction:** Many veteran eBay sellers swear by the ten-day auction. The extra three days of exposure (it can encompass two weekends) can easily net you more profit.

  If you're selling an esoteric collectible that doesn't appear on eBay often, run a ten-day auction to give it maximum exposure. Start the auction on a Friday, so it will cover the aforementioned two weekends' worth of browsers. See *eBay Timesaving Techniques For Dummies* (Wiley) for opinions on how long to run an auction and what day or time to begin it.

Your auction closes exactly 1, 3, 5, 7, or 10 days – *to the minute* – after you start the auction. Be careful not to begin your auctions when you're up late at night and can't sleep: You don't want your auction to end at two in the morning when no one else is awake to bid on it. If you can't sleep, make your time productive and prepare listings ahead of time with the TurboLister program to prepare your auctions and upload them for future launching when the world is ready to shop.

The specific day you close your auction can also be important. eBay.co.uk is full of weekend browsers, so including a weekend of browsing in your auction time is a definite plus. Often, auctions ending between Sunday afternoon and Monday morning benefit from this traffic and close with high bids.

Do some research to determine the best times to run your auctions and for how long. In Chapter 10, we show you how to combine your search engine research with a special kind of statistical counter to help you identify the best closing time for your items. (See Chapter 7 for the details about using the search engine as a valuable research tool.) The best person to work out the closing information for your auctions is you. Use the tools and over time you'll work out a pattern that works best for you.

Is there a definite time *not* to close your auctions? Yes, experience has taught many sellers never to close an auction on a bank holiday. It may be bonanza sales time for high street shops, but eBay auction items closing on this day go at bargain prices.

Marketing your auctions

How do you let people know about your auctions? What do you do if all 100 million-plus users on eBay.co.uk happen to not be on the site the week that your items are up for sale? You advertise.

Many mailing lists and newsgroups permit self-promotion. Find a group that features your type of items and post a bit of promotion. Advertising works best if you have your own Web site. Your site, which should be the hub for your sales, can give you an identity and level of professionalism that makes your business more official in the eyes of buyers. In Chapter 8, we detail the ins and outs of business sites on the Web.

TipLink buttons

eBay.co.uk supplies some nice link buttons (see Figure 2-8) that you can use on your Web site. Visit the following address to add these links to your site's home page:

```
http://pages.ebay.co.uk/services/buyandsell/link-
             buttons.html
```

Pirates of the Caribbean, er, Carribean?

Just before the *Pirates of the Caribbean* film premiered, Disneyland gave out exclusive film posters to their visitors. Ellen, savvy eBayer that she is, snagged several copies of the poster to sell on the site. She listed the posters (one at a time) when the film opened and couldn't get more than the starting bid, £4.99, for each of them.

When Ellen searched eBay for *pirates poster*, she found that the very same posters with a misspelled title, *Pirates of the Carribean*, were selling for as high as £20 each. Ellen immediately changed her auctions to have the more popular (misspelling) *Carribean* in the title and quickly saw those pound signs! After selling out her initial stock, Ellen found another seller who had 10 posters for sale – in one auction – with the proper spelling in the title. Ellen bought those posters as well (for £2 each) and sold them with misspelled titles on the site for between £8 and £15!

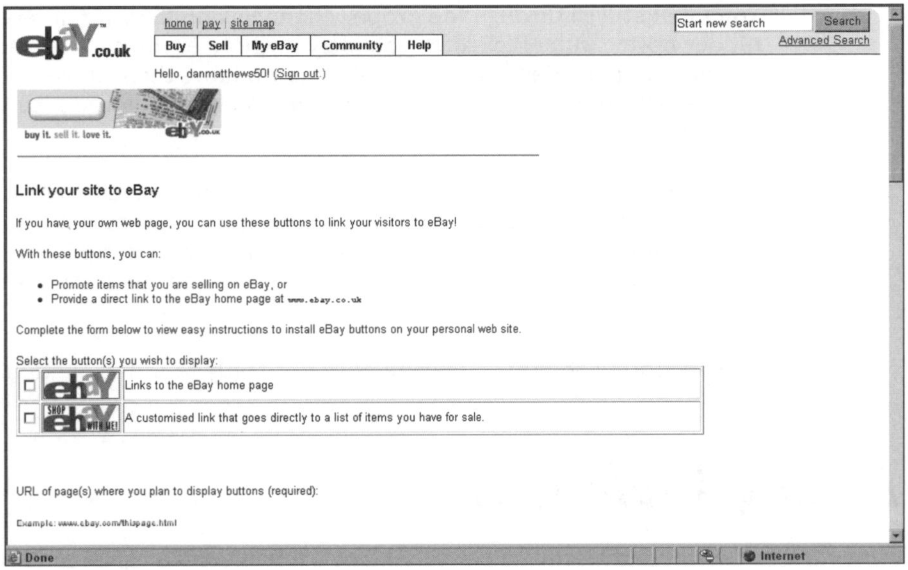

Figure 2-8:
The Shop
eBay.co.uk
with link
buttons.

We're guessing that you already know all about your About Me page, a handy tool for marketing your auctions. In Chapter 3, we discuss the values of the About Me page. Link to your Web site from your little home page on eBay.co.uk.

Here's a great way to market future auctions: When you're sending items after making a sale on eBay, include a list of items that you'll be selling soon (along with your thank you note, of course) – especially ones that may appeal to that customer. When you schedule your auctions, you're given the auction number before the item is listed.

Do not link your auction to your Web site – it's against eBay policy to possibly divert sales away from the auction site. *Do* link from your About Me page. See the 'Linking from your auctions' section, later in this chapter, to find out just what you can and cannot link to and from.

A second chance

The Second Chance feature on eBay.co.uk helps sellers legitimise something that previously went on behind closed doors and in violation of eBay policy. When a winner doesn't complete a sale, the Second Chance feature allows sellers to offer the item to the next highest bidder.

You must still go through the proper channels and file your non-paying bidder notice with eBay. After you file your notice, you can then send a Second Chance Offer to any under-bidder no more than 60 days after the end of the auction. Your final value fee is based on the price you receive when the offer is accepted.

In the Second Chance Offer scenario, the seller can leave two feedbacks: One for the winner (non-paying bidder) and one for the person who bought the item through the Second Chance Offer transaction. The bidder to whom you proffer your Second Chance Offer is covered by the eBay fraud protection programme.

The Second Chance Offer feature does not apply to Dutch auctions.

Listing Violations

eBay.co.uk does not sell merchandise – it is merely a venue that provides the location where others can put on a giant, e-commerce party (in other words, sell stuff). To provide a safe and profitable venue for its sellers, eBay must govern auctions that take place on its site. eBay makes the rules; we follow the rules. If we don't agree to follow eBay's rules, a safe and trusted eBay community can't exist.

Listing policies

eBay has some hard-and-fast rules about listing your items. You must list your item in the appropriate category (that makes sense), and we highlight here a few other rules that you should keep in mind when listing. What we discuss in this section isn't a definitive list of eBay listing policies and rules. Take time to familiarise yourself with the User Agreement (which details all eBay policies and rules) at the following:

```
http://pages.ebay.co.uk/help/policies/user-agreement.html
```

We recommend regularly checking the eBay User Agreement for any policy changes.

Choice auctions

Your auction must be for one item only: the item that you specifically list in your auction. Giving the bidder a choice of items, sizes, or colours is against the rules. eBay protects you with its Purchase Protection programme, which covers all online eBay transactions. When you give your bidders a choice, it's an illegal sale on eBay and isn't covered. Any transaction that's negotiated outside the eBay system can lead to either misrepresentation or fraud – don't get caught up in that sort of grief and misery.

If eBay catches you offering a choice, they'll end the auction and credit the insertion fee to your account.

Duplicate auctions

The theory of supply and demand is alive and well at eBay.co.uk. When people list the same items repeatedly, they drive down the item's going price while ruining all the other sellers' opportunities to sell the item during that time frame.

eBay.co.uk allows you ten identical listings at any time. If you list an item that many times, make sure you do so in different categories. Listing in different categories is a rule, but it also makes sense. Nothing drives down the price of an item faster than closing identical auctions, one after another, in the same category. eBay also requires that you list your auction in a category that's relevant to your item.

If you have multiple copies of an item, a better solution than listing in different categories is to run a Dutch auction for the total number of items you have for sale. Or perhaps you can run two Dutch auctions in different (but appropriate) categories.

If you're caught with more than ten identical auctions, eBay may end the additional auctions (any over ten) and it will credit the insertion fees.

Pre-sale listings

eBay doesn't like it when you try to sell something that's not in your hands (known as a *pre-sale listing*). Pre-sale listing is a dangerous game to play anyway. In many situations, being the first seller to put a very popular item up for sale can get you some pretty high bids. And if you can guarantee in your auction description that the item will be available to ship within 30 days of the purchase or the auction closing, you can run a pre-sale. However, we don't recommend even attempting a pre-sale listing if you're not completely sure that you'll have the item in time.

Pre-selling: Not worth the hassle

Jessica pre-sold Beanie Babies on eBay. She had a regular source that supplied her when the new toys came out, so she fell into a complacent attitude about listing pre-sales. Then one day, Jessica's supplier didn't get the shipment. Motivated by the need to protect her feedback rating (and by the fear that she'd be accused of fraud), Jessica ran all over town desperately trying to get the Beanies she needed to fill her orders. The Beanies were so rare that Jessica ended up spending several hundred pounds more than what she had originally sold the toys for, just to keep her customers happy.

---

eBay.co.uk charity fundraising

Tens of millions of pounds has been raised on eBay for charitable organisations. If you represent a legitimate charity, you may run auctions on eBay to raise funds. Just follow these simple steps:

1. **Register your charity as an eBay member.**

2. **Prepare an About Me page describing your charity.**

   Explain what your charity is, what it does, where the money goes, and so on. Set up the page to 'Show no feedback' and indicate for the page to 'Show all items'. eBay will link this page to the Giving Works area.

3. **Enter the following information to eBay. co.uk at** `http://pages.ebay.co.uk/ charity/information.html`

   ✔ User ID and e-mail address you registered with on eBay.co.uk

   ✔ The completed About Me page

   ✔ Your reference number as a registered charity

   ✔ The time frame in which you expect to run your auction

   ✔ A brief description of your organisation

   ✔ Examples of the items you'd like to list

   ✔ Name, e-mail address, and telephone number of the organisation's main contact person

   ✔ The Web site address for your organisation (if it has one)

   You'll hear back from eBay when your charity has been approved. Your charity will then appear on its Charity Fundraising home page (see Figure 2-9), and you can start planning your charity auctions. The eBay Charity Fundraising page is accessible from a link on the home page or directly through the following:

   `http://pages.ebay.co.uk/ charity/`

If you know that you'll have the item to ship – and it won't be lost on its way to you – you may list the item with the following requirement: You must state in your auction description that the item is a pre-sale and will be shipped by the 30th day from the end of the listing or purchase. You also have to use a little HTML here because the text must be coded with an HTML font no smaller than font size 3.

Keyword spamming

Keyword spamming is when you add words, usually brand names, to your auction description that don't describe what you're selling (for example, describing that little black dress as Givenchy-style when Givenchy has nothing to do with it). Sellers use keyword spamming to pull viewers to their auctions after viewers have searched for the brand name. To attract attention to their listings, some sellers use 'not' or 'like' along with the brand name, such as 'like Givenchy'.

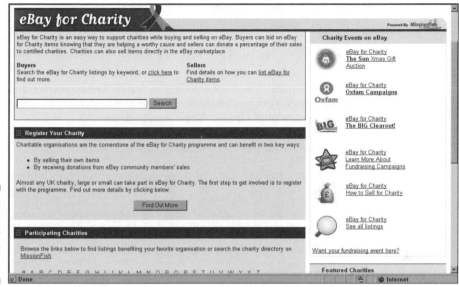

Figure 2-9:
The setup
screen for
eBay
charities.

Keyword spamming actually causes your auction to fall under 'potentially infringing' items for sale on eBay.co.uk. Keyword spamming is a listing violation, and we mention it here because it affects all listings. The wording you choose when you run this kind of auction manipulates the eBay search engine and prospective bidders. For a complete discussion of keyword spamming and its complexities as an item that is an infringement of eBay's policies, see Chapter 4.

Linking from your auctions

eBay.co.uk has some rules that govern linking, which we describe in this section.

In your auction item description, you *can* use the following links:

- ✔ One link to an additional page that gives further information about the item you're selling.
- ✔ A link that opens an e-mail window on the prospective buyer's browser so that the buyer can send you an e-mail.
- ✔ Links to more photo images of the item you're selling.
- ✔ Links to your other auctions on eBay.co.uk and your eBay Shop listings.
- ✔ One link to your About Me page, besides the link next to your user ID that eBay provides.

✔ Links to vendors' sites that help you with your auctions. eBay considers listing services, software, and payment services to be third-party vendors. You can legally link to these vendors as long as the HTML font is no larger than size 3; if you're using a logo, it must be no larger than 88 x 33 pixels.

Most third-party vendors are well aware of these restrictions. They don't want their credits pulled from eBay, so the information they supply as a link generally falls within eBay's parameters.

In your auction description, you *cannot* link to the following:

✔ A page that offers to sell, trade, or purchase merchandise outside the eBay site.

✔ Any area on the Internet that offers merchandise considered illegal on eBay. See Chapter 4 for information on illegal items.

✔ Any site that encourages eBay bidders to place their bids outside eBay.

✔ Sites that solicit eBay user IDs and passwords.

Linking from your About Me page

eBay rules pertaining to the About Me page are pretty much the same as the rules for the rest of the site. Because eBay gives you this page for self-promotion, *you* may link to your own business Web site from it (e-commerce or personal). Be sure not to link to other trading sites or to sites that offer the same merchandise for the same or lower price. Read more about the About Me page dos and don'ts in Chapter 3.

Chapter 3

Essential eBay.co.uk Tools

*e*Bay.co.uk offers you an amazing variety of tools. Because the site is constantly changing, few users know where these tools are, how to find them, or how to use them. Users often fall victim to the 'Oh, I didn't know I could do that' syndrome. Aside from the tools we tell you about in this chapter, the most important shortcut we can give you is to remind you to sign in and click the box that says 'Keep me signed in on this computer unless I sign out' before you attempt to do anything at eBay. Clicking this box permits you to do all your business at eBay without being bugged for your password at every turn.

If you have more than one user ID, or share a computer with other people, be sure to sign out when you're finished. The cookie system means your computer holds your sign-in information until you sign out. For your protection, you still have to type your password for actions involving financial information. To specify the tasks for which you want eBay to remember your sign-in information, go to the Preferences area of the My eBay.co.uk page.

Many eBay users frequently share with us some nugget of information that has helped them along the way. And now we share these nuggets with you.

eBay has developed some incredibly useful features, such as My eBay, which allows you to customise eBay.co.uk for your home page. Another feature, the About Me page, lets you tell the story of your business to the world as well as find out (with a click of the mouse) about the people you plan on buying from. To get the low-down on our favourite eBay tools, read on.

My eBay

Your own home page at eBay.co.uk can pop up on your screen every morning with a cheery, "My eBay – Hello, username", followed by your current feedback rating. My eBay is no longer a step-by-step list of what you're bidding on and selling, but a veritable Swiss army knife of eBay tools.

Access the My eBay page by clicking the <u>My eBay</u> button above the eBay.co.uk navigation bar. The navigation bar, which is shown in Figure 3-1, appears at the top of every eBay page. You can also click the <u>My eBay</u> link at the bottom of the eBay home or Search page. Why? I don't really know why anyone would take two steps instead of one, but you can if you want to.

Figure 3-1:
The eBay.co.uk navigation bar appears at the top of every eBay page.

Arriving at your My eBay page, you see a summary of the business that you have in progress on the site (see Figure 3-2). Each comment has a link, so you can investigate the progress of the transactions.

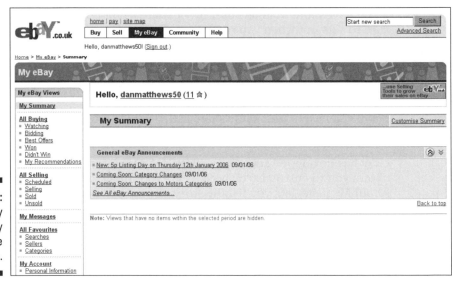

Figure 3-2:
A My eBay Summary entrance page.

My eBay is divided into five areas (My Summary, All Bidding, All Selling, All Favourites, and My Account), which you can visit by clicking links in the My eBay Views box on the left-hand side of the page. The top link of each My eBay area presents you with a summary of the activity in that area. The links below the top link take you to specific data, without having to scroll through a long page.

At the bottom of My eBay Views is a Related Links box with convenient links to services and to answers you may need while doing business at eBay (see Figure 3-3).

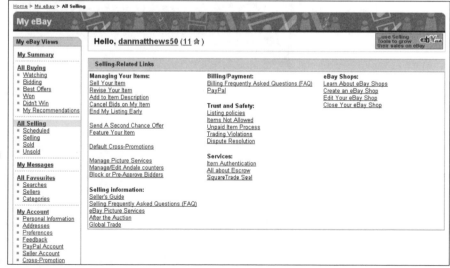

Figure 3-3:
The Related
Links box
on the My
eBay page.

The links in the Related Links box are different depending on the page, with buying-related links on the All Buying page, selling-related links on the All Selling page (as in Figure 3-4), account-related links on the My Account page, and favourites-related links on the All Favourites page. When you have a question regarding an eBay procedure, these links can be very handy.

Figure 3-4:
Selling-
related links
on the All
Selling
page.

At the top of each of the Views is a mini tote board, giving you a snapshot of your financial business dealings. In the Bidding area, the board displays the number of items you're bidding on and the cash amount of all your winning bids. In the Selling area, you see the number of items and the cash amounts bid. The other views have a similar summary tote at the top of the page.

All Buying

All Buying is the hub for keeping track of your bids, your wins, items you're watching, and any items you didn't win. Although you plan to sell more than buy at eBay.co.uk, we're sure you'll occasionally find something to buy if only to turn around and resell it. We've found many a bargain item at eBay that we've re-sold immediately at a profit. Plus, you can purchase most of your shipping supplies at eBay. (In Chapter 17, we reference a few eBay sources with great prices and fast shipping.)

Items I'm Bidding On

When you place a bid, eBay.co.uk automatically registers it in the Items I'm Bidding On area, like the one shown in Figure 3-5.

Figure 3-5:
Keeping
track of your
bidding at
My eBay.

Setting a desktop shortcut to your My eBay page

People often tell us they'd like a direct link from their computer desktop to their My eBay page. If you use Internet Explorer as your browser, just follow these steps:

1. **Sign in and go to your My eBay page.**

2. **In your browser's toolbar, choose File-Send-Shortcut to Desktop.**

Two steps and that's it – a clickable shortcut to your My eBay area is placed on your computer's desktop.

Make the bidding page a daily stop at eBay.co.uk so you can see the status of your bids:

- Bid amounts in green indicate that you're the high bidder in the auction.

- Bid amounts in red indicate that your bid is losing. To increase your bid, simply click the auction title to go to the auction.

- Dutch auctions appear in black. To determine whether you retain high bidder status in a Dutch auction, you need to go to the actual auction.

- The My Max Bid column reminds you of the amount of your highest bid; if you see a bid that surpasses your own, you know that you need to throw in another bid.

- The Bidding Totals box, at the top of the Bidding page, lists the current cash amount you're spending and the number of items you're currently winning in pending auctions. You can see the total amount you've bid and a separate total representing auctions you're winning.

- As auctions on which you've bid end, they automatically transfer to the Won and Didn't Win pages, based on your success or failure in the bidding process.

You can make notations on your bidding or item-watching, for example to help you organise your gift giving. (See the note we added in Figure 3-6.) Click to place a tick next to the item you want to annotate, click the Add Note button, and then add the information.

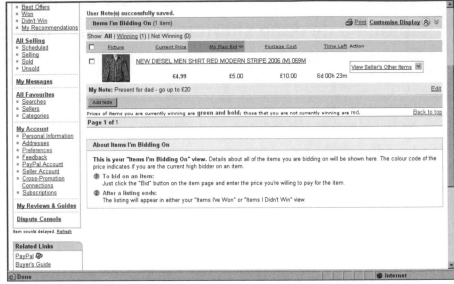

Figure 3-6:
A note reminding the bidder not to spend too much.

Items I've Won

Clicking the Won link in the bidding area displays all the items you've won as far back as the last 60 days. The default is 31 days, which should suffice for most transactions. The Items I've Won page is a great place to keep track of items that you're waiting to receive from the seller. This page is also a convenient way to keep track of your expenditures, should you be buying for resale. Helpful features on the Items I've Won page include the following:

- **Tick box:** Click the box to add a tick, and you can indicate that you'd like to add a note to your record or remove it from the list.

- **Seller's user ID:** Remembering the seller's name is useful, and this link sends you to the seller's Member Profile (feedback page) where you can send an e-mail to the seller.

- **Auction title:** A link to the auction. You can use this link when an item arrives to check it is exactly as advertised.

- **Item number:** The auction number for your records.

- **Auction sale date:** A convenient way to see whether your item is slow in shipping. After a week, dropping the seller an e-mail to check on the shipping status is good idea.

- **Sale price** and **quantity:** Helps you keep track of the money you've spent. Works with the totals in the tote board.

✔ **Action:** Displays different commands based on the status of your trans-action. You can click a link to pay for the item through PayPal, view the payment status on paid items, mark the item paid if you paid through other payment methods, or leave feedback after you receive the item and are satisfied that it's what you ordered.

✔ **Icons:** At the end of each item's listing are three icons that appear dimmed until the selected action is taken. A pound sign indicates whether you've paid for the item, a star indicates that you've left feedback, and a quote bubble indicates whether feedback has been left for you.

When you receive an item and leave feedback, click the box and then click the box next to it and press the Delete Selected Items button to remove the completed transactions from view.

Items I'm Watching

If you see an auction that makes you think, 'I don't want to bid on this at the moment, but I'd like to buy it if it's a bargain', one of the most powerful fea-tures of the My eBay area is just the tool to help you. Clicking the Watching link from the My eBay Views box brings you to the Items I'm Watching page (see Figure 3-7). This page lists each auction with a countdown (time left) timer, so you know exactly when the auction closes. When an auction on your watch list gets close to ending, you can swoop down and make the kill – if the price is right.

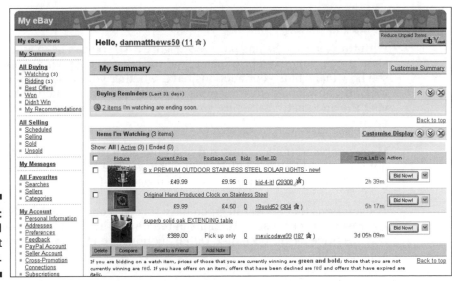

Figure 3-7:
Sit back and observe at My eBay.

Also a handy marketing tool, the Watching page allows you to store auctions from competitive sellers. That way, you can monitor the status of items similar to ones you plan to sell later and see whether the items are selling high or low, helping you decide whether now is a good time to sell.

You've probably seen the <u>Add to watch list</u> link at the top of each auction page. If you're watching items (eBay allows you to monitor 100 auctions at a time), you can see a notation on the page, indicating how many auctions you're currently watching.

Our number-one reason for using the watch list function is that it allows us to keep our bargain hunting quiet. Everybody – including the competition – knows when you're bidding on an item; nobody knows when you're watching the deals like a hawk. When you're looking for bargains to buy and resell, you may not want to tip off the competition by letting them know you're bidding.

All Selling

eBay.co.uk provides some smooth management tools on your Selling page. You can track items you currently have up for auction and items you've sold. This page is a quick way to get a snapshot of the value of your auctions, as they proceed. Although it isn't as good for marketing information (detailed counters are best – see Chapter 9), your Selling page is a pretty good way to tell at a glance how your items are faring.

Items I'm Selling

With the Items I'm Selling page (see Figure 3-8), you can keep an eye on your shop items, your fixed-price sales, and the progress of your auctions. You can see how many bids your auctions have, whether your reserves have been met, and how long before auctions close. By clicking an auction title, you can visit the auction to make sure your pictures are appearing or to check your counter.

Many people watch auctions and don't bid until the last minute, so you may not see a lot of bidding activity on your page. The # of Watchers feature can give you important information on the progress of your auctions.

The auctions that appear in green have received one or more bids (and met any reserves you've set). Auctions in red haven't received any bids or the set reserve price hasn't been met. Dutch auctions aren't colour-coded and appear in black.

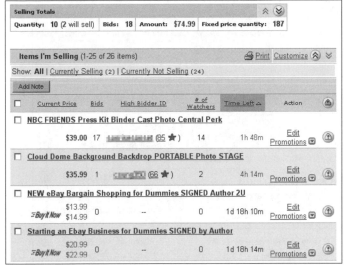

Figure 3-8:
The Items
I'm Selling
page at
My eBay.

At the top of the Items I'm Selling area, eBay lists the current price of all items, including bidding on items that haven't met your reserve. The total cash amount of the items that will sell when the auctions are over appears beneath these totals.

Items I've Sold

As you scroll down the All Selling page, you come to the Items I've Sold area. To avoid a lot of scrolling, you can reach an abbreviated version of this area (missing the detailed Selling Totals box) by clicking the Sold link in the Views box, under All Selling.

The Items I've Sold area keeps your sales in a concise place, as shown in Figure 3-9. You can use this area in lieu of fancy auction management software. If you're selling hundreds of items, your list will probably be too long to monitor individual auctions – but you can view the total current price of the items that will sell.

If you're selling more than 20 items a week, you may consider using eBay's Selling Manager to give you an even more complete auction management solution. See Chapter 9 for the low-down on how to make this tool work for you.

Figure 3-9:
The Items
I've Sold
page in
My eBay.

The Items I've Sold page has the following helpful features for completing your transactions:

- ✔ **Check box:** Click here to add a personal note to your record or to remove an item from your list.

- ✔ **Buyer's user ID** and **feedback rating:** The eBay ID of the winner of the sale. Click it to go to the User's Member Profile, where you can use eBay's e-mail server to contact the buyer.

- ✔ **Quantity:** If the sale was for multiple items, the number of items is displayed here.

- ✔ **Item title:** A direct link to the auction. You can click this link to check on your auction and see the other bidders, should you want to make a Second Chance Offer (see below).

- ✔ **Item number:** The auction number for your records.

- ✔ **Sale price:** The final selling price for your item.

- ✔ **Total price:** The final selling price plus the shipping amount.

- ✔ **Sale date:** Keep an eye on the end date to make sure you get your payment as agreed.

- ✔ **Action:** A hidden, drop-down menu is provided here that works with the icons to the left and offers links to various actions that you can take:

- **Mark paid:** If the customer hasn't paid using PayPal, you can indicate their method of payment (after you receive it).

- **View payment status:** See a copy of the payment receipt if the buyer paid using PayPal or a notation you inserted regarding other payment methods.

- **Print shipping label:** You can print a shipping label from here. See Chapter 14 for more professional options.

- **Leave feedback:** Leave feedback with a single click after you hear that the item arrived safely and your customer is happy. For more information on leaving feedback, check out the section 'Feedback: Your permanent record', later in this chapter.

- **Mark shipped**. After you ship the item, click here to indicate that it's on the way.

- **Second Chance Offer:** Click here to make a Second Chance Offer to one of your under-bidders if you have multiple items for sale.

- **Re-list:** Here you can re-list your item on the site.

✔ **Icons:** My eBay has several icons that appear dimmed until you perform an action with the Action command. You may also click the icons at the top of the list to sort your listings by actions completed, although most sellers prefer to keep the listings in the default chronological order.

- **Shopping cart:** The buyer has completed checkout (supplying a shipping address and planned payment method).

- **Pound sign:** The buyer has paid using PayPal, or you've used the drop-down menu to indicate that the buyer has paid with a different form of payment (such as a money order or a personal cheque).

- **Shipping box:** The item has shipped.

- **Star:** You've left feedback.

- **Comment bubble:** The buyer has left feedback. A plus sign (+) indicates a positive comment, and a minus sign (-) indicates a negative comment.

All Favourites

If you sell and have an interest in a few categories, look no further than the My eBay All Favourites page, which gives you some links for checking out what's hot and what's not. The All Favourites page helps you track trends and find some bargains to resell at eBay.co.uk.

Favourite Categories

eBay.co.uk allows you to store hot links for four categories. These links give you the chance to quickly check out the competition.

Before you list some auctions on a popular item, estimate the date and hour that other auctions selling that item will close. Then go into the category and check to make sure that your auction won't close during a flood of auctions for the same item. Nothing kills profits more than closing an auction in the middle of a series of auctions selling the same thing. You can watch the final values drop one at a time.

Favourite Searches

Another tool that comes in handy for sellers as well as buyers is My Favourite Searches (see Figure 3-10). You can list as many as 100 favourite searches; when you want to check one out, simply click the item link.

You can view saved searches, change them, delete them, or indicate that you'd like to receive e-mail notification when a new item is listed. To add an item to the list, run a search from any search bar on any eBay.co.uk page and click the <u>Add to Favourites</u> link that appears at the top of the search results. The next time you reload your My eBay All Favourites page, your new favourite will be listed.

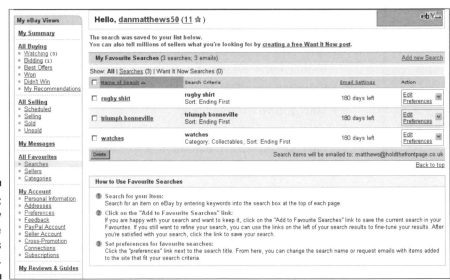

Figure 3-10: The My Favourite Searches page.

Keeping track of Favourite Searches is a valuable tool when you're looking for particular items to resell and want to find them at bargain prices. Take advantage of asterisks (wildcard characters) and alternate spellings so you can catch items with misspellings in the title – these tactics are your best bets for low prices. (See Chapter 7 for the low-down on the eBay.co.uk search engine and how it can help your sales.)

If you choose to receive e-mail when your search locates a new listing, you can request that you receive notification from 7 days to a year. You're allowed to receive new listing e-mails on 30 of your 100 searches. Just click the Edit Preferences link in the far-right column (refer to Figure 3-10). eBay sends its robot to check listings each night, so you'll get notification of a new listing the next morning.

Favourite Sellers

You can keep a list of people who sell items similar to what you sell using the Favourite Sellers tool. You can check up on these people and see what they're selling, when they're selling it, and for how much. You can also use this helpful tool to prevent you from listing an item right next to one of their auctions.

Favourite Sellers is also handy when your competition is selling an item that you plan to sell, but at a deeply discounted price. When that happens, don't offer your item until the competition sells theirs, at which time the price will probably go back up – supply and demand, remember? You can put wholesalers and liquidators under your Favourite Sellers, too, and search for job lots that you can resell at a profit.

To add a seller to your Favourite Sellers list, click the Add New Seller link on the right-hand side of the page. On the page that appears, type the seller's user ID. You may add a maximum of 30 sellers to your list.

My Account

Your eBay.co.uk account summary page (see Figure 3-11) lets you know how much you owe eBay and how much they will charge your credit card that month. This page is a quick and easy way to check your last invoice, payments and credits, and your account; all the links are located in one area.

You can also access your PayPal account to see, for example, when deposits were credited to your bank account. (For a complete picture of how to sign up and use PayPal, visit Chapter 13.)

Figure 3-11:
The My
Account
summary
page.

Personal Information

The Personal Information page holds all the links to your personal information at eBay.co.uk. This page is where you can change your e-mail address,
user ID, password, and credit card information, and edit or create your About
Me page. You can also change or access any registration or credit card information that you have on file at eBay.

The Personal Information page has a link for adding a wireless e-mail address
for your mobile phone or PDA. What a great idea: eBay can send End of
Auction notices right to your WAP-enabled mobile phone. Unfortunately,
sometimes these messages are sent out hours (days?) after the listing ends.
So don't count on always getting immediate updates.

eBay.co.uk Preferences

A nifty feature of the eBay Preferences page is the opportunity to customise
how you see your My eBay pages (see Figure 3-12). If you run many auctions,
you can show as many as 200 items on these pages.

Sign in preferences are special settings within My eBay that allow you to
determine how you remain signed in to eBay. To change your sign in preferences click the My eBay button at the top of any eBay page, then click the
Preferences tab of My eBay and click the <u>Show all</u> link. Then scroll down to
the Other general preferences section, in which you'll be offered the choice
to remain signed in permanently.

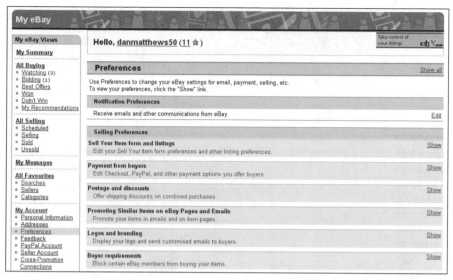

Figure 3-12:
Your eBay
Preferences
page.

The About Me Page

If you're on eBay.co.uk, you *need* an About Me page. eBay is a community and all eBay members are members of that community. Checking out the About Me page of people you conduct business with gives you an opportunity to get to know them. Because eBay is a cyberspace market, you have no other way to let prospective bidders know that you're a real person. Don't you buy things at some shops because you like the owners or people who work there? The About Me page takes a first step toward establishing a professional and trusted identity at eBay.

The About Me page enables you to personalise your business to prospective bidders. (See Figure 3-13 for an example.) Your About Me page also becomes your About the Seller page if you have an eBay shop.

An About Me page benefits you also when you buy. Sellers usually like to know about their bidders to build confidence in their trading partners, so if you've put up an About Me page, you're halfway there.

If you don't have an About Me page, put this book down and set one up immediately. This page doesn't have to be a work of art; just get something up there to tell the rest of the community who you are. You can always go back later and add to or redesign your About Me page.

Figure 3-13:
An example
of an About
Me page
from
member
Gadgets-
Ville.

When you plan your About Me page, consider adding the following and keep it succinct:

- Who you are and where you live.

- Your hobbies. If you collect things, here's where to let the world know.

- Whether you run your eBay business full time or part time and whether you have another career. This is more integral information about you; let the world know.

- The type of merchandise that your business revolves around. Promote it here; tell the reader why your merchandise and service are the best!

- Your most recent feedback and a list of your current auctions.

To create your page, click the <u>Me</u> icon next to any user's name, scroll to the bottom of the About Me page that appears, find the line that reads 'To create your own About Me page, <u>click here</u>', and click. You can also click the <u>About Me</u> link on the Personal Information page at My eBay; or go to the following:

```
http://cgi3.ebay.co.uk/ws/eBayISAPI.dll?AboutMeLogin
```

Then follow the simple preformatted template for your first page and work from there.

eBay.co.uk Seller Services

Most eBay.co.uk users don't know the extent of eBay's seller-specific services. And sometimes sellers are so involved with their auctions that they don't take the time to find out about new helper tools. So we've gone deep into the eBay pond to dig up a few excellent tools to help you with your online business. Even if you've used some of these tools before, consider revisiting them because eBay.co.uk regularly implements changes.

Bidder-management tools

Did you know that you don't have to accept bids from just anyone? Although you can include notices in your auction description attempting to qualify bidders ahead of time, this action doesn't always prevent undesirables from bidding on your auction. Alas, part of the business is watching your bidders. With bidder management tools, you can save yourself a good deal of grief.

Cancelling bids

You may have any number of reasons for wanting to cancel someone's bid. Perhaps an international bidder has bid in an auction in which you clearly state you don't ship overseas. Here are a few more legitimate reasons for cancelling a bid:

- ✔ The bidder contacts you to back out of the bid; choosing to be nice about it, you let him or her out of the deal.

- ✔ Your bidder has several negative feedbacks and hasn't gone through with other transactions that he or she has won.

- ✔ You're unable to verify the bidder's identity through e-mail or the phone.

- ✔ You need to cancel the auction (see following tip).

We don't recommend cancelling an auction unless you absolutely have to because doing so is just bad business. People rely on your auctions being up for the stated amount of time. They may be planning to bid at the last minute, or may just want to watch the action for a while. You may lose potential buyers by ending your listing early.

For whatever reason you're cancelling someone's bid, first e-mail that person and clearly explain why you're doing so. Your bid cancellation appears in the auction's bidding history and becomes part of the auction's official record. For that reason, we recommend that you leave a concise, unemotional, one-line explanation on the cancellation form as to why you've cancelled the bid.

To get to the bid cancellation form, start on your My eBay All Selling page and scroll to Selling Links. You can also get to the cancellation form directly by typing the following in your browser:

```
http://offer.ebay.co.uk/ws/eBayISAPI.dll?CancelBidShow
```

Ending your listing early

You may decide to end a listing early for any number of reasons. If any bids are on your auction before you end it, you are duty-bound to sell to the highest bidder. So before ending an auction early, politely e-mail everyone in your bidder list, explaining why you're cancelling bids and closing the auction. If an error in the item's description is forcing you to take this action, let your bidders know whether you're planning to re-list the item with the correct information.

After you e-mail all the bidders, you must then cancel their bids by using the bid cancellation form; for the link to this form, see the preceding section, 'Cancelling bids'.

Only after cancelling all bids can you go ahead and close your auction. To close your auction, use the more link at the bottom of your Selling Links box to get to the Managing Your Items box. Click the link there that says End My Listing Early. You can also go directly to

```
http://offer.ebay.co.uk/ws/eBayISAPI.dll?EndingMyAuction&s
              PageName=STRK:MESRL:005
```

Following are some legitimate reasons for closing your auction:

- ✔ **You no longer want to sell the item.** Your account may be subject to a 'Non-Selling Seller' warning unless you really have a good reason. (See Chapter 4 for more details.)

- ✔ **An error occurred in the minimum bid or reserve amount.** Perhaps your daughter said that she really loves that doll and you'd better get some good money for it, but you started the auction at £1.00 with no reserve.

- ✔ **The listing has a major error in it.** Maybe you misspelled a critical keyword in the title.

- ✔ **The item was somehow lost or broken.** Your dog ate it?

Blocking buyers

If you don't want certain buyers bidding on your auctions, you can remove their capability to do so. Setting up a list of bidders that you don't want to do business with is legal at eBay.co.uk. If someone that you block tries to bid on your auction, the bid doesn't go through. A message displays notifying the person that he or she is not able to bid on the listing and to contact the seller for more information.

You can block as many as 1000 users from bidding on your auctions. However, we recommend that you use this option only when absolutely necessary. Situations – and people – change, and you're best off to try to clear up problems with particular bidders.

You can reinstate a bidder at any time by going to the Buyer Blocking box at

```
http://offer.ebay.co.uk/ws/eBayISAPI.dll?BidderBlockLogin
```

Within the Buyer Blocking box, you can then delete the bidder's user ID and reinstate him or her.

Pre-approving bidders

Suppose that you're selling a big-ticket item and want to pre-qualify your bidders. Although eBay gives you the tools, you still have to do the research to determine whether you deem particular bidders trustworthy enough to bid on your special auction.

In your auction, state that bidders must pre-qualify by sending you an e-mail claiming their intent to bid. As you receive e-mails and approve bidders' intentions, you can build your pre-approved bidder list.

Your pre-approved bidder list is applicable only on an auction-by-auction basis. Using pre-approved bidders means that only bidders in the listings you indicate must be pre-approved. To use this feature, you must supply eBay.co.uk with the auction number. You can add approved bidders right up to the close of the auction. Access the form and type in the pre-approved bidders at

```
http://offer.ebay.co.uk/ws/eBayISAPI.
        dll?PreApproveBidders
```

If someone who isn't pre-approved tries to bid on your auction, eBay asks that bidder to contact you by e-mail before placing a bid. After you investigate the bidder to your satisfaction and are comfortable with that person bidding on your auction, you can add the bidder's name to your pre-approved bidder list for that auction.

Using the pre-approved bidder service can give you peace of mind when you're selling valuable items. But it also excludes a large chunk of potential customers who'll have to jump through hoops just to place a bid. We recommend using it for big-ticket items only.

Buyer Requirements

A new feature on eBay.co.uk, entitled Buyer Requirements, might be more useful to those of you who are selective about who gets to bid on your items. Found under the Seller Preferences section of My eBay, Buyer Requirements allows you to block bidders for a range of offences, including:

- ✔ Having a negative feedback score
- ✔ Having received two unpaid item strikes
- ✔ Not having a PayPal account

You can also block bidders who are unfortunate enough to live in a country that you don't post to or who are the winning bidder on a large number of your items. These caveats can be reversed at any time – should you have a change of heart.

Feedback: Your permanent record

Your eBay.co.uk feedback is meant to follow you forever at eBay. If you change your user ID, the feedback information is there; if you change your e-mail address, it's there.

When you click the feedback number next to a user's ID, the user's eBay ID card (see Figure 3-14) is displayed. The information shown tells you a lot about your bidder.

Figure 3-14: The eBay.co.uk Feedback page, with an overall profile and an ID card, summarising recent comments.

The most obvious tip-off to someone's feedback is the star you see next to the user ID. Different coloured stars are awarded as people reach milestones in their feedback ratings. To decipher the star colours and see what they mean, click the <u>help</u> link, and type the word *star*.

Your feedback means a great deal to people who visit your auctions. By glancing at your feedback page, they can see

- ✔ Whether you're an experienced eBay user
- ✔ Your eBay history
- ✔ When you started at eBay.co.uk
- ✔ How many bid retractions you've had in the past six months

This is valuable information for both the buyer and the seller because it helps to evaluate whether you're the type of person who would make a responsible trading partner.

Worried about negative feedback? Two possible ways exist for getting negative feedback expunged from your record. You can file for mediation with SquareTrade (see Chapter 4 on how to do this), or if both you and the other person are in agreement, you can file for Mutual Feedback Withdrawal by going to:

```
http://feedback.ebay.co.uk/ws/eBayISAPI.dll?MFWRequest
```

Enter the item number and continue filing the form. If the person who posted the feedback agrees to remove the negative feedback, eBay will oblige.

You can also apply to remove negative feedback in exceptional circumstance (for example, profanity) - see `http://pages.ebay.co.uk/help/policies/feedback-abuse-withdrawal.html` for details.

Leaving feedback

Everyone in the eBay.co.uk community is honour-bound to leave feedback. Sometimes when you've had a truly dreadful experience, you still hate to leave negative or neutral feedback, but if you don't, you're not helping anyone. The point of feedback is not to show what a great person you are, but to show future sellers or bidders where the rotten apples lie. So, when leaving feedback, be truthful and unemotional, and state just the facts.

Feedback is important, so leave some for every transaction you take part in. If a week has passed since you shipped an item, and you haven't heard from the bidder or seen any new feedback, drop that bidder an e-mail. Write 'Thanks for your purchase. Are you happy with the item?' Also emphasise that you'll be glad to leave positive feedback after you hear a reply, and ask for the same in return.

Never leave feedback on a sale until you're absolutely, positively sure that the buyer has received the product and is happy with the deal. Many inexperienced sellers leave feedback the minute they get their money, but experience can teach them that it ain't over till it's over. A package can get lost or damaged, or the bidder may be unhappy for some reason. A buyer may also want to return an item for no good reason, turning a seemingly smooth transaction into a nightmare. You get only one feedback per transaction, so use it wisely. However, you can follow up your feedback with an additional comment if something goes wrong.

eBay.co.uk provides so many different links to leave feedback that we could probably write an entire chapter on it. But we don't want you to fall asleep while reading, so here are only the most convenient methods:

- ✔ Go to your auction page and click the <u>Leave Feedback</u> link, which appears on the right.

- ✔ Click the number (in parentheses) next to the other user's name. When you're on that user's feedback page, click the <u>Leave Feedback</u> link.

- ✔ Click the <u>Leave Feedback</u> link next to the completed sale on your My eBay page.

- ✔ Visit the feedback forum (this link shows up on the bottom of every page) and click the link that shows you all pending feedback for the past 90 days. If you fall behind in leaving feedback, this is a super-fast way to catch up.

Responding to feedback

You may occasionally get feedback that you feel compelled to respond to although it is advisable not to respond in a negative manner. Did you know that you could do so? If the feedback is neutral or negative, cover yourself by explaining the situation for future bidders to see.

If you receive a negative feedback rating, a well-meaning admission of guilt can work. You can say something like, 'Unfortunately, shipping was delayed and I regret the situation'. Prospective bidders can see that you've addressed the problem instead of just letting it go.

To respond to feedback, follow these steps:

1. **In the My eBay Views box on your My eBay page, click the <u>Feedback</u> link under My Account.**

2. **On the feedback page, find Go to Feedback Forum at the top of the page, and click the <u>Reply to Feedback Received</u> link.**

   The Review and Respond to Feedback Comments Left for You page appears, as shown in Figure 3-15.

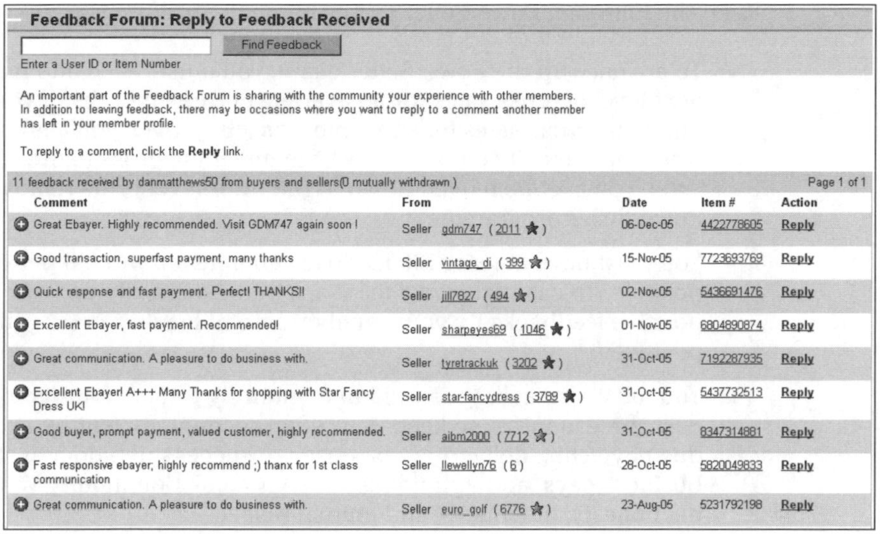

Figure 3-15:
Review and
respond
to your
feedbacks.

3. **Scroll to find the feedback comment that you want to respond to and click the Respond link.**

4. **Type your response, and then click the Leave Response button.**

The eBay.co.uk PowerSeller programme

We're sure you've seen that giant PowerSeller logo on auctions that you browse. eBay.co.uk PowerSellers represent the largest gross sales users at eBay. The following table outlines the requirements for becoming a PowerSeller:

PowerSeller Level	Gross Merchandise Volume (GMV)	Quantity of Items sold
Bronze	£750	100
Silver	£1,500	200
Gold	£6,000	300
Platinum	£15,000	400
Titanium	£95,000	500

Keep the following PowerSeller points in mind:

- To advance up the PowerSeller chain, you must reach and maintain the next level of gross sales for an average of three months. If you miss your minimum gross sales for three months, eBay gives you a grace period. After that time, if you don't meet the minimum gross figures for your level, you may be moved down to the prior level or be removed from the PowerSeller programme.

- You must have at least 100 feedback comments, with 98 per cent of them positive. To calculate your feedback percentage, divide your number of positive feedbacks by your number of total feedbacks (negatives plus positives).

- You must also average a minimum monthly total of four listings in the past three months, so keep your eBay account current by avoiding over-due payments, delivering responses to successful bidders within three business days, and upholding the eBay.co.uk Community Values, including honesty, timeliness, and mutual respect.

PowerSellers enjoy many benefits, particularly dedicated customer support as the following table indicates:

PowerSeller Level	Personal Phone	Fast Priority Email Support	Access to Dedicated Support Board	Invitations to eBay.co.uk PowerSeller Events
Bronze	no	yes	yes	yes
Silver	no	yes	yes	yes
Gold	yes	yes	yes	yes
Platinum	yes	yes	yes	yes
Titanium	yes	yes	yes	yes

Other benefits include a dedicated PowerSeller newsletter, a chance to be featured as a 'business of the month', and free business templates.

The best thing about being a PowerSeller is the fantastic level of customer service you receive, called Priority eSupport. When a PowerSeller dashes off an e-mail to a special customer service department, a reply comes back at the speed of light.

eBay.co.uk doesn't require you to show the PowerSeller logo in your descriptions when you attain that level. Some PowerSellers don't include the logo in their auctions because they'd rather be perceived as regular people at eBay. If you do want to add the PowerSeller logo instructions can be found at:

```
http://pages.ebay.co.uk/help/basics/
           f-powersellers.html#G10
```

eBay.co.uk auction software

eBay.co.uk has developed a fantastic software program called Turbo Lister, which is free and downloadable from the site. eBay also has an online Selling Manager to manage your auctions. For a breakdown of these software products and others to ease the seller's burden, skip to Chapter 9.

eBay.co.uk fraud protection

The minute an auction payment hits the postbox, or the moment that a winner pays with an online payment service, eBay.co.uk covers the buyer with its Standard Purchase Protection Programme. Most items bought on eBay are covered for up to £120 (minus £15 to cover processing costs). The maximum reimbursement for any claim is £105. For example:

- ✔ If the item price is £300, you are eligible for £105.
- ✔ If the item price is £100, you are eligible for £85.
- ✔ If the item price is £16, you are eligible for £1.

The Standard Purchase Protection Programme covers only fraud, not lost or damaged packages. The eBay.co.uk fraud protection programme covers eBay buyers only when they're defrauded, the item is never shipped, or the item is significantly different from the auction description. The policy does *not* cover sellers for anything – so don't ship that item until you're positive the cheque has cleared!

When you get down to the nuts and bolts of the Standard Purchase Protection Programme, it has a lot of ifs. Buyers can apply only if they did not pay with cash. Bidders, if they paid by credit card, need to first apply to their credit card companies to see whether they're covered through them. The insurance will not cover the bidder if the seller has a negative feedback rating. The bidder also can't file any more than three claims within a six-month period.

An example of fraud

Owing to the phenomenal success of eBay.co.uk, fraudsters are making a lucrative trade by ripping off both buyers and sellers. Watch out for e-mails (including ones received at work or on private non-eBay related accounts) threatening to suspend your access to eBay or PayPal if you don't update your details. People duped by the scams are tricked into inputting addresses and bank account details which are then used to fraudulently extract funds. These dodgy e-mails may read like this:

Dear valued eBay member: We regret to inform you that your eBay account has been suspended due to concerns we have for the safety and integrity of the eBay community. Please take 5 to 10 minutes out of your online experience and update your personal records. After doing so, you will not run into any future problems with the online service. Please update your records by 10 June. After you update your account records, your eBay session will not be interrupted and will continue as normal.

eBay will almost never contact you out of the blue, and you should always make contact through the site rather than clicking on links provided in any email. If you are worried or need to know more follow this link:

```
http://pages.ebay.co.uk/help/
    confidence/isgw-account-
    theft-spoof.html
```

eBay.co.uk education

eBay.co.uk offers many forms of training and education. No matter how advanced you are, going to eBay University and taking a refresher course on the basics can be fun. You can also find some great downloadable guides and online interactive tutorials as you make your way through eBay. Take a moment to watch these tutorials – you may just see one or two new features that you didn't know about. More information about eBay education is available at:

```
http://pages.ebay.co.uk/education/
```

eBay.co.uk Business Centre

For budding professionals, eBay.co.uk has created a new Business Centre, where you can find lots of great ideas to turn your hobby into a thriving business. Here you can find out how to register your business, set up a shop, and even get the low-down on global trading. Check out the Business Centre at:

```
http://pages.ebay.co.uk/businesscentre/
```

eBay.co.uk business registration service

eBay.co.uk has launched a new business registration system for smaller businesses to sign up to sell on the site. The service enables business owners to register their company details and payments details. (Until recently, you could only register a named individual's details.) The service also offers dedicated eBay customer support for registered business users.

Chapter 4

Practising Safe Selling

....

....

*T*he world abounds in *shoulds*. You *should* do this and you *should* do that. We don't know who's in charge of the *shoulds*, but certain things just make life work better. You may or may not take any of the advice on these pages, but they'll make your eBay.co.uk business thrive with a minimum of anguish.

In the real world, you have to take responsibility for your own actions. If you buy a DVD player for £25 from some guy selling them out of the back of a lorry, who do you have to blame when you take it home and it doesn't work? You get what you pay for, and you have no consumer protection from the seller of the possibly 'hot' DVD. Responsible consumerism is every buyer's job. People sue when they feel ripped off, but if you stay clean in your online business, you'll keep clean.

eBay.co.uk is a community, and the community thrives on the following five basic values:

✔ People are basically good.

✔ Everyone has something to contribute.

✔ An honest, open environment can bring out the best in people.

✔ Recognise and respect everyone as a unique individual.

✔ Treat others the way that you want to be treated.

eBay is committed to these values, and it says so on its Web site. eBay believes that community members should 'honour these values – whether buying, selling, or chatting'. So *should* everyone.

Is What You Want to Sell Legal?

Although eBay is based in California and therefore must abide by California law, sellers do business all over the world. Additionally, items sold at eBay.co.uk must abide by UK laws. As a seller, you're ultimately responsible for the legality of the items you sell and the way that you transact business on eBay. Yes, you're able to sell thousands of different items on eBay. But do you know what you aren't allowed to sell on eBay.co.uk?

The eBay User Agreement outlines all eBay rules and regulations regarding what you can and can't sell as well as all aspects of doing business at eBay. If you haven't read the User Agreement recently, do so; you can find it at the following address:

```
pages.ebay.co.uk/help/policies/user-agreement.html
```

These policies can change from time to time. As an active seller, make sure that you're notified of any changes. To request that you be notified when eBay makes changes to the User Agreement, as well as to control any correspondence you receive from eBay, follow these steps:

1. **In the My eBay Views section of the My eBay page, click the <u>eBay Preferences</u> link under My Account. Click the <u>Edit</u> link, next to Notification Preferences.**

   Alternatively you can go to the following address:
   ```
   cgi4.ebay.co.uk/ws/eBayISAPI.dll?OptinLoginShow
   ```

2. **Sign in with your user ID and password.**

   The Notification Preferences page appears.

3. **Scroll down to the Legal and Policy Notifications area (see Figure 4-1), and check or uncheck any option you want to invoke.**

   To receive important information that may affect how you run your auctions, click the User Agreement Changes option and Privacy Policy Changes option.

If you don't have a firm grasp of the rules and regulations for listing auctions, check out Chapter 2. But in addition to knowing the rules for listing items, you must consider the items themselves. In this section, we detail the three categories of items to be wary of: prohibited, questionable, and infringing. Some items are banned, full stop; others fall in a grey area. You're responsible for what you sell, so you need to know what's legal and what's not.

You may think *giving away* a regulated or banned item as a bonus item with your auction is okay. Think again. Even giving away such items for free doesn't save you from potential legal responsibility.

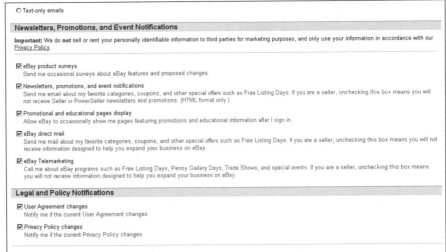

Figure 4-1:
The Legal
e-mails
area of the
Notification
Preferences
form.

Prohibited items

A *prohibited item* is banned from sale at eBay.co.uk. You can't sell a prohibited item under any circumstance. Take a look at the following list. A little common sense tells you there's good reason for not selling these items, including liability issues for the seller (what if you sold alcohol to a minor? – doing so is against the law).

The following is a list of items prohibited at the time of writing, so don't try to sell this stuff at eBay.co.uk.

- ✔ Aeroplane tickets
- ✔ Alcohol
- ✔ Animals and wildlife products
- ✔ Catalogue and URL sales
- ✔ Counterfeit currency and stamps
- ✔ Counterfeit and trademarked items
- ✔ Credit cards
- ✔ Drugs and drug paraphernalia
- ✔ Embargoed items, and items from prohibited countries
- ✔ Eurostar tickets
- ✔ Firearms and ammunition

- ✔ Fireworks
- ✔ Franking machines
- ✔ Football tickets
- ✔ Government IDs, licences and uniforms
- ✔ Human parts and remains
- ✔ Lockpicking devices
- ✔ Lottery tickets
- ✔ Mailing lists and personal information
- ✔ Offensive material
- ✔ Prescription drugs and materials
- ✔ Recalled items
- ✔ Satellite, digital, and cable TV decoders
- ✔ Shares and securities
- ✔ Stolen items
- ✔ Surveillance equipment
- ✔ Tobacco and tobacco products
- ✔ Travel vouchers
- ✔ Unlocking software

Check the following address for updates:

```
pages.ebay.co.uk/help/sell/questions/prohibited-items.html
```

Questionable items

A *questionable item* is iffy – determining whether or not you can sell it is tricky. Under certain circumstances, you may be able to list the item for sale at eBay.co.uk. To fully understand when and if you can list a questionable item, visit the links highlighted in Table 4-1. ***Note:*** Unless otherwise shown, all URLs listed in Table 4-1 begin with `pages.ebay.co.uk/help/community/png-`

Table 4-1	Questionable Items and Where to Find the Rules Regulating Them
Can I Sell This?	*Go Here to Find Out**
Adults only	pages.ebay.co.uk/help/policies/mature-audiences.html
Artifacts	pages.ebay.co.uk/help/policies/artifacts.html
Autographed items	pages.ebay.co.uk/help/policies/autographs.html
Batteries	pages.ebay.co.uk/help/policies/hazardous-materials.html
British titles	pages.ebay.co.uk/help/policies/britishtitles.html
CFC and HCFC refrigerants	pages.ebay.co.uk/help/policies/freon.html
Contracts and tickets	pages.ebay.co.uk/help/policies/contracts.html
Food	pages.ebay.co.uk/help/policies/food.html
Hazardous, restricted, and perishable Items	pages.ebay.co.uk/help/policies/hazardous-materials.html
Pesticides	pages.ebay.co.uk/help/policies/pesticides.html
Plants and seeds	pages.ebay.co.uk/help/policies/plantsandseeds.html
Police-related items	pages.ebay.co.uk/help/policies/police.html
Pre-sales listings	pages.ebay.co.uk/help/policies/pre-sale.html
Slot machines	pages.ebay.co.uk/help/community/png-slot.html

(continued)

Table 4-1 *(continued)*

Can I Sell This?	Go Here to Find Out*
Used clothing	pages.ebay.co.uk/help/policies/ used-clothing.html
Used medical devices	pages.ebay.co.uk/help/policies/ medical-devices.html
Weapons and knives	pages.ebay.co.uk/help/policies/ weapons.html

When alcohol becomes collectable

Many people collect rare and antique bottles of wine and other alcohol. Korbel bottles have featured artwork by designer Nicole Miller and comedienne Whoopi Goldberg as well as designs by Tony Bennett, Frank Sinatra, and Jane Seymour. People also collect Jack Daniels bottles, decanters and miniatures that are even more valuable when they're full. You *can* sell these on eBay.co.uk as long as you fulfil the following requirements:

✔ The value of the auctioned item is in the collectable container, not its contents. Thus bottles of wine are not permitted because their value is based on the wine in the bottle, and not the bottle itself.

✔ The auction description should state that the container has not been opened, but that any incidental contents are not intended for consumption.

✔ The item must not be available at any retail outlet, and the container must have a value that substantially exceeds the current retail price of the alcohol in the container.

✔ Sellers should take steps to ensure that the buyer of these collectables is of lawful age in both the buyer's and the seller's jurisdictions (generally 18 years old in the UK and Republic of Ireland and 21 years old in the US).

✔ Buyers and sellers must ensure that the sale complies with all applicable laws and delivery regulations in carrying out the transaction.

The Chanel-style purse

A lady once listed a quilted leather women's purse that had a gold chain strap, which she described as a Chanel-style purse. Within two hours, she received an Informational alert from the eBay listing police. She described the item to the best of her ability, but found that it became a potentially infringing item. Her use of the brand name *Chanel* caused her auction to come under the violation of keyword spamming (see more on that in the section 'Potentially Infringing items').

In its informational alert, eBay described the violation:

'Keyword spamming is the practice of adding words, including brand names, which do not directly describe the item you are selling. The addition of these words may

not have been intentional, but including them in this manner diverts members to your listing inappropriately.'

Ooops! You can see how her ingenuous listing was actually a violation of policy. Think twice before you add brand names to your auction description. Thankfully, the eBay police judge each violation on a case-by-case basis. Because her record is clear, she merely got a reprimand. Had her violation been more deliberate, she might have been suspended.

To see the Chanel (USA) statement on violations, visit the company's About Me page. The violations apply to many items that may be listed at eBay:

```
members.ebay.com/aboutme/
    chanelusa/
```

Potentially infringing items

Potentially infringing items follow a slippery slope. If you list a potentially infringing item, you may infringe on existing copyrights, trademarks, registrations, or the like. These items are prohibited for your own protection.

Items falling under the potentially infringing category are generally copyrighted or trademarked items, such as software, promotional items, and games. Even using a brand name in your auction as part of a description (known as keyword spamming) may get you into trouble.

Keyword spamming manipulates the eBay.co.uk search engine by including an unrelated item in the listing for a copyrighted or trademarked item, and then diverting bidders to an auction of other merchandise. This practice is frustrating for the person trying to use the search engine to find a particular item and unfair to members who've properly listed their items.

Keyword spamming can take many forms – some merely mislead the prospective bidder while others are legal infringements. A few of the most common keyword spamming tactics are:

- ✔ Superfluous brand names in the title or item description
- ✔ Using something like 'not brand X' in the title or item description
- ✔ Improper trademark usage
- ✔ Lists of keywords
- ✔ Hidden text – white text on a white background or hidden text in HTML code. The white text resides in the auction HTML, so it shows up in the search but is not visible to the naked eye. Sneaky, eh?
- ✔ Drop-down boxes

To get the latest on eBay.co.uk's keyword spamming policy, go to

    pages.ebay.co.uk/help/policies/keyword-spam.html

Repeating various un-trademarked keywords can get you in trouble as well. eBay.co.uk permits the use of as many as five synonyms when listing an item for sale. A permissible example of using words that mean the same thing might be: Purse, handbag, pocketbook, satchel, and bag. Adding many un-trademarked keywords causes the auction to come up in more searches.

Trading Violations

Both buyers and sellers can commit trading violations by attempting to manipulate the outcome of an auction or sale. Many of the violations aren't necessarily buyer- or seller-exclusive but apply to both. Regardless of the nature of a violation, such behaviour violates every member of the eBay community.

As a valued member of the community, you have some responsibility to look out for such violations – so that eBay.co.uk continues to be a safe community in which to do business. If you see a violation, report it immediately to the eBay Security Centre (see the section 'eBay.co.uk's Safety Centre', later in this chapter). In this section, we detail many common violations so that you can be on the outlook for them – and we'll just assume that you're not committing any yourself.

The eBay.co.uk Verified Rights Owners programme

eBay.co.uk can't possibly check every auction for authenticity. But to help protect trademarked items, eBay formed the Verified Rights Owners (VeRO) programme.

Trademark and copyright owners expend large amounts of energy to develop and maintain control over the quality of their products. If you buy a 'designer' purse from a bloke on the street for £20, it's probably counterfeit, so don't go selling it on eBay.

eBay works with VeRO programme members to educate the community about such items. eBay work also with verified owners of trademarks and copyrights to remove auctions that infringe on their products. If eBay doesn't close a suspicious or blatantly infringing auction, both you and eBay are liable for the violation.

To become a member of the VeRO programme, the owners of copyrights and trademarks must supply eBay.co.uk with proof of ownership. To view the VeRO programme information and download the application for membership, go to

```
pages.ebay.co.uk/vero/
```

Note: eBay co-operates with the law and may give your name and street address to a VeRO programme member.

To view a list of other VeRO members' About Me pages, go to

```
pages.ebay.co.uk/vero/
      participants.html
```

As part of the eBay community, you need to be a watchdog and protect other users. Don't feel like a squealer if you make a report. Remember that just one rotten apple can spoil the basket. So if you see a violation, do your duty and report it.

When the competition doesn't play fair

Unfortunately, you may sometimes encounter non-community-minded sellers who interfere with your auctions or sales. This interference can take several forms, such as sellers who illegally drive up bids or 'steal' bidders.

Again, should you fall victim to bad deeds, report the bad-deed-doer's actions immediately. (Check out the section 'Taking Action: What to Do When Someone Breaks the Rules', later in this chapter). eBay.co.uk will take some sort of disciplinary action. Penalties range from formal warnings and temporary suspension to indefinite suspension. eBay reviews each incident on a case-by-case basis before passing judgement.

Shill bidding

Shill bidding is the practice of placing a bid on an item to artificially inflate the final value. This practice is the bane of every eBay user (whether buyer or seller) and undermines community trust. Technically shill bidding is a criminal offence and not something to be toyed with!

The practice of shill bidding has been a part of auctions from their beginnings. To prevent the suspicion of shill bidding, honest eBay users in the same family, those who share the same computer, and people who work or live together should not bid on each other's items.

Should you ever even dream of participating in any sort of auction manipulation, we urge you to think twice. You may think you're smart by using another e-mail address and username, but doing so doesn't work. Every time you log onto your ISP, your connection carries an IP address. So no matter what name or computer you use, your connection identifies you. eBay can use this number to track you through its site.

Shill bidders are fairly easy to recognise, even for the eBay user who isn't privy to things such as IP addresses. By checking a bidder's auction history, you can easily determine a user's bidding pattern. A bidder who constantly bids up items and never wins is suspicious.

Spurious sellers often employ shill bidding to increase the number of bids on an item to more quickly make it a hot item. This increased bidding doesn't mean that all hot auctions are products of shill bidding, it means that hot auctions are desirable and pull in lots of extra bids (due to the herd mentality). Rogues want all their auctions to be hot and may take any road to ensure that they are.

Transaction interference

Have you ever received an e-mail from an eBay.co.uk seller offering you an item that you're currently bidding on for a lower price? This practice is called *transaction interference*, and it can prevent sellers from gaining the highest bid possible.

Transaction interference also occurs when a troublemaker who has it 'in' for a particular seller e-mails bidders participating in the seller's current auctions to warn them away from completing the auction. Tales of woe and much bitterness usually accompany such e-mails. If a bidder has a problem with a seller, that bidder can and should file a report with eBay.co.uk and leave negative feedback for that seller. This e-mail barrage can potentially fall under the category of libel and isn't a safe tactic to practise. If you receive an e-mail like this, ignore its message but report it to eBay.co.uk.

Transaction interception

They say the criminal mind is complex; when it comes to transaction interception, it certainly is! *Transaction interception* occurs when an eBay.co.uk scoundrel keeps track of closing auctions and then, when the auction is finished, e-mails the winner as if the scoundrel were the seller. The e-mail often looks official and is congratulatory, politely asking for payment. Interceptors usually use a PO box for such mischief. This behaviour goes beyond being a trading violation – these people are stealing.

To protect yourself from such miscreants accept payments through a payment service, such as PayPal, by using a <u>Pay Now</u> link. For more about setting up a payment service account, see Chapter 13.

Fee avoidance

Fee avoidance is the practice of evading paying eBay.co.uk fees by going around the eBay system. There are many ways to commit fee avoidance – sometimes without even realising it. Read this section carefully so that you don't commit this violation by mistake.

You're guilty of fee avoidance if you:

- ✔ Use information that you receive from an eBay member's contact information in an attempt to sell a listed item off the system.

- ✔ Close your auction early because a user e-mails you offering to buy an item you are auctioning, and you accept the offer.

- ✔ End your auction before it legally closes by cancelling bids, to sell the item to someone who e-mails you with an offer of a higher price.

- ✔ Use an eBay member's contact information to sell an item from one of your closed auctions off the eBay site in which the reserve wasn't met.

- ✔ Offer duplicates of your item to the unsuccessful bidders in your auction, unless you use the Second Chance option.

Take a look at the discussion on listing policies in Chapter 2 for listing violations that also may fall into this category.

Non-selling seller

Refusing to accept payment from the winning bidder and refusing to complete the transaction is simply wrong. This practice is very, very bad form!

You are legally and morally bound to complete any transaction into which you enter.

Baaad bidders

Nothing can ruin a seller's day like a difficult bidder, such as someone who asks questions that are clearly answered already in your auction description or someone who asks you to close the auction so that he or she can buy the item offline. Honestly – you'd think no one read the rules. From the non-paying bidder to the unwelcome and shady, you may, unfortunately, encounter the buyers we describe here.

Bid shielding

When two or more eBay.co.uk members work together to defraud you out of real auction profits, they're guilty of *bid shielding*. One member, let's call him Joe, places an early bid on your item, with a proxy bid. Immediately, the accomplice, (we'll call her Sophie), places a very high proxy bid to drive the auction to the max or beyond. If legitimate bidders bid, they only ratchet up the second bidder's bid – they don't outbid the high bidder's proxy. When the auction is coming to a close, the high bidder (Sophie) retracts her bid, thereby granting the winning bid to her mate (Joe), the original low bidder. The ultimate point of bid shielding is that it increases the bid to such a high level that normal bidding by authentic bidders is discouraged.

This illegal bidding process is used not only to get bargain-priced merchandise but also to drive bidders away from competitors' auctions by artificially inflating the high bid level. The clever people at eBay.co.uk have realised this and have decided to ban bid retractions within 12 hours of the auction's end. It's not a perfect remedy but it is, at least, making it trickier for the fraudsters.

Unwelcome bidder

In the auction business, you may think that you couldn't possibly regard anyone as an *unwelcome bidder*, but you just might. Remember how you painstakingly explain your terms in your auction description? That information is lost on people who don't take the time to read those descriptions or choose to ignore them. Consider the following points:

- ✔ You state in your description that you ship only within the United Kingdom, but you see a bidder with an e-mail address that ends in .jp (Japan), .au (Australia), .ie (Ireland), – or whatever. E-mail that bidder immediately to emphasise your domestic-only shipping policy.

✔ You state in your description that you don't want bidders who have a negative feedback rating or more than one negative rating in a six-month time span, but someone fitting that description bids on your auction. You may want to contact this bidder, who may be new to the eBay system and may not understand the legal connotations of making a bid.

✔ You decide to cancel a bid for one of the previous two reasons, but the bidder continues to bid on your auction.

✔ You block a particular bidder (see Chapter 3), but the bidder uses a secondary account to bid on your auctions.

If you encounter any of the previous situations, contact eBay.co.uk immediately to report the unwelcome bidder; see the section 'eBay.co.uk's Safety Centre', later in this chapter.

Alternatively, you can use the Buyer Preferences function, which allows you to decide who can bid for your items. It's located under Seller Preferences in My eBay.

Using Buyer Preferences you can block buyers for a range of reasons including those who are:

✔ Registered in countries that you don't post to

✔ Have a a negative feedback score

✔ Have received two Unpaid Item strikes in the last 30 days

✔ Don't have a PayPal account

Non-paying buyers

A non-paying buyer (NPB) is simply not tolerated at eBay.co.uk. eBay reminds all bidders, before they place a bid, that 'If you are the winning bidder, you will enter into a legally binding contract to purchase the item from the seller'. You'd think that reminder was clear enough, but sadly, many people out there think bidding and buying on eBay is a game. If you see a high bidder on your auction who has a very low or negative feedback, dropping a line reiterating eBay policy never hurts.

How you, as a seller, communicate with the high bidder is also important. Often a well-written, congenial, businesslike e-mail can cajole the basically good person into sending payment. To see some samples of reminder e-mails that get the job done, visit Chapter 12.

We've been selling and buying at eBay for nearly 10 years. During that time, we've had to file only five non-paying buyer alerts (see the steps a bit later in this section). Non-paying buyers tend to bid on certain types of items. After you've seen some NPBs, you'll get an idea of which items they tend to bid on. Our NPB items? A gas-powered scooter, a video game, and some teletubbies. Serious collector or business items have never been an issue.

To reduce the number of non-paying buyers, eBay has established that all eBay users are indefinitely suspended if they have too many complaints filed against them. An *indefinite suspension* is a suspension of members' privileges to use the eBay site for more than 60 days, with no definite reinstatement date. If users attempt to re-register at eBay and use the system under new IDs, they risk being referred to the strong arm of the law.

Before filing a non-paying buyer alert – eBay.co.uk calls them Unpaid Item Disputes – give the winner a second chance to send payment. If you still don't receive payment, follow these steps to recoup your Final Value Fees and be eligible for the non-paying buyer re-list credit:

1. **As soon as you have a winner, contact him or her.**

2. **If you don't hear from the winner within three days of the auction's end time, send a payment reminder:**

    a. **Go to the My eBay Views area on the My eBay page. Under Selling, click the <u>Sold</u> link.**

    b. **Click the <u>View Payment Status</u> link next to the pertinent auction.**

    c. **Click the <u>Send a Payment Reminder</u> link.**

    You may send a reminder between 3 and 30 days after the auction closes.

If you still don't hear from or receive money from your high bidder, you need to swing into action and file an alert.

You must file the Unpaid Item Dispute no earlier than 7 days and no later than 45 days after the auction has ended.

Sellers can file a dispute at `feedback.ebay.co.uk/ws/eBayISAPI.dll?CreateDispute` with eBay for each item that has not been paid for. eBay will issue a 'strike' on the account of the buyer who does not honour their obligation to pay (unless the buyer and seller mutually agree not to complete the transaction).

If a buyer gets too many strikes within a short period, their account will be suspended indefinitely. In some cases, limits may be placed on the buyer's account in advance of suspension.

After you file the alert, eBay begins sending online and e-mail prompts to the buyer reminding him or her that it is time to pay and allowing for structured communication with the seller. The seller can file a 'Mutual Agreement Not to Proceed', which prompts the buyer to confirm the agreement. After the buyer does so, eBay issues a Final Value Fees credit to the seller. The seller also receives a Final Value Fees credit if the buyer fails to respond in 7 days – and the buyer receives a strike against his or her account.

When you file for a Final Value Fee credit, you also have the option of blocking that buyer from your auctions.

If you work things out with the winner, you may remove the non-paying buyer alert within 90 days of the close of the auction. eBay sends an e-mail to notify the winner that the alert has been removed at your request. Find the link to remove the warning from your buyer's record at

```
feedback.ebay.co.uk/ws/eBayISAPI.dll?ViewDisputeConsole&
               DisputeType=1
```

In the case of Dutch auctions, you may file a non-paying buyer alert only *once* per listing. You may file against as many bidders as necessary in that one alert, but you can't go back and file more alerts later. You may remove a non-paying buyer warning at any time.

Accessing contact details

Most eBay.co.uk users employ user IDs rather than expose their e-mail addresses for all to see. However, you must supply eBay with your contact information. When you register at eBay, its software immediately checks your primary phone number area code against your postcode to verify that the two numbers are from the same area. If you supply incompatible codes, the eBay servers recognise that and ask you to re-input the correct codes.

If for some reason a buyer or seller fails to get in contact with you, you can search for a member's phone number (see Figure 4-2) by going to the following address:

```
search.ebay.co.uk/ws/search/AdvSearch?sofindtype=8
```

Remember to be sensitive; your buyer or seller may not be able to get in touch for legitimate reasons – because he or she is ill, for example. Don't unnecessarily bite off someone's head!

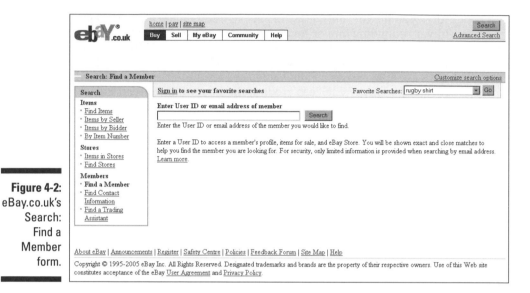

Figure 4-2:
eBay.co.uk's
Search:
Find a
Member
form.

To be on the up-and-up at eBay (and to keep others honest, too), make sure that you:

- **Have your current phone number on file at eBay:** If a bidder can't reach you, you're in violation of the False Contact Information policy and you *can* be disciplined.

- **Have your current e-mail address on file:** If your bidder continually gets e-mail bounced back from your e-mail address, you can get in big trouble.

- **Report all underage bidders:** If you suspect that a bidder in one of your auctions is underage (eBay requires that all users be over 18), eBay may close the account. Underage bidders may be using their parent's credit card without permission, or perhaps even a stolen card, for registration.

- **Verify e-mail purportedly coming from an eBay employee:** If someone e-mails you claiming to work for eBay, check it out before replying. When eBay employees conduct personal business on the site, company policy requires that they use a personal, non-company e-mail address for their user registration. If you suspect someone is impersonating an eBay employee for harmful purposes, contact the Safety Centre.

Taking Action: What to Do When Someone Breaks the Rules

Take a business-like approach to problems at eBay.co.uk, whatever those problems may be. In previous sections of this chapter, we outline eBay's many rules, as well as the bad deeds and bad seeds you're likely to encounter while doing business at eBay.co.uk.

As a member of the eBay community, you have the responsibility of knowing and abiding by eBay's rules and regulations. This responsibility includes notifying eBay when someone tries to sell an illegal item (see 'Is What You Want to Sell Legal?', earlier in this chapter), an integral part of keeping eBay a safe and lucrative place to do business. In this section, we discuss who to call when someone breaks the rules and what to do when a third party is necessary.

Don't be lured by phishing

Fraudulent e-mail has become a common occurrence. Without warning, a request for confirmation of your personal details arrives allegedly from your bank, Internet ISP, credit card company, PayPal, or even eBay. These e-mails are *phishing* for your personal information and passwords to defraud you of your money or your identity.

These e-mails look just like a legitimate e-mail from the company that holds your data. If you follow the links in the e-mail to 'update' your information, you're typically brought to a Web page that duplicates a legitimate Web page.

How can you protect yourself from these scammers?

✔ **Look for personalisation.** Your bank, eBay, or PayPal will address the e-mail to your proper name, not, for example, to *Dear PayPal Member*.

✔ **Never go to the Web site in question from the link in the e-mail.** Open up a new browser and type the URL that you normally use to enter the site. After you log in, you'll know whether there's a problem with any of your information.

✔ **Always look for secure Web site information.** If you're logged onto a secure Web site, the URL will begin with `https://` rather than the standard `http://`. You'll also see a lock symbol in the status bar at the bottom of your browser window.

(continued)

(continued)

- ✔ **Regularly log onto your Internet accounts.** By keeping in regular contact with your providers, you'll know about issues with your accounts before they have a chance to cause a problem.

- ✔ **Report the e-mail.** If you receive an e-mail supposedly from PayPal, forward the e-mail to spoof@paypal.co.uk straight away. Forward an e-mail purportedly from eBay to spoof@ebay.co.uk in the same way.

You can take things into your own hands by checking the suspicious e-mail's underlying code. You can check the code if you use Internet Explorer and Outlook, by opening the e-mail, right-clicking it, and choosing View Source. When you view the HTML code, you can see the actual URL of the site that would get your response if you click the link, as shown in the figure.

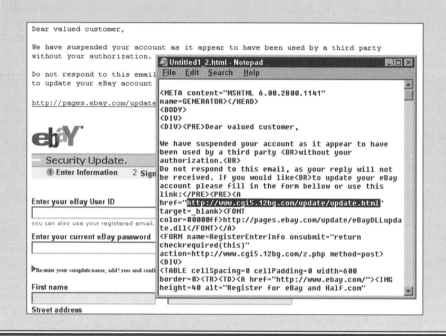

Here are the basic steps you can follow:

- ✔ **Contact the buyer:** If you're involved in a transaction, get the buyer's contact information by using the following:

```
search.ebay.co.uk/ws/search/AdvSearch?sofindtype=8
```

Call the buyer to see whether you can diplomatically resolve the situation.

✔ **Seek out eBay safety:** Use the Safety Centre to report any shady actions, policy violations, or possible fraud, such as a community member impersonating an employee or a suspicious auction. Likened to the front desk at your local police station, eBay's Safety Centre report form gets results. Click the Safety Centre link, which appears at the bottom of most eBay pages, and then click the bright green Report a Problem link. Alternatively, you can go directly to

```
pages.ebay.co.uk/safetycentre/?ssPageName=f:f:UK
```

An all-purpose security form is provided on this page to help you in your eBay transactions. These forms will be routed to the right department for action.

✔ **Apply for online resolution:** SquareTrade offers online dispute resolution services and mediation for eBay members. See the following section on how to involve SquareTrade.

✔ **Contact the Report Auction Fraud Service**: Established in 2002, this organisation acts to address the problem of credit card fraud experienced by businesses trading online. To really bring down wrath on your nemesis, report them at the following address:

```
www.reportauctionfraud.com
```

✔ **Contact the local police:** If you become the target of a cheque-bouncer, contact the local police in your bidder's home town. eBay.co.uk supplies any information necessary to help the police clear the world of fraud. Provide eBay with the name of the local police officer, telephone number, and police report number. Also include the offending user's ID and the auction item's number.

SquareTrade to the rescue

Threats of suing each other, filing fraud charges, and screaming back and forth don't really accomplish anything when you're in the middle of a dispute at eBay.co.uk. Back in the olden days of eBay, when you weren't able to respond to feedback, users threw negative feedback back and forth willy-nilly, which resulted in some vile flare-ups.

These days you have SquareTrade, one of the best services that you can use as a seller. When you're selling regularly at eBay.co.uk, you will undoubtedly run into a disgruntled buyer or two. SquareTrade, a Web-based dispute resolution company, waits in the wings to pull you out of the most difficult situations.

If you find yourself in an inexorably difficult situation with one of your bidders, and want to take the situation up a notch, go to the following page, shown in Figure 4-3:

```
www.squaretrade.com/cnt/jsp/odr/overview_odr.jsp?marketpla
        ce_name=ebay
```

After you click the <u>File a Case</u> link on this page and answer a few questions regarding the situation, SquareTrade generates and sends an e-mail to the other party, giving instructions on how to respond. From this point, the case information and all related responses appear on a private, password-protected page on the SquareTrade site.

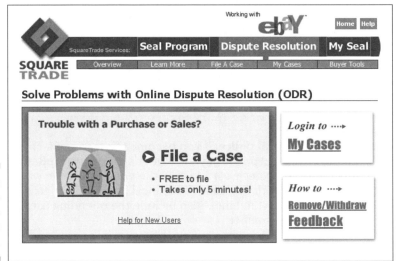

Figure 4-3: SquareTrade Dispute Resolution start page.

SquareTrade offers three main services to eBay members, which we discuss in this section:

✔ Online dispute resolution through direct negotiation

✔ Professional mediation

✔ SquareTrade seal

Online dispute resolution

Online dispute resolution is a fast, private, and convenient way to resolve your auction disputes – and the service is *free*. You and the buyer work together through the SquareTrade Web-based system. Online dispute resolution (ODR) works whether your transaction is in the UK or another country. Every day, several hundred buyers file cases with the ODR service.

The SquareTrade Web-based negotiation tool is automated, and you and the other party get to communicate on neutral ground. When (and if) the buyer responds, the two of you can work out the situation online and without human interaction. If you're unable to reach a solution, you need to move on to professional mediation (see the following section).

SquareTrade states that problems are usually solved in 10 to 14 days and 85 per cent of all cases are resolved without going to mediation. The process can run a quicker course if both people in the transaction are at their computers and answer e-mail during the day.

Participation in ODR is voluntary. If a buyer is set on defrauding you, he or she probably isn't going to engage in a resolution process. If you get no response to your ODR, report your situation to the Safety Centre.

Professional mediation

If push comes to shove, and in auction disputes it certainly can, you may have to resort to professional mediation. A *mediator*, who is neither a lawyer nor a judge but an impartial professional, works with both parties to bring the situation to a convivial conclusion. This service is available for a reasonable fee of about £11 at the time of writing, but the exact fee varies per issue.

If both parties participating in dispute resolution agree to mediation, each party communicates with only the assigned mediator, who communicates with both parties through the same case page. Your case page shows only your communications with the mediator. The mediator reviews both sides of the story to find a mutually acceptable solution to the problem. The mediator tries to understand the interests, perspectives, and preferred solutions of both parties, and tries to help both parties understand the other's position.

The mediator is there to disperse highly charged emotions commonly associated with disputes and recommends a resolution only if both parties agree to have the mediator do so. By using the mediation service, you do not lose your right to go to court if things aren't worked out.

SquareTrade seal

A SquareTrade seal lets prospective bidders know that you deal with customers promptly and honestly. Should you choose to get a SquareTrade seal, SquareTrade inserts it into your auctions automatically. (Each seal icon contains a digital watermark with an encrypted expiration date.) You can use the seal in your auctions only if SquareTrade approves you.

Your SquareTrade seal approval is based on several points:

- ✔ **Identity verification.** SquareTrade verifies your identity using the information you provide through a third party.

- ✔ **Superior selling record.** SquareTrade runs your eBay feedback history through five individual checks. It has an advanced system based on its extensive experience of dispute resolution that allows it to evaluate the quality and quantity of eBay feedback.

✔ **Dispute resolution.** SquareTrade checks whether you have a history of resolving disputes.

✔ **Commitment to standards.** You pledge to meet the SquareTrade standards regarding selling and to respond to disputes within two business days.

After you have a seal, you must continue to uphold SquareTrade standards and maintain an acceptable feedback rating. If approved, the nifty little personalised seal icon appears on each of your auctions. Users can click the icon to access your own Seal Display page on the SquareTrade site.

Recently, SquareTrade did a study of 623 SquareTrade seal members, comparing their feedback for the four months after they became a seal member to their feedback in the prior four months. They found that after a seller became a SquareTrade seal member, negative feedback was reduced by 43 per cent. The ratio of negative to positive feedback went from 1 in 60 before receiving the seal to 1 in 280 after.

The SquareTrade seal (shown in Figure 4-4) currently costs around $7 (£4) per month – an affordable and good idea if you're in this business for the long run. The seal tells prospective buyers that you care about good customer service and don't tolerate fraudulent activity. The seal also says that you abide by the SquareTrade selling and customer service standards, which dictate that you will:

✔ Disclose contact information and credentials

✔ Provide clear and accurate descriptions of goods and services in your auctions

✔ Clearly disclose pricing, including all applicable fees

✔ List clear policies on after-sales services, such as refunds and warranties

✔ Maintain privacy policies

✔ Conduct transactions on only secure sites

✔ Respond to any disputes filed against you within two business days

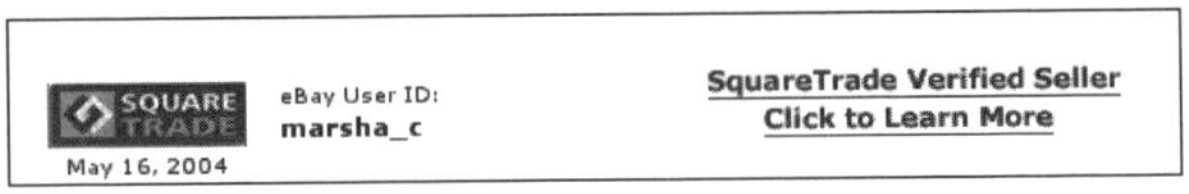

Figure 4-4:
The
SquareTrade
seal.

SquareTrade
eBay User ID:
marsha_c
May 16, 2004

SquareTrade Verified Seller
Click to Learn More

To provide an additional security feature for your buyers, you can bond your auctions. Doing so also protects you. See Chapter 10 for more information.

eBay.co.uk's Safety Centre

The Safety Centre is the eBay.co.uk version of the Special Branch. By rooting out evildoers, the Safety Centre serves and protects – and puts up with an immense amount of e-mail from users.

If you see an item on eBay that isn't allowed (see the earlier section 'Is What You Want to Sell Legal?'), make eBay aware of the auction. The Community Watch team then takes over and investigates the item and, when necessary, ends the auction and warns the seller.

When you click the Safety Centre link, which is at the bottom of most eBay pages, you see the page shown in Figure 4-5. Click the Report a Problem button to get action.

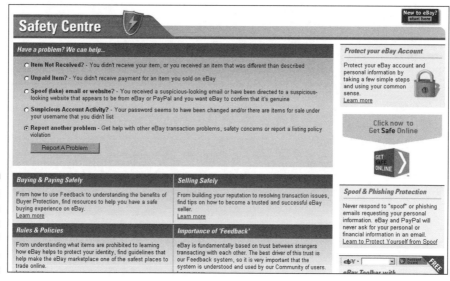

Figure 4-5: The eBay.co.uk Safety Centre.

You then fill out a step-by-step customer service report, which is shown in Figure 4-6.

Alternatively, you can get to the Safety Centre Customer Service reporting form at

`pages.ebay.co.uk/help/contact_us/_base/index.html`

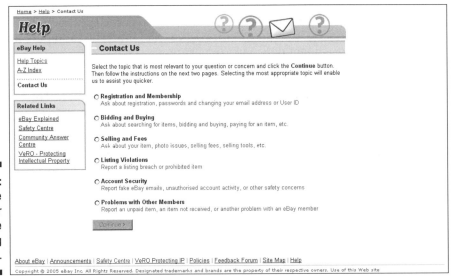

Figure 4-6:
The
Customer
Service
reporting
form.

Chapter 5

Opening a Shop, Virtually

*I*f you're doing well selling your items on eBay.co.uk auctions, why open a shop? Have you used the eBay Buy It Now feature in one of your listings? Did this enticement work? In an eBay shop, all items are set at a fixed price and online until cancelled (or listed at least 30 days), so the shop is rather like a giant collection of Buy It Now featured items. Get the idea?

When you're opening a shop, you have just three main rules to remember and apply: Location, location, location. If you were opening a bricks-and-mortar shop, you could open it on the high street, in a shopping centre, or even somewhere out of town. You'd decide in what location your shop would do best; that goes for an online shop as well. Loads of locations exist for an online shop, including online shopping centres (when you can find them) and sites such as Amazon, Yahoo!, and, of course, eBay.

You have to pay rent for your online shop, but opening and running an online shop isn't nearly as expensive as a shop in the real world (where you also have to pay electrical bills, maintenance bills, and more). Plus, the ratio of rent to sales makes an online shop a much easier financial decision, and your exposure can be huge.

In this chapter, we show you step-by-step how to get business booming by opening your own eBay shop.

Online Shops Galore

Amazon, Yahoo!, and eBay make up the big three of online shops – they're the top locations and get the most visitors. According to US-based Web site tracker comScore Media Metrix, in April 2004 these sites garnered an astounding number of *unique* visitors (that counts *all* of one person's visits to the sites just *once* a month):

- ✔ Yahoo!: 113,190,000 (it's a search engine; we must hit it ten times a day – but we rarely visit the auctions)
- ✔ eBay: 60,016,000
- ✔ Amazon: 39,083,000 (it sells books, CDs, DVDs, and lots of other merchandise)

No doubt feeling competition from Yahoo! and Amazon, eBay decided to open its doors to sellers who wanted to open their own shops. The fixed price shops were a normal progression for eBay in its quest to continue as the world's marketplace. And eBay Shops make sense: They're a benefit to all current eBay sellers and open doors to new shoppers who don't want to deal with auctions.

eBay.co.uk is an online shop that specialises in selling *your* stuff, not *theirs*. This shop doesn't stock merchandise, and it isn't in competition with you. In addition to its staggering number of visitors, eBay offers you the most reasonable shop rent. To see what we mean, check out the sample rents in Table 5-1.

Table 5-1	Online Starter Shop Monthly Costs	
	eBay	*Amazon Marketplace (Pro-Merchant)*
Basic rent	From £6 per month	£28.75 per month
Listing fee	£0.05	none
High final value fee	From 5.25% of item value	17.25% of value (8.05% for electrical items)

 For more information on current rankings, go to the Hitwise Web site at www.hitwise.co.uk and search for *eBay*. This site keeps a monthly scorecard of unique visitors to the UK's top Internet sites. Have a look at the comScore site now and then to see where the online industry is going.

We don't think you need a rocket scientist to convince you that having a space in eBay Shops (see Figure 5-1) is a better bargain than setting up shop anywhere else. We know the shops aren't based on auctions, but Buy It Now items are as easy to handle as auctions. To review prices and rules before opening your shop, go to

```
pages.ebay.co.uk/help/sell/storefees.html
```

Choosing Your eBay.co.uk Shop Name

You are taking the plunge and opening an eBay.co.uk shop. Do you have an eBay user ID? Have you thought of a good name for your shop? Your shop name doesn't have to match your eBay user ID, but they're more recognisable if they relate to each other. You can use your company name, your business name, or a name that describes your business. We recommend that you use the same name for your eBay shop that you plan to use in all your online businesses. By doing so, you begin to create an identity (or as the pros call it, a *brand*) that customers will come to recognise and trust.

Your online eBay shop shouldn't replace your Web site (see Chapter 8); it should be an extension of it. When people buy stuff at your eBay shop, take the opportunity to also make them customers of your Web site through your shop's About the Seller page (which is also your About Me page on eBay). Bargain!

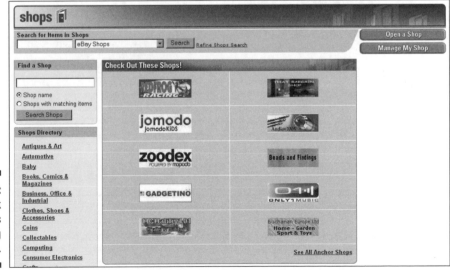

Figure 5-1:
eBay.co.uk
Shops
opening
page.

Minding your underscores and hyphens

If you want to use your eBay.co.uk user ID for your shop name, you can – unless it contains a hyphen (-) or an underscore (_). While eBay recommends that you break up words in your user ID with a dash or an underscore, that's no good for an eBay shop name. Without the underscore, your user ID may translate into a user ID that someone else has already taken, which means you can't use it. Also, your user ID may not be an appropriate name for a shop. If so, find a name instead that suits your merchandise to a T.

Setting Up Shop

To get down to business, go to the eBay Shops hub and click the <u>Open a Shop</u> link in the upper–right-hand corner of the screen (refer to Figure 5-1). Doing so takes you to the Seller's starting point of eBay Shops, as shown in Figure 5-2.

Figure 5-2: The Open Your eBay Shop welcome page.

Before you click that link to open your shop, ask yourself two questions:

✓ **Can I make a serious commitment to my eBay shop?** A shop is a commitment and it won't work for you unless you work for it. You need the merchandise to fill your shop and the discipline to continue listing shop and auction items. Your shop is a daily, monthly, and yearly obligation. When you go on holiday, you need someone else to ship your items or your customers may go elsewhere. You can close your shop for a holiday, but eBay.co.uk reserves your shop name for only 30 days. After that time, you have to come up with a new name (and your competition may have taken over your famous shop name).

✓ **Will I work for my eBay shop even when I don't feel like it?** You need to be prepared for the times when you're ill or just don't feel like shipping, but orders are waiting to be shipped. You have to do the work anyway; it's all part of the commitment.

eBay.co.uk gives you the venue, but making your mercantile efforts a success is in your hands. If you can handle these two responsibilities, read on!

If you're serious and ready to move on, click the <u>Open Your eBay Shop</u> link on the left-hand side of the page (refer to Figure 5-2). Because you're always signed in on your home computer, you're escorted to a page reminding you that eBay shops fall under the same User Agreement that you agreed to when you began selling on eBay. Click the Continue button to access the Open Your Shop pages (see Figure 5-3).

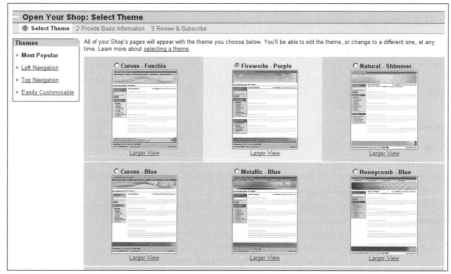

Figure 5-3:
Select your
shop theme.

You need to make a few decisions to create a good shop. So before building your shop, read the following sections.

1. Choose a colour theme.

EBay.co.uk provides some elegant colour and graphics themes. You can change the colour scheme or layout later, so until you have time to go berserk and design a custom masterpiece, choose one of the 14 clearly organised layouts, either pre-designed or with easily customisable themes. Don't select something overly bright and vibrant – a colour scheme that's easy on the eyes is more conducive to a comfortable selling environment.

You have the option of selecting a shop theme that doesn't require you to insert a custom logo or banner but we highly recommend against it. You need to establish a unifying brand for your online business.

2. Click Continue.

3. Type your new shop's name (see Figure 5-4).

Your eBay shop name can't exceed 35 characters. Before you type your chosen name, double-check that you aren't infringing on anyone's copyrights or trademarks. You also can't use any permutation of eBay trademarks in your shop's name.

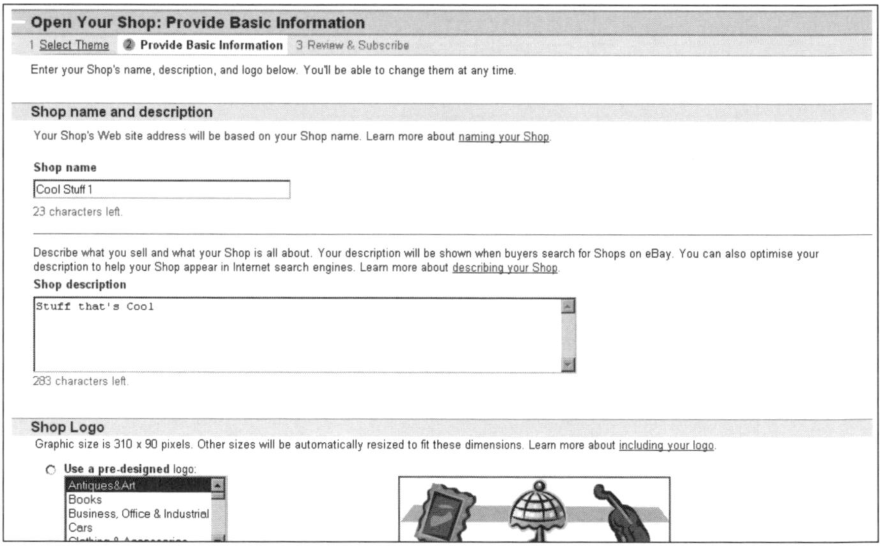

Open Your Shop: Provide Basic Information

1 Select Theme   ② **Provide Basic Information**   3 Review & Subscribe

Enter your Shop's name, description, and logo below. You'll be able to change them at any time.

Shop name and description

Your Shop's Web site address will be based on your Shop name. Learn more about naming your Shop.

Shop name

Cool Stuff 1

23 characters left.

Describe what you sell and what your Shop is all about. Your description will be shown when buyers search for Shops on eBay. You can also optimise your description to help your Shop appear in Internet search engines. Learn more about describing your Shop.

Shop description

Stuff that's Cool

283 characters left.

Shop Logo

Graphic size is 310 x 90 pixels. Other sizes will be automatically resized to fit these dimensions. Learn more about including your logo.

○ **Use a pre-designed** logo:

Antiques&Art
Books
Business, Office & Industrial
Cars
Clothing & Accessories

Figure 5-4:
Type your shop's name and description.

---

4. Type a short description of your shop.

When we say short, we mean *short*. The paragraph you're reading now is 270 characters, and you have only *300* characters to give a whiz-bang, electric description of your shop and merchandise. You can't use HTML coding to jazz up the description, and you can't use links. Just write the facts please, plus a little bit of dazzle.

This description is hugely important. When people search eBay.co.uk shops and descriptions, the keyword information you put here is referenced. Also, if the shop header contains your description (as in the Classic style themes), search engines such as Google and Yahoo! look in this description for the keywords to classify and list your shop.

Write your copy ahead of time in Word. Then, still in Word, highlight the text and choose Tools➪Word Count. Word gives you the word count of the highlighted text. Check the character count with spaces, to be sure your text fits.

5. **Select a graphic to jazz up the look of your shop.**

   You can use one of eBay's clip-art style banners or create a custom 310 x 90 pixel size one. If you use one of eBay's graphics, you must promise (hand on heart) that you won't keep it there for long. (See the text after this set of steps for info on designing your own graphics – or hiring someone to do it for you.)

6. **Click Continue.**

   At this point, your eBay shop looks something like what you see in Figure 5-5. You are about to open an eBay shopfront (drum roll, please).

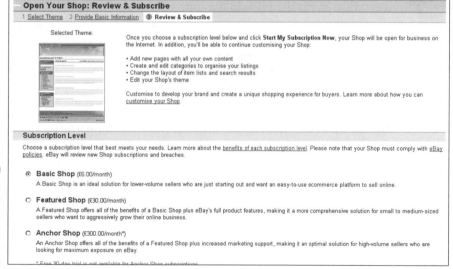

Figure 5-5:
Verify your choices and become a shop owner.

Open Your Shop: Review & Subscribe

1 Select Theme   2 Provide Basic Information   ③ **Review & Subscribe**

Selected Theme:

Once you choose a subscription level below and click **Start My Subscription Now**, your Shop will be open for business on the Internet. In addition, you'll be able to continue customising your Shop:

• Add new pages with all your own content
• Create and edit categories to organise your listings
• Change the layout of item lists and search results
• Edit your Shop's theme

Customise to develop your brand and create a unique shopping experience for buyers. Learn more about how you can customise your Shop.

Subscription Level

Choose a subscription level that best meets your needs. Learn more about the benefits of each subscription level. Please note that your Shop must comply with eBay policies. eBay will review new Shop subscriptions and breaches.

⦿ **Basic Shop** (£6.00/month)

A Basic Shop is an ideal solution for lower-volume sellers who are just starting out and want an easy-to-use ecommerce platform to sell online.

○ **Featured Shop** (£30.00/month)

A Featured Shop offers all of the benefits of a Basic Shop plus eBay's full product features, making it a more comprehensive solution for small to medium-sized sellers who want to aggressively grow their online business.

○ **Anchor Shop** (£300.00/month*)

An Anchor Shop offers all of the benefits of a Featured Shop plus increased marketing support, making it an optimal solution for high-volume sellers who are looking for maximum exposure on eBay.

* Free 30-day trial is not available for Anchor Shop subscriptions.

7. **Sign up for the basic shop (£6.00 a month), and click the Start My Subscription Now button.**

    Your shop is now LIVE on the Internet with nothing up for sale – yet.

8. **Click the supplied link to customise your shop further.**

You decide in which category your shop is listed on the eBay Shops home page. eBay.co.uk checks the items as you list them in the standard eBay category format. For example, if you have six books listed in the Books: Fiction and Non-fiction category and five items in the Cameras & Photo category, you'll be in the listings for both of those categories. Your custom shop categories (read on) will be used to classify items only in your shop.

If you use one of eBay's prefab graphics, people buying things at your eBay shop will know that you aren't serious enough about your business to design a simple and basic logo. We've had many years of experience in advertising and marketing, and we must tell you that a custom look beats clip art any day. Your shop is special – put forth the effort to make it shine.

If you have a graphics program, design a graphic with your shop's name. Start with something simple; you can always change your design later when you have more time. Save the image as a GIF or a JPG, and upload it to the site where you host your images (your own Web site, your ISP, or a hosting service). Jump ahead to Chapter 8 for help choosing a hosting service.

Many talented graphic artists make their living selling custom Web graphics on eBay.co.uk. If you aren't comfortable designing, search eBay for *web banner* or *banner design*. Graphic banners on eBay sell for about £10 to £20 – certainly worth the price in the time you'll save.

Improving Your Offering

You can customise your shop at any time by clicking links in the Shop Design area of the Manage My Shop box, which is at the bottom of your shop's page and in the upper right-hand corner of the eBay Shop's hub page. The page shown in Figure 5-6 appears, with headings describing important tasks for your shop.

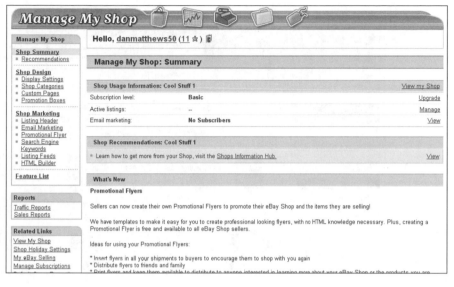

Figure 5-6:
You can
perform
all the
necessary
tasks for
running a
shop here.

Shop design and marketing

In the Shop Design and Marketing list, you can perform the major tasks required for your store:

✔ **Display Settings:** You can go to Display Settings (the shop set-up area) to change the name of your shop or the theme of your pages. You can also change the way your items are displayed: Gallery view (as in Figure 5-7) or list view (as in Figure 5-8). Neither view is inherently better, but we like the gallery view because it shows the thumbnails of your items.

You can also select the order in which your items will sort, for example Highest priced first, Lowest priced first, Items ending first, or Newly listed first. Choosing Ending first as your sort is a good idea, so that buyers can get the chance to swoop in on items closing soon.

✔ **Custom pages:** Most successful eBay sellers have a shop policies page – Figure 5-9 shows you an example. When you set up a policies page, eBay.co.uk supplies you with a choice of layouts. Go to Custom Pages and click the <u>Create New Page</u> link to see the template that you want to use, as shown in Figure 5-10. Don't freak out if you don't know HTML, eBay helps you out with an easy-to-use HTML generator (as in the Sell Your Item form – see Chapter 3).

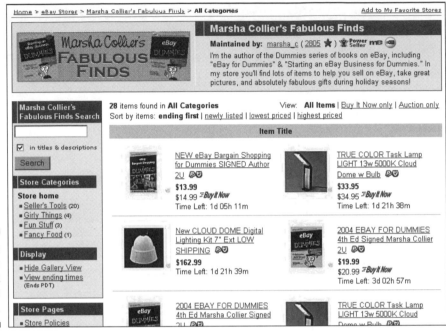

Figure 5-7:
An
eBay.co.uk
shop in
gallery view.

Figure 5-8:
AireGuitars'
eBay.co.uk
shop in list
view.

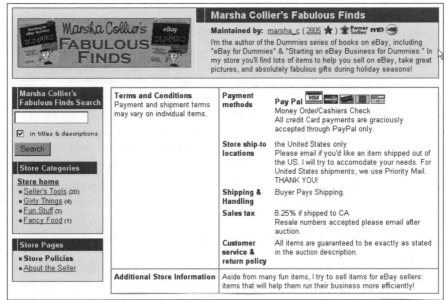

Figure 5-9:
Example
eBay.co.uk
shop
policies
page.

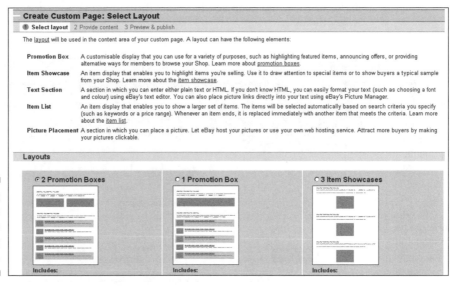

Figure 5-10:
eBay Shop
page
customising
templates.

Following are some important policies to include:

- Indicate to what locations you ship.

- State your customer service and return policy. Fill in the information regarding how you handle refunds, exchanges, and so on. If you're a member of SquareTrade (see Chapter 4), mention here that you subscribe to its policies. Also include whatever additional shop information you think is pertinent.

You can also set up a custom home page for your shop, but doing so is not a popular option. Letting your visitors go straight to the page listing what you're selling is a better idea, don't you think?

✔ **Custom categories:** You really make your shop your own here. You may name up to 19 custom categories that relate to the items you sell for your shop.

✔ **Custom listing header:** The custom listing header display is one of the best tools you can use to bring people into your shop – so use it! Click the link and select the option to show your custom listing header on all your eBay auctions and fixed-price sales. Doing so encourages shoppers to visit your eBay shop when they browse your eBay listings.

When customising, include your shop logo as well as a shop search box. In Figure 5-11, you can see how the shop header looks at the top of an eBay listing.

Figure 5-11:
Super promotion on your auctions: Add a link to your eBay.co.uk shop and the capability to search the shop.

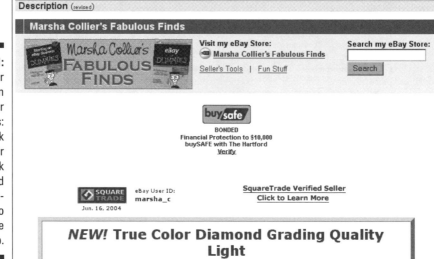

Creating an About the Seller page

If you haven't already created an eBay.co.uk About Me page, do so now! The About Me page becomes the About the Seller page in your shop. This page is a primary tool for promoting sales. (See Chapter 3 for more on About Me pages.) You can put your About the Seller page together in about ten minutes with eBay's handy and easy-to-use templates!

Managing your items

We assume you've listed items on eBay.co.uk, so we won't bore you with a tutorial on how to list your items here (although we do give you some listing and photo image tips in Chapter 11). Following are the main differences between listing an item in your shop and listing an auction on eBay.co.uk:

- ✔ You have to assign your item to one of the prescribed shop categories that you designated while setting up your shop. If your new item falls into a category that you haven't defined, you can always go back to your shop and add a category (as many as 19) or put it in the eBay-generated Other Items category.

- ✔ You don't place a minimum bid or a reserve price on your shop items because everything you list in your eBay shop is a Buy It Now item.

- ✔ Listings in an eBay shop can be put up for sale for 30 or 90 days, or GTC (Good 'Til Cancelled). The listing fees are shown in Table 5-2. Finally, you can buy something for 5p!

Table 5-2	Shop Inventory Insertion (Listing) Fees		
Duration	*Insertion Fee*	*Surcharge*	*Total*
30 days	£0.05	N/A	£0.05
90 days	£0.05	£0.10	£0.15
Good 'Til Cancelled	£0.05 / 30 days	N/A	£0.05 / 30 days

The items you list in your eBay.co.uk shop *will not* appear in the regular eBay site title search. Your items *will* be seen if one of your buyers does a Seller or Shops search from the eBay.co.uk search page, which is why you pay only 5p per listing for 30 days. You *must* put a link in your auctions to your eBay shop (see the next section) – and tell the auction browsers that you have more stuff for them that they 'can't find in a regular eBay search'.

Promotions

eBay.co.uk has added some excellent ways to promote your shop. As an eBay shop owner, you have access to promotional tools that other sellers can't use. The most valuable of these tools is cross promotions – using it is free, too! The cross-promotion box appears after a buyer places a bid on or purchases an item from an eBay seller.

The beauty of having a shop is that the cross-promotion box appears *twice*: Once with your regular listings and again with a different assortment of items (if you want), after someone buys an item. Best of all you get to select which items are shown with your individual auctions.

Figure 5-12 shows you a cross-promotion box that appears when someone views an auction.

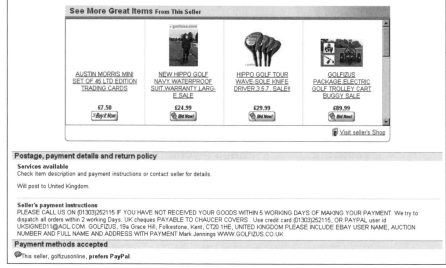

Figure 5-12:
A cross promotion in an eBay.co.uk auction.

You can set up the promotions so that they default to show other items from related shop categories, or you can go in and set them up yourself for individual auctions. Again, every listing has two sets of options: One for when a user views your listings, and the other for when someone bids or wins your item.

Marketing Your Wares

eBay.co.uk has more tempting options that you can use to spruce up your shop items. These options work exactly like the ones eBay offers for your auctions (see Chapter 10). When choosing whether to use these options, remember that your eBay shop items only appear when someone searches in the eBay shops. eBay shop items don't appear in a regular eBay search, so the Gallery option may be the most beneficial option at this time. Check out Table 5-3 for a rundown of optional feature fees.

Table 5-3	eBay Optional Shop Features		
eBay Picture Services Fees			
Feature	*30 days*	*90 days*	*Good 'Til Cancelled (recurring 30-day listing)*
First picture	Free	Free	Free
Each additional picture	£0.12	£0.12	£0.12/30 days
Supersize image	£0.60	£0.60	£0.60/30 days
Picture Show	£0.15	£0.30	£0.15/30 days
Picture Pack	£0.90	£0.90	£0.90/30 days
Listing Upgrade Fees			
Feature	*30 days*	*90 days*	*Good 'Til Cancelled (recurring 30-day listing)*
Gallery	£0.05	£0.05	£0.05/30 days
Item subtitle	£0.35	£0.35	£0.35/30 days
Listing designer	£0.07	£0.07	£0.07/30 days
Bold	£0.05	£1.50	£0.05/30 days
Highlight	£2.50	£2.50	£2.50/30 days
Featured in search	£9.95	£14.95	£9.95/30 days
Scheduled listings	£0.06	£0.06	£0.06/30 days

eBay.co.uk Shops versus Auctions

From the buyer's point of view, shopping at an eBay.co.uk shop is different to winning an auction. eBay shops feature fixed-price sales; the buyer gets the merchandise as soon as you can ship it (instead of waiting for the auction to run its course). Even though your auctions show up on your shop's home page, all regular listings in your eBay shop are Buy It Now items.

When a buyer makes a purchase from your eBay shop, this is what happens:

1. **The buyer clicks the Buy It Now button on the listing page.** The Review Payments page appears, where the buyer can review the purchase. This page contains the shipping amount that you specified when you listed the item.

2. **The buyer provides shipping information (required).** When eBay notifies you that a sale has been made, you have all the information you need. You don't have to scurry around looking for the return address on the envelope when the payment arrives.

3. **The buyer reviews the transaction and then clicks the Confirm button.** The information about the sale is e-mailed to you, and the buyer receives confirmation of the sale.

Your eBay shop can be an essential back-up to your auctions. You can use your shop to sell out-of-season items, accessories for the items you sell actively, and even consignment items between re-listings. Considering the price of an eBay shop, you only need to make a few sales per month to pay for it – and when your sales start to build, your efforts will be greatly rewarded!

Part II
Setting Up Shop

"There's been a mistake here — we ordered 12 <u>tins</u> not 12 tons of salmon from fishathome.co.uk."

In this part . . .

Your hobby is what you love, and I'm betting you have a household of duplicate items – the perfect stuff to sell on eBay.co.uk! Or why not buy from other collectors locally and become a specialist on eBay.co.uk? Or perhaps you'd like to sell inventory from an existing business or from others on consignment. Or maybe you want to start buying wholesale merchandise like the bog boys.

As you can see, the options are endless. In this part, we talk about how to find merchandise to sell, the best way to sell it, and your ever-important Web site.

Chapter 6

Stocking Your Shop

· ·

· ·

You're probably wondering just how you can possibly get enough merchandise to list as many as twenty items a day. But you're going to have to if you want to keep up with top eBay.co.uk PowerSellers! Maybe you're thinking that there aren't possibly enough sources out there to fulfil that kind of volume? Success on eBay isn't easy. Many hours and a good deal of perspiration – along with loads of inspiration – are necessary to make a good living selling online. You *can* see your profits soar – if you apply the same amount of effort in acquiring merchandise.

One of my mottoes is 'Buy off-season, sell on-season'. You can get great bargains on winter merchandise in the heat of summer. January's a great time to stock up on Christmas decorations, cashmere jumpers, too! In the winter, you can get great deals on end-of-line summer sports merchandise. Using this stocking-up tactic is all in the timing.

How are you going to acquire the products you need? We've spent hours, days, weeks, okay, even months trying to work out the best ways to stock an eBay.co.uk business. Ultimately, your stocking strategy depends on you, your personality, and the type of merchandise you plan to sell. We've tried many of the tactics that we discuss in this chapter, as have other eBay sellers we know, so here we pass on all the secrets and caveats that each of us discovered along the way.

Sourcing on a Budget

Pound shops come in all shapes and sizes. These places can be filled with tat or treasure, and a practised eye is needed to separate the wheat from the chaff. Try going in to a pound shop with a teenager, and see whether he or she reacts to any of the items for sale. Sometimes only one in five visits works out, but you'll know when you see the item – and at these prices you can afford to buy loads! Stock at these shops doesn't stay on the shelf for long; if you pass on an item, it may not be there when you return for it the next day. Maybe another savvy eBay.co.uk seller grabbed the bargain.

Poundstretcher

Probably the most successful 'budget business' is Poundstretcher. These shops are now common sights on high streets up and down the country and fly in the face of the theory that people nowadays have more sophisticated tastes and are only interested in branded products. Go to www.poundstretcher.co.uk to find your nearest outlet.

The bulk of the items sold at pound shops are closeouts or special opportunity buys. When a company changes its labels, for example, it might sell all remaining stock with the old labels to pound shops. We've found some profitable books, Olympics memorabilia, and pop culture items at shops like these. The market for budget goods is expanding rapidly, so keep your eyes open for a pound shop opening near you. Otherwise, pull out the phone book (or bother the 118 operators) and see what you can find.

Pound shop warehouses can sell direct to a retailer (that's you!). Find out where the distribution warehouse is for your local pound shop chain and make contact. Being nice can go a long way here. Befriend the office or warehouse manager, who may then call you when merchandise that matches your speciality comes in.

The Trader

The Trader is a UK magazine that essentially lists every type of wholesale business you can think of. *The Trader* provides you with phone numbers and Web sites so you can check out stock or book a visit. Going straight to a wholesaler may seem daunting, but some allow you to buy small amounts of stock early on – especially if they think you'll come back again.

Many wholesalers listed in *The Trader* offer crates of merchandise for a flat fee or sell you ranges of items (say, jeans in every conceivable size). Some wholesalers let you pick and choose your items.

Cash & Carry

Cash & Carry stores take the 'stack 'em high sell 'em cheap' motto to its natural conclusion. Lots of different Cash & Carry businesses exist, including Peggy Sue, CR, and Bestway, but in general these places are big warehouses full of industrial-size containers of stuff for you to buy and sell on.

Be careful what you buy in Cash & Carry stores. eBay.co.uk restricts the sale of some food and drink items (see Chapter 3) so you don't want to end up with a job lot of something you're not allowed to sell!

Car Boot Sales

Car boot sales are a Mecca for bargain hunters because you get great items on the cheap. The trick at these events is to differentiate between things that will sell and things that are cheap tat. But remember: An item that one person thinks is worth £1, another may be prepared to spend £5 on.

Finding a car boot sale in your area is probably easy – they happen all over the place! Many car boot sales are advertised in your newspaper, online, and in brochures published by local clubs and societies. After you find one, make sure you turn up early to hoover up the best items. Also, be sure to take plenty of small change because traders are often reluctant to break £20 (or larger) notes.

When an item catches your eye, haggle over the price. Bargaining is expected at car boot sales, and while some people drive a hard bargain, they won't turn you away just because your opening offer was too low.

Costco

Marsha is a big Costco fan: One day she was wheeling her cart around Costco and right in front of her was a huge display with women jumping and grabbing at the merchandise. She glanced above to read the sign: Fendi Baugette Handbags $199.99. Marsha and her daughter elbowed their way (in not too ladylike fashion) through the crowd and saw the regularly $450 priced purses, stacked like they were bin bags. In those days, the Baugette was new and sold on eBay for around $350. Needless to say, they bought all that their credit cards could handle.

In the first edition of this book, Marsha talked about a special on the Costco Web site (you can find the UK version by logging on to `www.costco.co.uk`), for a new *Snow White & the Seven Dwarfs* DVD. For $18.49, you could pre-order the Snow White DVD and get a second Disney DVD for *free*. When there's an offer like this, you can sell two items on eBay.co.uk for the price of one. If she had bought a case of this deal and held some for future sales, she'd be in the money today. It seems that Disney movies are released for a limited time only. Now, that original DVD set sells on eBay for around $40.

When an item is new but has some collectability, we suggest you buy in bulk, sell some of the item off to make up your investment, and save the balance for later. This has paid off for us a good many times with Disney films, Barbies, and Andy Warhol dinnerware.

Garage Sales

While these are a bigger deal in the US than in the UK, garage sales neverthe-less provide fertile ground for bargain hunters. Buy your local newspaper or check its classified ads online (just search on Google for the name of your local newspaper), and print maps of the sale locations from StreetMap or Yahoo! If you know the neighbourhoods, make a route from one sale to the next that makes sense.

Neighbours often take advantage of an advertised sale and put out some stuff of their own. Bring a friend; you can cover more ground faster if two of you are attacking the sales.

A few tips on shopping at garage sales:

- Fancier neighbourhoods have better stuff than poor or middle class ones. We know that sounds unfair, but rich people's cast offs *are* better than ours.

- Look for sales that say 'Early Birds Welcome' and make them the first on your list so you can get them out of the way. Some sales start as early as 7 am, so get up early if you want the best bargains!

- Keep an eye out for 'moving to a smaller house' sales. These sales are usually held by people who have brought up their children, accumulated a houseful of stuff (collectables? old toys? designer vintage clothes?), and want to shed it all so that they can retire to a bungalow in Bournemouth.

Any toys people are selling while downsizing are usually good ones.

✔ Sales that feature 'kids' items and toys' are generally held by young couples (with young children) who are trying to raise money or are moving. More often than not, these people are keeping the good stuff and are simply shedding the excess.

Going-Out-of-Business Sales

Going-out-of-business sales can be a bonanza, but be careful and don't be misled. Find out whether the business is *really* going out of business and not just trying to tempt more customers. Some shop ads may read 'Going Out for Business' or some similar play on words, so make sure that you're going to the real thing. When a retailer is liquidating its stock, you get the best buys. A retailer often runs the sale week by week, offering bigger discounts as time goes by. If a company is really going out of business, don't be afraid to make a manager an offer on a larger quantity of items.

A chain of children's wear went out of business a while ago. This chain also carried a smattering of popular dolls. A seller we know made an offer for all the remaining dolls and subsequently purchased them at a great price. Throughout the following year, this seller then sold the dolls on eBay.co.uk for three to four times what she had paid.

Auctions

Two types of auctions where you can pick up bargains are liquidation and estate auctions. (We also discuss charity auctions, where you may be able to find bargains while donating to a good cause.) You can find perfectly saleable and profitable items in all types of auctions, but each type has its idiosyncrasies.

Before you go to any auction, double-check payment terms and find out whether you must bring cash or can pay by credit card. Also, before you bid on anything, find out the *hammer fee*, or *buyer's premium*. These fees are a percentage that auction houses add to the winner's bids; the buyer has the responsibility of paying these fees.

Have you seen this spam headline before?

'Make Hundred$ of thou$ands in profits by reselling items from Government auctions!' Yes, we've received this spam too. You send someone money, and they let you in on the big 'secret'.

And the secret is: You can find out about many government auctions at these sites:

✔ **www.governmentauctionsuk.co. uk:** This site provides news and information about government auctions around the UK. It specialises in auctions featuring items from local councils. You can sign up to receive a newsletter that gives you the dates of the auctions.

✔ **www.ganews.co.uk:** An online resource of news and guides helping you to approach government auctions the right way. Subscribers also receive a regular newsletter.

✔ **www.government-auctions.co.uk:** This site bills itself as the 'most comprehensive auctions resource in the UK' and tells you where to find auctions involving goods seized by Her Majesty's Revenue and Customs (HMRC), the Police, bailiffs, and the Courts.

✔ **www.edisposals.com/:** The website of the Disposal Services Agency, which gets rid of equipment for the Ministry of Defence. Don't worry, you can't buy anything that goes bang here, but there are interesting vehicles and gadgets – even ships!

✔ **www.bumblebeeauctions.co.uk:** This official site of UK Police property disposal features live auctions of items including watches, electrical equipment, toys, and jewellery.

✔ **www.dvla-som.co.uk/home/en/ Auction:** At prestigious locations around the UK, the DVLA holds around seven auctions a year featuring the more distinctive and appealing car number plates.

For other sites, search online for *government auction*, *seized property*, *tax sales* and *confiscated property*. Remember, if you're asked for payment to get the information, the site is probably not official.

Liquidation auctions

When a company gets into serious financial trouble, its debtors (the people to whom the company owes money) obtain a court order to liquidate the company to pay the bills. The liquidated company then sells its stock, fixtures, and even buildings and land. Items can sell for next to nothing, and you can easily resell many of them on eBay.co.uk. A special kind of auctioneer handles these auctions. Get on the mailing lists of auctioneers so you always know when something good comes up for sale.

Charity auctions

We're sure you've been to your share of silent auctions for charity. A school or an organisation gets everyone from major corporations to the local gift shop to donate items. The items are then auctioned off to the highest bidder, sometimes in a silent bidding format.

You can find many a great item at charity auctions. Aside from new merchandise, collectors may feel good about donating some collection overflow to a charity. Our friend purchased the keystone of her Star Trek action figure collection at a charity auction: The very rare tri-fold Borg (one of perhaps only 50 in existence). This figure has sold as high as £500 on eBay.co.uk, and our friend paid just £35, all while donating to a charity.

At charity shops, such as Oxfam and the Red Cross, you sometimes uncover treasure while other times you find only junk. Befriend the manager who sees the merchandise as it comes in, knows just what you're looking for (because you said so in a friendly conversation), and can call you *before* the items hit the shelves. This type of relationship can save you from making fruitless trips.

Freebies

Freebies come in all shapes and sizes and – best of all – they're free, of course. Freebies are usually samples or promotion pieces that companies give away to introduce a new product, service, or media event. Even carefully trimmed ads from magazines can fetch high prices from collectors.

When you go to the cosmetic counter and buy a way-too-expensive item, ask for tester-sized samples. Cosmetic and perfume samples of high-priced brands sell very well on eBay.co.uk. Also, look for *gift with purchase* deals. If the free gift is a speciality item, you can usually sell it on its own to someone who'd like to try a sample rather than plunge headlong into a large purchase. Less special items can be grouped together as lots. Make sure you put the brand names in the title.

Fast food giveaways, especially models connected with films or popular cartoons, can be as popular as old corgi toys. The bigger the film, the more collectable the related toy, so start buying up those Happy Meals and Bargain Buckets!

When *Return of the Jedi* was re-released in the US in 1997, the first 100 people to enter each cinema got a Special Edition Luke Skywalker figure. These figures are still highly prized by collectors, especially since the latest Star Wars trilogy was released.

In 1995, Paramount network premiered a new show, *Star Trek Voyager.* In selected markets, Paramount sent a promotional microwave popcorn packet as a Sunday newspaper insert. These packets are still selling well (when you can find them), although the value rises and falls according to current interest in Star Trek.

Before you pass by a freebie, reconsider its possible future resale value.

Salvage: Liquidation Items, Unclaimed Freight, and Returns

Salvage merchandise is retail merchandise that has been returned, exchanged, or shelf-pulled (see below) for some reason. Generally, this merchandise is sold as-is and where-is and may be in new condition. To buy this merchandise, you must be prepared to pay the shipping to your location.

Available all over the country, the liquidation business has been a well-kept secret for years. As long as you have space to store salvage merchandise and a way to sell it, you can acquire it for as low as 10p in the pound. When we say you need storage space, we mean lots of space. To buy this type of merchandise at bottom-of-the-barrel prices, you must be willing to accept lorry-loads of merchandise at a time. If you have access to the more than 10,000 square feet of warehouse that you need to unpack and process this amount of merchandise, you're in business.

Several types of salvage merchandise are available:

✔ **Unclaimed freight:** When a trucking company delivers merchandise, a *manifest* (a document containing the contents of the shipment) accompanies the freight. If, for some reason, a portion of the shipment arrives incomplete, contains the wrong items, or is damaged, the entireshipment may be refused by the merchant. The trucking company is now stuck with as much as a lorry-load of freight. The original seller may not want to pay the freight charges to return the merchandise to his or her warehouse (or accept blame for an incorrect shipment), and so the freight becomes the trucker's problem. The trucking companies arrive at agreements with liquidators to buy this freight in the various areas that the liquidators serve. This way, truckers are never far from a location where they can dump, er, drop off merchandise.

✔ **Returns:** Did you know that after you buy something and decide that you don't want it and return it to the shop or mail-order company, it is not usually sold as new again? The merchandise is often sent to a liquidator who agrees in advance to pay a flat percentage for goods. The liquidator must move the merchandise to someone else. All major retailers liquidate returns, and much of this merchandise ends up on eBay.co.uk.

If you're handy at repairing electronics or computers, you can do very well with a specialised lot. You may easily be able to revitalise damaged merchandise, often using parts from two unsaleable items to come up with one that you can sell in like-new working condition.

✔ **Liquidations:** Similar to the liquidation auctions that we mention in a previous section on auctions, these liquidators buy liquidation merchandise by the lorry-load and sell it in smaller lots. The merchandise comes from financially stressed or bankrupt companies that need to raise cash quickly.

✔ **Seasonal overstocks:** Remember our motto, 'Buy off-season, sell on-season'? At the end of the season, a shop may find its shelves overloaded with seasonal merchandise (such as bikinis in August) that it must get rid of to make room for the autumn and winter stock. These brand-new items become salvage merchandise because they're seasonal overstocks.

✔ **Shelf-pulls:** Have you ever passed up one item in the shop for the one behind it in the display because its box was in better condition? Sometimes the plastic bubblewrap or the package is dented, and you'd rather have a pristine one. That box you just passed up may be destined to become a *shelf-pull*. The item inside may be in perfect condition, but it's cosmetically unsaleable in the retail store environment.

We scoured the Internet and found loads of liquidators. The following are some sites that stood out and offered a wide variety of deals:

```
www.wesco-wholesale.co.uk
```

```
www.drakus.com
```

```
www.gemdiscounts.co.uk
```

```
www.uk-wholesaler.co.uk
```

```
www.xcataloguewarehouse.co.uk
```

Drop shipping to your customers

Some middlemen, wholesalers, and liquidators specialise in selling to online auctioneers through a *drop-ship service.* Some crafty eBay.co.uk sellers make lots of money selling lists of drop-shipping sources to eBay sellers – we hope not to you. Dealing with a drop shipper means that you don't ever have to take possession of (or pay for) the merchandise. You're given a photo and, after you sell the item, you give the vendor the address of the buyer. They charge your credit card for the item plus shipping, and they ship the item to your customer for you.

This way of doing business costs *you* more and lowers your profits. If you're in business, your goal is to make as much money as you can.

Because the drop shipper is in business too, they'll mark up the merchandise they sell to you (and the shipping cost) so they can make their profit.

Be careful when using a drop shipper. Ask for references. See whether loads of sellers are selling the same merchandise on eBay – and not getting any bites. Also, what happens if the drop shipper runs out of an item that you've just sold? You can't just say 'oops' to your buyer without getting some nasty feedback. Your online reputation is at stake. If you find a solid source and believe in the product, order a quantity and have it shipped to your door. Don't pay for someone else's mark-up for the privilege of shipping to your customers.

Be careful before signing up for a newsletter on some of these sites – your spam woes may grow to massive proportions. To preserve your privacy, sign up for a free Yahoo! or Hotmail account and use it for these types of promotional offers.

A proportion of liquidation items, unclaimed freight, and returns may not be saleable for the reasons that we discuss in the rest of this section. Although you can acquire many gems that stand to bring you profit, you may also be left with a varying percentage of useless items. Read on carefully.

Items by the pallet

Some suppliers take the risk and purchase salvaged merchandise by the lorry-load. These suppliers then break up each lorry-load and sell the merchandise to you a pallet at a time. You can probably find some local liquidators who offer this service, or you can go online to find one. The rub in this scenario is: finding the right person to buy from.

As in any business, you can find both good-guy liquidators and bad-guy liquidators. The world is full of e-mail scammers and multi-level marketers who are in business to take your money. No one trying to sell you merchandise can possibly *guarantee* that you'll make money, so beware of liquidators who offer this kind of promise – we don't care who they are or what they say. Carefully research whomever you choose to buy from. Use an Internet search engine and search for the words *salvage*, *liquidation*, and *pallet merchandise*.

Some liquidation sellers sell their merchandise in the same condition that it ships in to their location, so what you get is a lucky dip. You may lose money on some items while making your money back on others. Other sellers who charge a bit more will remove less desirable merchandise from the pallets. Some may even make up deluxe pallets with better quality merchandise. These loads cost more, but if they're filled with the type of merchandise that you're interested in selling, you'll probably write better descriptions and subsequently do a better job selling them.

Getting a pallet of merchandise shipped to you can be very expensive, so finding a source for your liquidation merchandise that's close to your base of operations is a good idea. Notice that many liquidation sites have several warehouses, which translates to lower shipping costs for the buyer. (They can then also accept merchandise from places close to the various warehouses.) You may see FOB (freight on board) and a city name listed, which means that when you buy the merchandise, you own it in the city listed. You're responsible for whatever it costs to ship the merchandise to your door. Search around; you may have to go through many sources before you find the right supplier of liquidation merchandise for you.

When you find a source from which you want to buy merchandise by the pallet, check out a few things before spending your hard-earned cash:

- Do they sell mostly to flea marketers (you may not want that kind of merchandise because you're looking for *quality* at a low price) or close-out shops (more retail-orientated)?

- Did you get a reply within 24 hours after calling or e-mailing?

- Does anyone you speak to appear to care about what you want to sell?

- Are the available lots within your budget?

- Are the lots general or have they been sorted to include only the type of merchandise that you want to sell?

- How long has this liquidator been in business and where does its merchandise come from?

- Does the source guarantee that you *will* make money or that you *can* make money by buying the right merchandise? Remember: No one can guarantee that you'll make money.

- Does the supplier offer on its Web site references that you can contact to find out some usable information on this seller's items and the percentage of unsaleable goods in a box or pallet?

- Is a hard sell involved? Or is it a matter-of-fact deal?

Before you are dazzled by a low price on a lot and click the Buy It Now button, check the shipping cost. Many so-called wholesalers lure you in with bargain-basement prices, only to charge you three times the normal shipping costs. Do your homework before you buy!

Job lots

Manufacturers often have to get rid of merchandise, too. Perhaps a particular manufacturer made five million nodding-head dogs and then sold only four million to retailers. This manufacturer has to quickly unload this merchandise (known as *job lots*) so that it can have the cash to invest in next season's array of items. Job lots often consist of hundreds or thousands of a single item. Make sure you enjoy what you're selling because you'll be looking at the stuff for a while.

Remember supply and demand – don't ever flood the eBay.co.uk market. Doing so makes your item valueless.

Many Web sites specialise in job lots, but you have to visit them often because the deals are constantly changing. One worth checking out is Misco, shown in Figure 6-1. Visit this site at www.misco.co.uk.

Figure 6-1: www.misco.co.uk has regularly updated lots of liquidation merchandise.

Wholesale Merchandise by the Case

If you want to buy direct from a manufacturer, you can. Unfortunately, manufacturers often have a monetary minimum for the amount of your order, which may be more than you want to spend (and you'd get more of a particular item than you'd ever want at once). To remedy that, see whether you can find some independent retailers who buy in quantity and who perhaps will let you in on some quantity buys with manufacturers.

Sometimes the liquidators that we discuss in the preceding section get cases of perfectly saleable goods in their loads. Pallets break up into many cases, and liquidators will often sell these cases individually on eBay.co.uk. What a great way to acquire goods for your eBay business.

Resale Items on eBay.co.uk

We'll keep this eBay.co.uk buying technique short and sweet: Use the magic search engine! But be careful; many a get-rich-quick schemer uses boldface keywords in their auctions to attract your attention. Look only for good quality merchandise to resell. Remember that the only way to make a living on eBay is to sell quality items to happy customers so that they come back and buy from you again. Search eBay.co.uk auction titles for the following keywords: resale, resell, "case of", "case quantity", "lot of", "pallet of" (see Figure 6-2), closeout, and surplus. Be sure to use the quotes anywhere that we include them here because doing so forces the search engine to find the words in the exact order you write them inside the quotes. Alternatively, you can just go to the Wholesale & Job Lots section on eBay.co.uk at `wholesale.ebay.co.uk` (see Figure 6-3).

Figure 6-2: Results of "case of" search.

		Item Title	Bids	Price	Postage	PayPal	Time Left ▲
		CASE OF TAPES	-	£2.99 £3.00			1h 55m
		The Case Of The Mukkinese Battle-Horn Goons on DVD plus Running Jumping Standing Still & Sellers Profile	2	£4.95 £1.50			1h 59m
		SPECIMEN CASE OF BUTTERFLY S OR MOTHS? NO RESERVE	2	£6.50 --			2h 27m
		The Strange Case of Dr Jekyll and Mr Hyde	1	£1.00 £2.00			3h 46m
		Sherlock Homes, The case of the Silver Earring.	1	£1.99 £2.00			4h 06m
		THE STRANGE CASE OF POT-MICHAEL SCHOFIELD-AS NEW	-	£1.50 --			4h 14m
		VHS A CASE OF HONOUR VIETNAM 1988	-	£0.99 £1.90			5h 09m
		Vintage case of "SOLILA" Dental Hypodermic Needles	-	£2.99 £1.00			5h 14m
		A CASE OF ASSORTED DRY AND WET FLIES 50 OF EACH	-	£14.99 £3.00			5h 16m
		sherlock holmes and the case of the rose tattoo	5	£3.20 £2.00			5h 23m

346 items found for "case of"
Located in: United Kingdom Show all

Add to Favourite Searches

List View | Picture Gallery   Sort by: Time: ending soonest   Customise Display

Matching Categories
Books, Comics & Magazines (96)
 • Fiction Books (56)
 • Non-Fiction Books (18)
 • Children's Books (13)
   more ....
Music (42)
 • CDs (20)
 • Records (9)
 • Cassettes (1)
   more ....
DVD, Film & TV (34)
 • DVDs (17)
 • Videos: VHS/ PAL (UK) (13)
 • Film Memorabilia (4)
 See all categories...
Buying Guides
 • Health & Beauty
 • Computers & Networking
 See all buying guides ....
Search Options
Location:
☐ European Union
☐ Items within 200
 miles of Postcode
Show only:

Figure 6-3:
The
Wholesale &
Job Lots
page on
eBay.co.uk.

eBay.co.uk has set up wholesale subcategories for almost every type of item. You can find the wholesale items in the category list on the left-hand side of the page after performing a search, or just go to the eBay home page, scroll down the list of categories, and click Wholesale & Job Lots. Doing so takes you to the Wholesale hub page, as shown in Figure 6-3. Just click the category of your choice to find some great deals.

Consignment Selling

Consignment sales are the up-and-coming way for you to help newcomers by selling their items on eBay.co.uk. Lots of sellers do consignment sales, and several retail locations base their business on this. You take property of the item from the owner and sell it on eBay. You're responsible for taking photos and marketing the auction on eBay – for a fee. In addition to the money you earn selling on consignment, you also get excellent experience for future auctions of your own merchandise.

To set up your business for consignment sales, follow a few guidelines:

1. Design a consignment agreement (a contract), and send it to the owners of the merchandise before they send you their items. Doing so ensures that all policies are set up in advance and that no questions will arise after the transaction has begun.

Becoming an eBay.co.uk Trading Assistant

After you have 50 feedbacks under your belt on eBay.co.uk (and have sold at least four items in the past 30 days), you can become a registered eBay.co.uk Trading Assistant. Check out `tradingassistant.ebay.co.uk/ws/eBayISAPI.dll?TradingAssistant&page=main`

eBay.co.uk publishes a directory of consignment sellers that you can search by telephone area code, postcode, or country. Check out whom in your area is a registered Trading Assistant. Read these consignment sellers' terms and fees. Consignment sellers charge varied amounts based on their geographic location (some areas can bear higher fees than others).

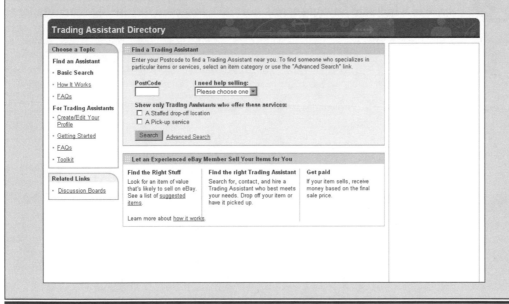

2. Have the owners sign and send the agreement to you (the consignor) along with the item.

3. Research the item based on past sales so that you can give the owners an estimated price range of what the item may sell for on eBay.

4. Photograph the item carefully (see Chapter 11 for some hints) and write a thoughtful, selling description.

5. Handle all e-mail inquiries as though the item were your own; after all, your fee is generally based on a percentage of the final sale.

What do you charge for all your work? We can't give you a stock answer for that question. Many sellers charge a flat fee for photographing, listing, and shipping that ranges from £5–£10, plus as much as a 30 per cent commission on the final auction total (to absorb eBay fees). Other sellers base their fees solely on the final sale amount and charge on a sliding scale, beginning at 50 per cent of the total sale, less eBay and payment service fees. You need to decide how much you think you can make on an item.

Traditional auction houses handle consignment sales in a similar fashion.

When you reach the next level of your eBay enterprise and are looking to spend some serious money on your merchandise, check out *eBay Timesaving Techniques For Dummies* by Marsha Collier (Wiley). That book delves into the type of wholesale-buying secrets normally reserved for the big-time retailers.

Chapter 7

Knowing Your Merchandise

· ·

In This Chapter

▶ Searching eBay.co.uk for comparative pricing

▶ Finding publications in your area of interest

▶ Using online appraisal services

▶ Authenticating your merchandise

· ·

*1*f you don't know what your item is worth, you may not get the highest price in any market. If you don't know how to make your item easy to find, it may not be noticed by even the hardiest of collectors. If you don't know the facts or what to say, your well-written title and detailed description (combined with a fabulous picture) may still not be enough to get the highest price for your item.

Knowing your item is a crucial part of successful selling at eBay.co.uk, which is why we suggest in Chapter 1 that you specialise in a small group of items so that you can stay on top of ever-changing trends. An item may be appraised or listed in a book for a high value, but what you care about is the price at which the item will actually sell. Imagine someone uncovering a hoard of your item and, not knowing the value of it, dumping loads on eBay with low Buy It Now prices. This scenario would drive down the value of the item within a couple of weeks.

The values of collectables go up and down. Star Wars items are a perfect example; values skyrocketed during the release of *Episodes I to III* a few years back, but now prices have settled to a considerably lower level. A published book of value listings is valid only for the *moment* the book is written. If you stay on top of your market in a few specialities, you'll be aware of these market fluctuations.

You no doubt *will* purchase the occasional gem and will want to make the most money possible, so in this chapter we examine the different ways you can find out just how much something is worth. We start with the easiest and most accurate method and work up to the most laborious. We hope you can get your answer the easy way.

Benchmarking eBay.co.uk Rivals

The best tool for evaluating your items is right under your nose. The eBay.co.uk search tool is the best and quickest link to finding your pricing information. To see how items like yours have been selling, search the completed auctions. You can also search these results to see in which categories to list your item and at what time of day the high bidders for your type of item jumped in and won.

Every type of item has a different type of bidder – which makes sense. Would a person searching for collectable dolls have the same shopping habits as a coin collector? Probably not; coins tend to be more expensive than collectable dolls. Although generalities can be dangerous, *profiling* your item's buyer is worthwhile. After you check out the completed auctions for items like yours, the buying patterns of shoppers in different categories can become amazingly clear. After you arm yourself with this knowledge, you'll know not only how much your items should go for but also the best time to end your auctions.

If you're selling a common item, check to see how many other sellers are selling the same item – and when their auctions close. Nothing can kill your profits like being the second or third auction closing with the same piece of merchandise. Space your auctions apart from the others to avoid the law of supply and demand kicking in – and kicking you in the wallet.

Make sure you know how to use the search system. Almost every eBay page has a small box for searching. Initially you may find going to the search page easier, but if you know the search engine *syntax*, or shorthand, you can pinpoint your items with amazing accuracy.

Here are some pointers to help you get the most out of the eBay search engine:

- ✔ The search engine isn't case sensitive, so you don't have to worry about using capitalisation in your search.
- ✔ To find more needles in the haystack, select the Search Titles and Descriptions option.
- ✔ To find historical pricing (what the item has sold for in the past), check the box to search Completed listings as well as current.
- ✔ If you're looking for a popular item, don't search only auction titles and descriptions; search by category, too. For example, suppose that you're searching for a Winnie the Pooh baby outfit. Type *Pooh outfit* and you get loads of results. Look to the left of the page, and see the category that more closely matches your search. In Figure 7-1, the matching category is Baby. Click the link below for the Baby Clothes subcategory. Now you can see the search results in the appropriate category.

Figure 7-1:
The
eBay.co.uk
search
results
with the
Matching
Categories
refinement
box.

> ✔ Don't use conjunctions (*or, and*) or articles (*a, an, the*) in your search; the search engine may misconstrue these *noise* words as part of your search. Some sellers use the ampersand (&) in place of the word *and*, so if you include *and* in your search, you don't find auctions that use the ampersand. In addition, some sellers, due to the 55-character limit, may not place *the* in their title; the same goes for *a, or,* and *and*.

Advanced searching commands

If you need to pinpoint a particular item or just want to weed out bogus responses, try the following advanced search methods. You can use these shortcuts in any of eBay.co.uk's search windows.

If you're searching for items with two or more keywords, type in the keywords with a space between them.

> **Example search:** Wedgwood cups blue

> **Returns:** Items with all three words in the title in any order

If you're searching for items containing words in a particular order, place quotation marks around the group of words.

> **Example search:** "Gone With the Wind"

> **Returns:** Items with titles containing Gone With the Wind, but not those just containing wind, gone or Gone With Wind

If you're searching for items that *don't* contain a certain word, place a minus sign (actually a hyphen) before the word to be excluded.

Example search: bib overalls -baby

Returns: Items with titles containing the words bib and overalls but not containing the word baby

If you're searching for items that don't contain several words, place a minus sign (again, a hyphen) before the list of words separated by commas (with no spaces) and put in parentheses.

Example search: Wedgwood -(black,green,purple)

Returns: Items with titles containing the word Wedgwood but not containing black, green or purple

If you're searching for items where one word or another is present, type the keywords in parentheses separated by commas. (No space after the commas.)

Example search: (Wedgwood,Lenox)

Returns: Items whose titles contain either the word Wedgwood or Lenox

If you're searching for items that contain words starting with a particular sequence of letters, type in the letter sequence followed by an asterisk.

Example search: chin* buddh*

Returns: Items whose titles contain words starting with 'Chin', such as China, Chinese, Chinois, Chinook, and chintz, as well as words starting with 'Buddh', including Buddha, Buddhas, Buddhist, Buddhism

If you're searching for items containing a particular word in addition to an advanced search command, use a plus sign (+) before the required word.

Example search: (Wedgwood,Lenox) +cup

Returns: Items whose titles contain cup and either Wedgwood or Lenox

Now that you know how to finesse the search engine, head to the search page and see if you can work some magic.

If you have the item number, you can type or paste it into any of the eBay search boxes to get to that item.

Using eBay.co.uk Advanced Search

By clicking on the Advanced Search link under the search box that appears on most pages, you can access eBay.co.uk's advanced search options. With the advanced search, you can narrow your search to check out the competition (who's selling items similar to yours). In the basic search, you also have a few options:

- ✔ **View results:** You can choose whether you want to see a mini gallery of photos. Although this may not ordinarily help when you're doing research, information is key; you may just see a variation of the item in photos that you didn't know about.

- ✔ **Search in categories:** You can narrow your search to one of the 29 major categories at eBay.co.uk. If your product is made for men, women, or children, you may get more efficient results by looking in the category that applies directly to your item. Strangely, when searching for a ladies watch, we found the following synonyms and abbreviations for *ladies: lady's, ladys, lds,* and *femmes.*

- ✔ **Completed listings only:** Check this box to go directly to completed listings for your item research.

- ✔ **Sort by:** You can find items by auctions that end first (default), newly listed items first, lowest prices first, or highest prices first. You can also search for items by seller, bidder, shop, and member.

When you click the Advanced Search link below the previously described options, you can narrow your search even further:

- ✔ **Payment:** You can isolate your search to only those sellers who accept PayPal. Utilising this search option may enlighten you as to whether buyers of this product pay higher prices if they have the option to pay with credit cards. (Although the PayPal exclusion does not include other methods of credit card payments, it still speaks strongly for credit card users.)

- ✔ **Locate items near you:** If you're selling something big that you can't (or don't want to) ship, you need to deliver it or get the buyer to pick it up. This option allows you to check out the competition only in your closest major metropolitan eBay trading area.

- ✔ **Multiple item listings:** This option allows you to search by quantity or lot.

So how can you search completed auctions to find bidding patterns on items like yours? Follow the instructions below to dig out all the details you need.

Perform a search on the item for which you want information on the Search: Find items page. When the results appear (see Figure 7-2), you see how many other sellers are selling your same item. That way, you can determine whether now is the right time to sell. (If all active auctions for your items have high bids, now is the time to sell – but don't list your auction to end at a similar time as another one.)

To dig into the details for historic pricing, also perform the completed items search from the advanced search options page:

1. **Click the link on the basic Search page to expand the advanced options.**

2. **Click the Completed listings only option box near the top.**

3. **To sort by price, go to the Sort By drop down menu at the bottom of the page and click the <u>highest prices first</u> option.**

4. **Click Search.**

   The results of completed auctions of your particular item for the last 14 days appear sorted by highest prices first (see Figure 7-3). Pull out your calendar and make note of what days your item landed the highest bids. More often than not, you find that a pattern appears. Your item may see more action on Sunday or Monday or Thursday or whenever.

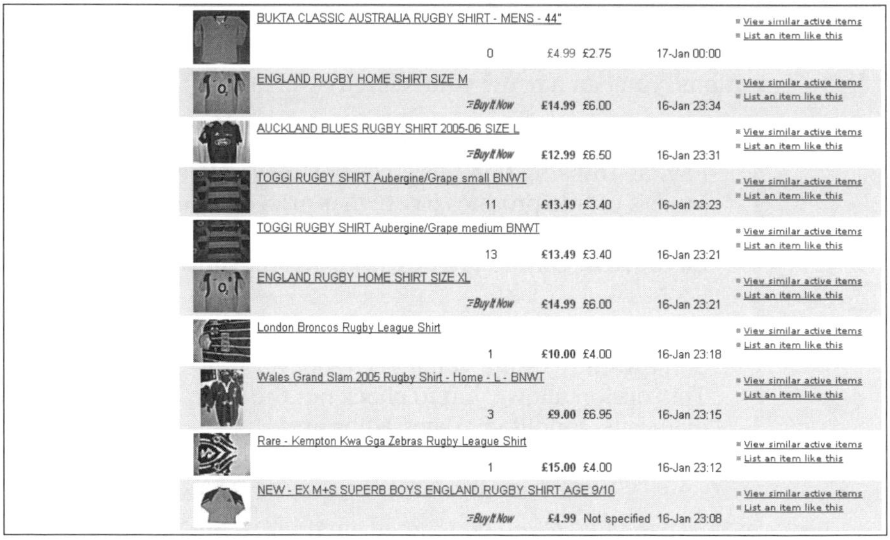

Figure 7-2: Results of an investigatory search.

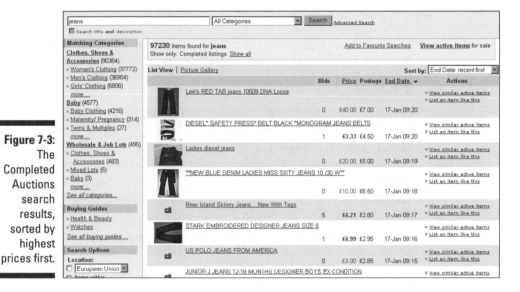

Figure 7-3:
The
Completed
Auctions
search
results,
sorted by
highest
prices first.

eBay also has a superior tool for checking your competitor's auctions. After a while, you can identify the sellers that frequently sell items similar to yours. Aside from keeping them in your favourite sellers list on your My eBay page (for more on that, see Chapter 3), the following is a way to see whether one of your competing sellers has an item like yours up for sale:

1. **Go to the Search area, and click the <u>Items By Seller</u> link on the left.**

2. **Enter the seller's user ID in the box provided.**

   To search the seller's completed listings, select the time frame in which you want to search. To search their current listings, just go to the bottom and click the Search button.

Useful Publications

So what if your item isn't for sale on eBay.co.uk and hasn't been for 30 days? The first thing you need to do is check out your local newsagent for one of the many publications devoted to collecting. Alternatively, do a search online: Searching for 'action figure collector' from Google brings up loads of interesting sites for you to research for more information on publications, dealers, and collecting trends.

Here's a list of some popular reference publications:

- ✔ *The Collector:* One of the UK's best guides to antiques and general collectables. Published alternate months, principally listing specialist antiques dealers alphabetically by area and specialisation, this magazine is available online at www.artefect.co.uk
- ✔ *Classic Record Collector:* Magazine dedicated to the (very) golden oldie music industry. Go online at www.classicrecordcollector.com
- ✔ *Model Collector Magazine:* From Dinky to Corgi, this publication has all the information you need about people who go crazy for models. Check out www.modelcollector.co.uk
- ✔ *Stamp Magazine:* Reporting on the world of philately since 1934, this publication is available online at www.stampmagazine.co.uk
- ✔ *Dolls House World:* A weekly magazine featuring news and features about dolls and miniatures and the people that collect them. Go online at www.dollshouseworld.com

Online Sources of Information

In this section, we give you a few more fun online sources where you may be able to get more insight about your items.

Web sites

Many Web sites devoted to different collectable areas list prices at recently completed auctions. These auctions are the best evaluation of an item's value because they're usually directed towards specialists in the specific collectable category. Most of the participants in these auctions *really* know their stuff.

You may have to poke around the following Web sites to find the prices realised at auction, but after you do, you'll have the holy grail of estimated values. Look for links that point to auction archives. Many of these sites consign your item from you as well and sell it to their audience:

- ✔ Art Market intelligence: www.invaluable.com/
- ✔ Wholesale research: www.ukonlinewholesalers.com/
- ✔ Autographs: www.frasersautographs.com

✔ Football gear: www.bidfootball.co.uk

✔ Technology: www.Itseller.com

✔ Rock and roll memorabilia: www.rockvault.co.uk

✔ Sports memorabilia and cards: www.mullockmadeley.co.uk

Online appraisals

At first glance, online appraisals seem quite tempting. At second glance, though, you realise that unless the person doing the appraisal can actually *see* and *feel* the item, an accurate appraisal can't be performed. Also, you have no guarantee that the person at the other end is really an expert in the field that relates to your item.

If you have an item of real value and worth appraising, get the item appraised in person. Most large cities have auction houses, and many of those auction houses have regular valuations of private items and collections (a way for auction houses to get merchandise for their future auctions). If you bring an item to the auction house, you aren't legally bound to have the house sell your item for you, but it may not be a bad idea. All you get is a free verbal appraisal; the auction house doesn't fill out any official paperwork, but at least you get an idea of what your item is worth. Real appraisals are expensive, are performed by licensed professionals, and come with a formal appraisal document.

Authentication Services

Some companies provide the service of *authenticating* (verifying that an item is the real deal) or authenticating and *grading* (determining a value based on the item's condition and legitimacy). To have these services performed on your items, you have to send them to the service and pay a fee.

Following are a few excellent sites for grading coins:

✔ Robert Matthews Coin Authentication:
www.coinauthentication.co.uk/

✔ Chard coin valuing: www.24carat.co.uk

✔ Predecimal: www.predecimal.com

Stamp collectors (or those who have just inherited a collection from grandpa) can get their stamps authenticated by the British Philatelic Trust. Visit www.ukphilately.org.uk for more information.

You can find links to authentication discounts for eBay.co.uk users at

```
pages.ebay.co.uk/help/community/auth-overview.html
```

Loads of sports cards and sports memorabilia authentication services exist, but they're based outside the UK. If you got your autograph or memorabilia direct from the player or team, you can assure its authenticity. Having the item authenticated may or may not get you a higher price at eBay.co.uk. Try these sites:

- ✔ **Professional Sports Authenticator (PSA):** Offers eBay users a discount at www.psacard.com/cobrands/submit.chtml?cobrandid=23
- ✔ **Sportscard Guarantee (SCG):** Has an eBay discount on card authenticating at www.scgcard.com/new/grading.html
- ✔ **Online Authentics:** Reviews autographs by scans online or by physical review. Look at its services at www.onlineauthentics.com

The best way to find a good authenticator in your field is to search the items at eBay to see who is the most prominent authenticator listed in the descriptions. For example, note in the coins area that certain grading services' coins get higher bids than other services. You can also go to an Internet search engine (Google or Yahoo!) and type the keywords **coin grading** (for coins). You come up with a host of choices; use your common sense to see which one suits your needs.

Remember that not all items need to be officially authenticated. Official authentication does add value to the item, but if you're an expert on your items, you can comfortably rate them on your own in your auctions. People will know from your description whether you're a specialist. Your feedback will also work for you by letting the prospective bidder or buyer know that your merchandise from past sales has been top-drawer.

Chapter 8

Establishing a Base:
Your Web Site

● ●

In This Chapter

▶ Finding free Web space

▶ Choosing a host

▶ Deciding on the perfect name

▶ Registering the perfect name

▶ Marketing your piece of the Web

● ●

*Y*our eBay.co.uk shop is important to your business, but it doesn't replace an e-commerce Web site. Yes, eBay is an important site (duh) for your sales and store, but so is your own business Web site. You should establish your own presence on the Web. And although you can – and should – link your site to eBay.co.uk, don't miss out on the rest of the Internet population.

You don't have a Web site yet? The space for a Web site comes *free* from your ISP. This site can be the practice site for your business so use it to post pictures of items you're selling.

You do have a Web site? Have you taken a good look at it lately to see whether your information is up to date? Does your site link to your eBay auctions, eBay shop, and the gallery that we discuss in Chapter 5?

Most small and medium businesses are increasing their online revenue. In spring 2004, Interland, one of the leading Web hosting providers, took a survey of some of their shared hosting customers to measure the barometer of online activities. They found that 63 per cent of respondents have five or fewer employees – does that sound like you? Figure 8-1 shows how important a Web site is to these companies' business.

An overwhelming majority of small business owners said online resources would be very or somewhat important for business success in the coming year.

99.5% Online identity
(i.e. have a Web site, business e-mail)

67% Site interactivity
(i.e. web-based business forms, blogs, interactive maps and e-newsletters)

62% Online promotions
(i.e. search engine optimization, keyword advertising and e-mail marketing)

55% Online transactions
(i.e. e-commerce, online catalogs and coupons and selling via a third-party site like Amazon or eBay)

Source: Interland's Spring 2004 Business Barometer of Online Activities

Figure 8-1:
A revealing graph from Interland.

Whether or not you have a Web site, this chapter has something for you. We provide a lot of detail about Web sites, from thinking up a name to choosing a host. If you don't have a site, we get you started on launching one. If you already have a site, we give you some pointers about finding the best host. For the serious-minded Web-based entrepreneur (that's you), we also include some ever-important marketing tips.

Free Web Space – a Good Place to Start

Although we love the word *free,* in real life nothing is *really* free. *Free* generally means something doesn't cost you too much money – but may cost you a bit more in time. When your site is free, you aren't able to have your own direct URL (Universal Resource Locator) or domain name. Most likely, a free Web site has an address such as one of the following:

```
www.netcom.com/~marshac
```

```
home.socal.rr.com/marshac
```

```
members.aol.com/membername
```

Having some kind of site at least gives you the experience in setting one up. When you're ready to jump in for real, you can always use your free site as an extension of your main business site.

To access the Internet, you had to sign on with an Internet Service Provider (ISP), which means you more than likely already have your own Web space. Most ISPs allow you to have more than one e-mail address per account. Each e-mail address is entitled to a certain amount of free Web space. Through the use of *hyperlinks* (small pieces of HTML code that, when clicked, route the clicker from one place to another on the page or on other Web site), you can combine all the free Web space from each e-mail address into one giant Web site. Table 8-1 compares some popular ISPs.

Table 8-1	ISPs Who Give You Free Web Space	
ISP	*Number of E-Mail Addresses*	*Total Space per Account*
Freeola	unlimited	unlimited
Abel Gratis	1	50MB
Wanadoo	1	nine pages
Freewire	unlimited	50MB
Lycos	50	1000MB
Yahoo! GeoCities*	1	15MB

*Yahoo GeoCities isn't an ISP, but it is a reliable online community that gives each member online Web space. Membership is free. Extra megabyte space is available for purchase.

Many ISPs have their own page-builder (HTML-generating) program that's free to their users.

Poke around your ISP's home page for a Community or Your Web space link. For example, if you poke around Freeola ISP's home page (http://freeola.com/), you can find and click the Hosting link, which leads you to a page offering various options. You'll find a Free Website link, which takes you to a page that walks you through setting up your own home page. After agreeing to the Terms and Conditions, you can simply log on and set up your home page. Freeola comes highly recommended – especially for beginners – because it is reliable and easy to use.

We highly recommend FrontPage, but if you want all its benefits, you need a site that uses FrontPage *extensions* (portions of the FrontPage program that reside on the server and enable all the HTML magic to happen automatically – and you don't have to write in the code). Save FrontPage extensions for *hosted* Web sites (the ones you pay for) when you have a good deal of allotted space. Installing Microsoft FrontPage extensions on a small Web site like the one that Road Runner provides takes up too many of your precious megabytes. (Yahoo!, however, has extensions installed for the GeoCities sites, and doesn't count them as part of your allotted megabyte count.)

Why learn HTML when Web page editors can do it for you?

If you need some help designing those first pages, try looking for inexpensive HTML Web software. There are basic templates and software packages currently being sold on eBay.co.uk for under £5! Lots of Web page editors are available; the key is to find one that includes a graphical (WYSIWYG, or what-you-see-is-what-you-get) interface that allows you to preview your pages as you design them. You can also use an older version of Microsoft FrontPage (without the extensions) to design simple Web pages.

In lieu of getting involved in a huge (and expensive) program such as FrontPage, you may want to consider using a quick and easy HTML generator such as CuteHTML. If you're not looking to get extra fancy, this is the program for you. We often use CuteHTML to put together eBay auctions when using tables (to put pictures next to the text). You can download a free trial; the price to buy the program is only £14. You can find CuteHTML on the GlobalSCAPE Web site at

```
www.globalscape.com
```

If you find it offered, use FTP (File Transfer Protocol) to upload your pages and images. You can still design pages in Microsoft FrontPage – just don't use the fancy features. If your ISP doesn't supply an FTP program for you, go to the following and download a free trial of CuteFTP:

```
www.globalscape.com/o/912
```

Cute FTP is a small, simple program that helps you get your pages and images to your site. Your first Web pages may be simple, and that's okay. You have to get used to having a Web site before you can really use it for commerce. Put up a home page that links to a few product-related pages and your eBay auctions and, voila, you're in business. If you're feeling more adventurous about your Web site, check out the next section, where we describe a handful of Web site hosts.

Paying for Your Web Space

If you're on the Internet for any length of time, you may be bombarded by hosting offers through your daily spam. A Web hosting company houses your Web site code and electronically doles out your pages and images to Web page visitors.

If you take advantage of PayPal's free Pay Now buttons or Shopping Cart, you can turn a basic-level hosted site into a full-on e-commerce shop without paying additional fees to your hosting company. The PayPal tools are easily inserted into your pages with a snippet of code provided by PayPal. See information later in this chapter.

Before deciding to spend good money on a Web hosting company, thoroughly check it out. Go to that company's site to find a list of features they offer. If you still have questions after perusing the Web site, look for a freefone number to call. You won't find any feedback ratings like you find on eBay, but the following are a few questions to ask (don't hang up until you're satisfied with the answers):

- ✔ **How long have they been in business?** Avoid a Web host that's been in business only a few months and operates out of a garage. Deal with a company that's been around the Internet for a while and, hence, knows what it's doing. Is the company's Web site professional looking? Does the company look like it has enough money to stay in business? You don't want it disappearing mysteriously with your money.

- ✔ **Who are some of their other clients?** Poke around to see whether you can find links to sites of other clients. Take a look at who else is doing business with them and analyse the sites. Visit several of their client sites. Do the pages and links come up quickly? Do all the images appear in a timely manner? Web sites that load quickly are a good sign.

- ✔ **What is their downtime-to-uptime ratio?** Does the Web host guarantee *uptime* (the span of time its servers stay operational without going down and denying access to your site)? Expecting a 99 per cent uptime guarantee is not unreasonable; you're open for business – and your Web host needs to keep it that way.

- ✔ **How much Web space do you get for your money?** Most ISPs offer cheap web hosting packages and occasionally you'll come across those that offer it for free. Generally, you don't get much space with the latter – so be prepared to put your hand in your pocket if you require more than, say, 30MB of space.

- ✔ **What's their data transfer limit?** *Data transfer* is a measurement of the amount of bytes transferred from your site on the server to the Internet. Each hit transfers a certain amount of bytes (kilobytes, megabytes) from your host's servers to the viewer's computer.

- ✔ **Do they offer no-charge technical support?** When something goes wrong with your Web site, you need it fixed immediately. You must be able to reach technical support quickly without hanging around on the phone for hours. Does the Web host have a technical support area on its Web site where you can troubleshoot your own problems (even in the middle of the night)?

Whenever you're deciding on any kind of provider for your business, take a moment to call their technical support team with a question about the services. Take note of how long you had to hold and how courteous the techs were. Before plunking down your hard-earned money, be sure that the provider's customer service claims aren't merely that – just claims.

✔ **What's the policy on shopping carts?** In time you're probably going to need a shopping cart interface on your site. Does your provider charge extra for that? If so, how much? In the beginning, a convenient and professional-looking way to sell items on your site is to set up a PayPal shopping cart or PayPal Pay Now buttons. When you're running your business full time, however, a shopping cart or a way to accept credit cards is a must.

✔ **What kind of statistics do you get?** Visitors who go to your Web site leave a bread-crumb trail. Your host collects these statistics, so you can know which are your most and least popular pages. You can know how long people linger on each page, where they come from, and what browsers they're using. How your host supplies these stats to you is important. One of the best reporting formats is provided from a company called WebTrends (www.webtrends.com/worldwide).

✔ **Are there any hidden fees?** Are they charging exorbitant fees for set-up? Charging extra for statistics? Imposing high charges if your bandwidth suddenly increases?

✔ **How often does the Web host back up your site?** No matter how redundant a host's servers are, a disaster may strike and you need to know that your Web site won't vaporise. *Redundancy* is the safety net for your site. You may be interested in how many power back-ups a company has for the main system. Perhaps it has generators (more than one is good) and more.

If you have a Web site you're probably always looking for other hosts that offer more pizzazz for your pound. Looking behind the glitzy promotional statements and finding out the facts behind each company takes time. Go to uk.tophosts.com/ and click the link to their current Top 25 Web hosts. You may want to also check out www.webhostdir.com/webhostawards. This company checks out Web hosting companies monthly. Take a look at who's listed and then go to check out the host's own Web site.

There are literally hundreds of ISPs out there – far too many to list here – so make sure you put in some research. To help, Table 8-2 provides a comparison of some host service costs. In the rest of this section, we go into greater detail about some further companies you might consider trying. . Make sure you check out these hosting companies' Web sites, however, to get the most current information.

Table 8-2	Comparing Entry-level Hosting Costs			
Feature	*Fasthosts*	*Hostway*	*Netcetera*	*NetPivotal*
Monthly plan cost	£3.99	£4.95	£3	£3.95
Yearly discount rate	None	£49.50	£30	£39.50
Disk space storage	750MB	150MB	500MB	2,000MB
Data transfer/month	Unlimited	3GB	1GB	80GB
24/7 cost-free tech support	Yes	Yes (e-mail only)	Yes	Yes
E-mail aliases	Unlimited	100	30	1,000
FrontPage capability	Yes	Yes	Yes	Yes

Keep in mind that 200MB disk storage space can host as many as 6000 HTML pages.

UKFast.net

UKFast.net (`www.ukfast.net`) is an industry favourite. As the winner of ISPA's Best Hosting Provider 2005 and Future's Best Business ISP 2004, it provides complete dedicated hosting solutions that ensure your business is fast and efficient, with little or no downtime. UKFast.net currently operates four data centres (one in London and three in Manchester), providing managed server solutions as well as reseller packages and ADSL. Figure 8-2 shows UKFast.net's home page.

Donhost.co.uk

Donhost's unique hosting platform, shown in Figure 8-3, was written in-house by their team of qualified and experienced specialists. This hosting platform is one of the fastest, most reliable, feature packed, and economical hosting solutions available.

For smaller businesses, many companies offer *shared hosting*, which is probably what you'll use for quite a while. With shared hosting, your site resides with others on a single server, sharing all resources.

Figure 8-2:
The
UKFast.net
home page.

Figure 8-3:
The
Donhost.
co.uk home
page.

If your Internet sales gross more than a £100,000 a year, you may have to look into *dedicated hosting*, in which your site is on a server of its own and is managed by the technical experts at your hosting company.

Hosting companies offer you many levels of entry. Beyond a basic do-it-yourself level, companies may also offer the services of their crack team of professional Web designers to help you get up and running. Having the assistance of a professional always helps when you're just staring out.

What's in a Web Site Name: Naming Your Baby

What to name the baby, er, Web site? Choosing a Web site name is almost as much of a dilemma as deciding on your eBay user ID or eBay shop name. If you don't have an existing company name that you want to use, why not use the same name as your eBay shop? (Check out Chapter 5 for details about eBay shops.) Lock your name up now so that you can keep your brand forever.

Name your site with a name that identifies what you do, what you sell, or who you are. And make sure you like the name you choose, because once its yours and you begin operating under it and establishing a reputation, it'll be with you 20 years from now when you're still selling online!

A few Web sites offer wizards to help you decide your domain name. You can find a particularly intuitive one at:

```
www.namesarecheap.com/wizard.shtml
```

In a small, Web-based form, you input your primary business type and keywords that describe your business. The wizard then displays a large number of options and also lets you know whether the options are available – very convenient.

Before you attempt to register a name, check it isn't anyone else's trademark. To search an updated list of registered trademarks, go to the following and use the electronic trademark search system:

```
www.patent.gov.uk/search
```

After a search, you may want to trademark your site name. Again, `www.patent.gov.uk` is the online service that can help you with that. The site also offers online trademark applications.

Registering Your Domain Name (Before Someone Else Takes It)

Choosing a select *registrar* (the company that handles the registering of your site name) is as important as choosing the right Web host. Remember that the Internet is still a little like the wild west, and that Billy the Kid may be waiting to relieve you of your hard-earned cash. One of the ways to protect yourself is to understand how the registry works (knowledge *is* power), so read on.

The early Internet – known as 'the Arpanet' – was established 30 years ago in the US. In the 1980s, a parallel UK system, the Joint Academic Network (JANET), was set up. Emerging Internet service providers became involved with the network in the 1990s, providing domain names in exchange for a fee. Soon the ISPs established a naming committee to vet all domain name applications.

When the World Wide Web came into being in 1994, people started to grasp its moneymaking potential. Soon the committee became swamped with applications for new domain names and the need for a professional registry was realised. Nominet was established as the official registrar for domain names ending in .uk in 1996.

Before you decide on a registrar for your domain name, take a minute to see whether the registrar is accredited by ICANN (Internet Corporation for Assigned Names and Numbers – the international governing body for domain names) or is reselling for an official ICANN-accredited registrar. (Ask who they register with.) The Accredited Registrar Directory is updated constantly, so check the following for the most recent list:

```
www.internic.com/regist.html
```

Domain parking

Suppose that you come up with a brilliant name for your site and you get really big and famous. Then someone else uses your Web site name but registers it as a `.net` – while yours is `.co.uk`. To avoid this situation, when you're ready to register your site, make sure you register the three main domains (`.com`, `.co.uk`, and `.net`) and park them with your registrar. For example, `www.ebay.net` and `ebay org` are registered to (guess who?) ebay.com. You can check the owner of any domain name at any of the Web hosting or registrar sites.

Making your personal information private

CANN requires every registrar to maintain a publicly accessible WHOIS database displaying all contact information for all domain names registered. Interested parties (or fraudsters) can find out the name, street address, e-mail address, and phone number of the owner of the site by running a *whois* search on the domain name. You can run a whois search by going to `www.whois.net` and typing in the domain name in question.

This information can be very useful to spammers who spoof your e-mail address as their return address to cloak their identity, identity thieves, stalkers, and just about anyone up to no good. To see the difference between private and public registrations, run a whois search on these two Web sites: `www.coolebaytools. com`, and `www.ebay.com`.

Good registrars should offer private registration for no extra charge. In some cases you can simply decline to fill in certain private details when buying the domain. Check to see whether your registrar offers this service. For updated information on private registration, visit `www.coolebaytools.com`.

For a comparison of registration fees, see Table 8-3.

Table 8-3	Comparing Yearly Domain Name Registration Fees	
Registrar	*Registration Fee*	*URL Forwarding*
easyspace.com	£4.75	Free
netnames.co.uk	£25.00	Included
lowcostnames.co.uk	£7.50	Free
nominate.net	£18	Free

You usually get a substantial discount from the more expensive registrars when you register your domain name for multiple years – a good idea if you plan on staying in business. Also, if you register your name through your hosting service, you may be able to cut the prices in Table 8-3 in half! The only drawback to doing so is that your prepaid registration may go out of the window if you choose to change hosting companies.

If you're registering a new domain name but already have a site set up with your ISP, you need a feature called URL, or Web address, forwarding. *URL forwarding* directs any hits to your new domain name from your existing long URL address. Some registrars offer this service, but watch out for hidden surprises, such as a free offer of the service, which means they probably smack a big fat banner at the bottom of your home page. Your registrar should also have some available tech support. Trying to troubleshoot DNS issues – don't worry, we don't understand what this means either – is a job for those who know what they're doing! Remember, sometimes you get what you pay for.

Marketing Your Web Site (More Visitors = More Business)

You've set up your Web site – now let the world know about it. Having spent many years in the advertising business, we can spot businesses that *want* to fail. These businesses open their doors and expect the world to beat a path to them and make them rich. Unfortunately, this marketing plan doesn't work – ever.

You must take an active approach to letting the world in on the goodies you have for sale. Getting your business known means spending a good deal of time promoting your site by running banner ads and getting your URL into a search engine. There are no shortcuts.

Loads of people out there want to take your money for advertising your Web site. As with all transactions regarding your Web site, knowing who you're dealing with is key. If you want to run your banner on someone else's site, don't spend money; ask to do an exchange. The more advertising that you can get for free, the better. If you decide you want to pay for advertising, wait until after you make a profit selling merchandise from your site.

A simple link to your Web site from your eBay.co.uk About Me page draws people to your site initially. You'll be pleasantly surprised.

Banner ad exchanges

The way banner ad exchange services work is simple. You design a banner ad in your graphics program to a designated size following certain standards (see the following list), and the service displays the banner on other sites. When Web surfers click your banner, they're taken to your site, where they see all the great stuff you have for sale. You can even target what type of sites you want your banner to appear on as well. Remember that this is an *exchange*. Someone else's banner appears on your pages in exchange for showing yours on other sites.

Here are the standard specs for a banner ad:

468 pixels wide by 60 pixels high

GIF format (no JPEGs)

Nontransparent

File size less than 10K (10240 bytes)

If animated, the animation stops at seven seconds and doesn't include loops

Banner design

If you think that designing an eye-catching banner ad (see Figure 8-4 below) is beyond your graphic talents, you'll be happy to know that many excellent graphic artists on the Internet can produce one for you. Type *banner design* into any search engine, and you come up with lots of listings. To find a designer who matches your needs, look at samples (and pricing) on their Web sites.

Figure 8-4:
An
animated
banner ad.

On eBay.co.uk, search for *web banner* or *banner design*. We found 77 listings of banner ad designers with reasonable prices; we're sure you can find one who meets your needs.

Microsoft Banner Advertising

Microsoft Banner Advertising is one of the largest and most effective networks on the Net. They rotate your banner throughout their 70,000 sites and give you great stats on how often your banner is viewed, your page visits, and your clickthrough ratio (the number of times people click your banner and visit your site to the number of times your banner is displayed). Follow this link to find out more: www.microsoft.com/smallbusiness/online/banner-advertising/detail.mspx

Google.co.uk Adwords

While we're at it, if you're looking for cost-effective advertising, Google Adwords is a popular choice for online businesses. Your ads appear on websites that offer a complimentary service to your own and you only pay when someone clicks through to your shop.

Getting your URL into a search engine

For people to find your site (and what you're selling), they must be able to locate you. Most people locate what they're looking for by searching with a search engine – so submit your site to search engines. Go to the search engines that interest you and look for a link or a help area that enables you to submit your site. Be sure to follow any specific instructions on the site; some may limit the amount of keywords and the characters allowed in your description.

To submit your URL to search engines, a little work is necessary (nothing's easy, is it?). Write down 25–50 words or phrases that describe your Web site; these are your *keywords*. Now, using as many of the words you came up with, write a description of your site. With the remaining words, create a list of keywords, separating each word or short phrase by a comma. You can use these keywords to add meta tags to the header in your HTML document for your home page. *Meta tags* are identifiers used by search engine *spiders,* robots that troll the Internet looking for new sites to classify on search engines. Meta tags are used like this:

```
<META NAME = 'insert your keywords here separated by
            commas' CONTENT = 'short description of your
            site'>
```

If you have a problem coming up with keywords, check out Yahoo! GeoCities handy meta tag generator, which you can use for free:

```
geocities.yahoo.com/v/res/meg.html
```

Submit It!

Submit It!, part of Microsoft's Small Business Center in the US, handles your site submissions to hundreds of online search engines automatically, saving you the trouble of going from site to site. This is perfect for those of you who plan to sell abroad, but not for those who plan to sell exclusively in the UK. For $49 (about £28) a year, the service submits as many as ten URLs as often as you like. Submit It! even sends you a regular report letting you know of progress. Your site will also be listed in the Microsoft Small Business Directory as part of your subscription. Using Submit It! is money well spent.

Google

Google crawls the Internet regularly with its spider, Googlebot, looking for new sites to index on Google Search. If Googlebot has missed your site, go to the following and let Google know that you're site is ready for listing:

```
www.google.co.uk/addurl/?continue=/addurl
```

Google doesn't guarantee that your site will be listed, but the process takes less than a minute so what could it hurt?

Yahoo.co.uk Search!

Yahoo! is one of the more difficult sites to list with, although you *can* get a free listing if you fill out all the forms correctly and wait six to eight weeks. Instructions for the free listing are at the following:

```
uk.search.yahoo.com/freesubmit/submit
```

Part III
Serious Business!

"Next time you order something from remindsmeofengland.com, choose it yourself, don't let them choose it for you."

In this part . . .

Now it's time to delve into the pounds and sense of your eBay.co.uk business. In this part we discuss automating your business by using online and offline tools, jazzing up your auctions, setting up your home photo studio, and handling shipping (the bane of most businesses). We also give you the lowdown on two other important aspects of your business: working with customers and collecting payments.

Chapter 9

Software Built for Online Auctions

In This Chapter

▶ Figuring out what tasks you can automate

▶ Finding online auction management services

▶ Exploring auction management software

*N*ow that eBay.co.uk has become a world marketplace, a single-page auction or item listing is an increasingly valuable piece of property. Thousands view your sale, and the more auctions and fixed-price items that you can list, the better your chance to make a good living. Time is money: You need to post your auctions quickly and accurately.

Auction posting, record keeping, inventory cataloguing, photo managing, and statistic gathering are all tasks that you can automate. The more your business grows, the more confusing things can become. Automated tools can help you keep your business admin straight. But remember that the more tools you use, the more expense you may be adding to your business. Always keep your bottom line in mind when evaluating whether to use fee-based software and services.

In this chapter, we discuss how to automate different tasks, software that you can use to automate, and Web sites that offer services to make your daily chores considerably more bearable. After you read this chapter, you'll be well-equipped to decide whether or not you want to automate your business.

As luck would have it, many of the products and services that can help with your eBay.co.uk listing are only provided by companies across the pond in the US. We've checked that the products and services featured in this chapter will work for eBay.co.uk users.

Even so, products change over time and it's best to lodge an enquiry with the software company before buying. Ask whether their stuff is compatible with your business. You might also like to check out Auction Software Review – a US Web site found at www.auctionsoftwarereview.com.

Take the time to get in touch with any US company to find out whether their products or services will work for you in the UK before you purchase.

Considering Tasks for Automation

You have to perform certain office tasks, no matter how few or how many auctions you're running. Depending on your personal business style, you may want to automate any or all of the following tasks. You may choose to use a single program, a manual method, or some features from one program and some from others. If you aren't ready for the automated plunge, we offer alternatives. Where appropriate, we insert references guiding you to where in this book or on the Web you can find more information about the automated services we discuss.

Setting up images for automatic FTP upload

You have several ways to store the display images in your auctions. If you're using an auction management service or software (such as MarketWorks.com or Auction Wizard, both of which we discuss later in this chapter), an *uploader* is usually included as a part of the software. Many online services merely fetch the photos from your hard drive without the need for additional FTP software. To upload your photos, you use a screen similar to eBay.co.uk's Sell Your Item Page, shown in Figure 9-1.

Figure 9-1:
Uploading images from your hard drive.

| eBay Picture Services | Your own Web hosting |
| Let eBay host your pictures | Enter your picture URL |

Upgrade to our free full-featured version
It's faster, lets you upload pictures of any size, and enables you to preview

Picture 1 (Free)
[   ] Browse...

To add pictures to your listing, click Browse.
Picture 2 ($0.15)
[   ] Browse...

Picture 3 ($0.15)
[   ] Browse...

Picture 4 ($0.15)
[   ] Browse...

Picture 5 ($0.15)
[   ] Browse...

Picture 6 ($0.15)
[   ] Browse...

Picture 7 ($0.15)
[   ] Browse...

With this format, you merely click the Browse button to access the Open File window, and then find the location of the image on your hard drive. When you locate the images that you want to upload (one per line), click the Upload button and the images will be on their way to the service's servers.

If you choose to keep images on your own Web site (which makes the images available for your Web site, too), you have to use some sort of FTP software. You probably aren't using close to the total space that your hosting service allots to you for your Web site, making for plenty of room to store a separate folder of eBay images. ISPs often also give you several megabytes of storage space (see Chapter 8).

A straightforward, standalone FTP software program should be part of your auction arsenal, even if you use a service or other software. (We like to have a backup method.) Our personal favourite is CuteFTP from GlobalSCAPE, shown in Figure 9-2.

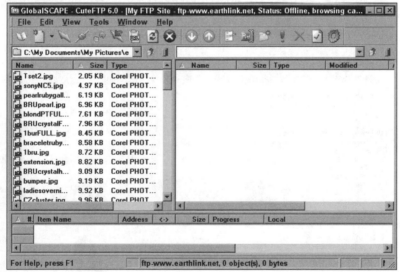

Figure 9-2:
CuteFTP
Home
Edition.

CuteFTP is so simple to use, we've never read the instructions. To send files to a site, type the location and your username and password. Click Connect, and CuteFTP automatically connects to the site. From this point, you merely drag and drop to move a file from the screen on the left (your hard drive) to the screen on the right (your Web site). A 30-day free trial is downloadable from

www.globalscape.com/o/912

You can register the program for only US$39.95 – just over £20.

Setting up an auction photo gallery

Until you establish your own eBay.co.uk shop, setting up an online photo gallery is a great alternative. If your customers have a high-speed connection, they can browse your auctions through photographs. Some auction management sites host your gallery. Some sites charge for this service; others do not. You can produce your own gallery without any fancy programs or auction management software and at no additional cost.

To make your own gallery on eBay without installing fancy scripts in your listings, you need to do three things. You must include eBay gallery photos with all your listings. (You're doing that anyway, aren't you?) Next, test the following URL in your browser, substituting your own user ID where indicated in *bold italic*:

```
search-desc.ebay.co.uk/search/search.dll?
        MfcISAPICommand=GetResult&query=youreBayuserID&
        ht=1&srchdesc=y&SortProperty=MetaEndSort&st=1
```

Figure 9-3 shows you a sample of what you'll see.

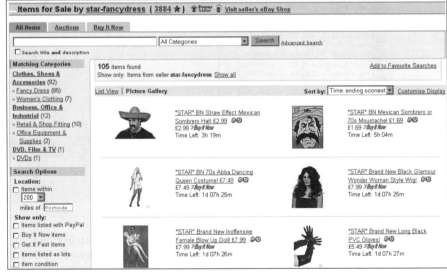

Figure 9-3:
A star-fancydress'
homemade
gallery
linked page.

Now that you have seen a sample of your gallery, insert the following HTML into each auction to include a link to your gallery.

```
<a href="   search-desc.ebay.co.uk/search/search.dll?
           MfcISAPICommand=GetResult&query=youreBayuserID&
           ht=1&srchdesc=y&SortProperty=MetaEndSort&st=1">
           <B>Click <I>here</I> to view yourebayuserID
           Gallery</B> <img
           src="http://pics.ebay.couk/aw/pics/ebay_my_butt
           on.gif" alt="My Gallery on eBay"></a >
```

As you can see in Figure 9-4, this HTML snippet also inserts the custom eBay button.

Figure 9-4:
A link
from your
auctions to
your own
gallery.

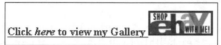

Sorting auction e-mail

A vital function of any auction software or system is the ability to customise and send e-mails to your winners. Many sellers use the default letters in these programs, which tend to be a bit – no, incredibly – impersonal and uncaring. (To see some examples of customer-friendly e-mails and tips on drafting your own, head to Chapter 12.) You need to decide whether you want the program to receive e-mail as well.

Most computer-resident auction management programs have their own built-in e-mail software as part of the program. When you download your winner information from eBay.co.uk, the program automatically generates invoices and congratulatory e-mails.

How to handle your auction-related e-mail is a personal choice. Although we currently use eBay's Selling Manager to send auction related e-mails, we receive auction e-mail through Outlook, using a separate folder titled Auctions that contains subfolders for eBay Buy and eBay Sell.

Automating end-of-auction e-mail

If you want to set up e-mails to be sent automatically after an auction ends, you need to use a software application to do so. The software should download your final auction results, generate the e-mail, and let you preview the e-mail before sending it out. Many of the online sites that we discuss later in this chapter (see the section 'Online auction management sites') send out winner confirmation e-mails automatically when an auction is over; set your preferences to preview the e-mail before sending, if you want to use this option.

Keeping inventory

Many eBay.co.uk PowerSellers depend on the old clipboard or notebook method – crossing off items as they sell them. If that system works for you, great. Others prefer to use an Excel spreadsheet to keep track of inventory.

Most of the auction management packages that we detail later in this chapter (see the section 'Auction management software') can handle inventory for you. Some packages automatically deduct an item from inventory when you launch an auction. You have your choice of handling inventory directly on your computer or keeping your inventory online with a service that's accessible from any computer, wherever you are.

We handle our inventory on our desktop through QuickBooks. When we buy merchandise to sell and post the bill to QuickBooks, it automatically puts the merchandise into inventory. When we input our sale, QuickBooks deducts the items sold from the standing inventory. We can print a status report whenever we want to see how much merchandise we have left – or have to order.

Generating HTML

Fancy auctions are nice, but fancy doesn't make the item sell any better. Competitive pricing and low shipping rates work in your favour. Also, a clean listing with as many photos as necessary goes a long way to sell your product. Some software and services offer a large selection of templates to jazz up your auctions. But think of your customers – some of them are still logging on with dial-up connections, which are notoriously slow. The use of simple HTML doesn't slow the loading of your page, but the addition of miscellaneous images (decorative backgrounds and animations) definitely makes viewing your auction a chore for those dialling up. And forget the background music – it *really* slows things down!

Don't fret; you can make do by repeatedly incorporating two or three simple HTML templates, cutting and pasting new text as necessary. Most auction management programs offer you several choices of template. Stick with a couple of templates that are similar, giving a standardised look to your listings, just the way major companies give a standardised look to their advertising and identity. Your customers will get used to the look of your auctions and feel comfortable each time they open one.

You can use CuteHTML to generate much of your code for auction descriptions. An important line of code that everyone seems to forget is the one that inserts a picture into your auction description. On the Sell Your Item page, click the tab to view in HTML mode, and insert the following line below where you'd like your image to appear in your description:

```
<img src="http://www.yourserver.co.uk/imagename.jpg">
```

Make sure you substitute your own server and image name. If you want to put one picture on top of another, just type <P> between the lines of code – repeat the HTML line with a different image name for each image that you want to display.

If you're in a rush and need a quick and easy HTML generator, go to www. coolebaytools.com and click Tools. *eBay Timesaving Techniques For Dummies* by Marsha Collier (Wiley) has sample HTML code for auction descriptions as well as a chart of all the code you'll ever need for an eBay auction.

One-click re-listing and selling similar items

Using an auction software or service speeds up the process of posting or re-listing items. After you input your inventory into the software, posting or re-listing your auctions is a mouse click away. All the auction management software packages that we detail later in this chapter include this feature.

If you buy your items in bulk, you may want to take advantage of eBay.co.uk's free re-listing tool. By clicking the <u>Sell Similar</u> link on any successful listing, you can automatically re-list your items. Sell Similar starts the listing as new, so if the item doesn't sell you can avail yourself of the Re-list feature. This way, if the item sells the second time, your listing (insertion fees) for the first listing will be credited.

Although eBay says that Sell Similar is for re-listing items, it also works when listing a duplicate of an item that has sold successfully. The only difference is that you aren't credited for the unsold auction listing fee.

 You can use the eBay Sell Similar feature to post new auctions. You merely click the <u>Sell Similar</u> link, and then cut and paste your new information into the existing HTML format. That way, your auctions all have the same feel and flavour.

Scheduling your listings for bulk upload

If you want to schedule the unattended launch of your auctions without incurring eBay.co.uk's fee, you need to use an online management service (check out the 'Online auction management site' section, later in this chapter). If you can be at your computer to send your auctions to eBay singly or in bulk, you can use the Turbo Lister application, which eBay offers at no charge. (For details, see the 'Turbo Lister' section, later in this chapter.)

Researching your statistics

So many questions exist when you're selling on eBay.co.uk. What is the best time to end my auction? What day should I start my listing? Is it better to run a five-day or a seven-day auction? Now an online service can help you separate the rumours from the facts.

Lots of eBay *experts* out there give you hard-and-fast rules to guarantee success with your listings. These people's advice is a load of bunk. Every category and every type of item may draw shoppers at different times of the day and different days of the week.

The best experts are those who are selling every day on eBay, day in and day out. These people are usually PowerSellers and do their own research for their listings. They don't have the time to spout off and give you secrets. We're regular sellers on eBay (we're PowerSellers too), and we've noticed distinct variations in our sales through a fantastic online service called ViewTracker from Sellathon.

Sellathon tracks your listings using a small piece of code that you insert in your auctions. The site gives you loads of information about your visitors, without violating anyone's privacy. Here are some of the things you can find out:

✔ How many times someone has visited your auction

✔ The date and time the visitor arrived at your auction and what city and country your visitor is from

✔ Whether the reserve price was met when the visitor arrived

✔ When the item receives a bid (and how many bids have been placed up to that moment)

✔ Whether the visitor has chosen to watch this listing in his or her My eBay page

✔ Whether the visitor browsed a category, searched a category, searched all of eBay, used eBay's Product Finder utility, came from 'See Seller's Other Items' or some other page and what category they were browsing

✔ If they were searching, what search terms they used to find your item and did they search Titles Only or Titles and Descriptions

✔ Whether the user elected to view Auctions Only, Buy it Now, or both

You get all this information and more. Sellathon offers a 30-day free trial at www.sellathon.com. After that time period, the service is US$4.95 (about £2.80) a month or $49.00 (about £27.50) a year.

To end an old wives' tale about what days your auctions get the highest hits, Figure 9-5 shows you a chart from a Sellathon account, showing how many visits 26 listings got each day. Verrry interesting.

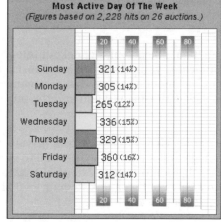

Figure 9-5:
Sellathon
chart
showing
2,228 hits on
26 auctions
in 7 days
worth of
listings!

Most Active Day Of The Week
(Figures based on 2,228 hits on 26 auctions.)

Day	Hits
Sunday	321 (14%)
Monday	305 (14%)
Tuesday	265 (12%)
Wednesday	336 (15%)
Thursday	329 (15%)
Friday	360 (16%)
Saturday	312 (14%)

Photo hosting

If all you need is photo hosting, and you've checked out your ISP and they don't give you any free Web space to use (please check Chapter 8 for a list of ISPs and the amount of Web storage space they give to their customers), you can always use eBay.co.uk's picture services to host an additional picture in each auction at 12p an image.

However, if you run more than 40 auctions a month, a better alternative is Auctionpix.co.uk, offering a reasonably priced package, the FTP Account, which is tailored for eBay sellers. For £10 every three months (or £40 a year) you get 5MB of storage space to hold your eBay images, auction templates, and a handy feedback organiser, which allows you to track who hasn't given you feedback and, if necessary, chase them up. New users can buy more storage space for £1 per MB. There are also some free services available. For more information, visit

```
www.auctionpix.co.uk/
```

Automating other tasks

You can automate a few more tasks. Having so many options is like being in a sweet shop: You may want it all, but that may not be good for you. For example, if you use online postage, you may not want to print your labels because that doubles your work. Take a serious look at the options you're offered and see whether they fit into your particular work style.

Checking out

When someone wins or buys an item, eBay.co.uk's checkout integrates directly with PayPal and also indicates your other preferred forms of payment. If you're closing less than 100 auctions a day, that arrangement is all you need. eBay and PayPal also send an e-mail to you and the buyer so that you can arrange payment.

Some online auction management services offer your own private checkout area, which costs you a percentage of your sale, so you need to decide whether your business warrants this option – many do not. A personalised winner's notification e-mail can easily contain a link to your PayPal payment area, making a checkout service unnecessary.

Tracking buyer information

Keeping track of your winners isn't rocket science. You can track buyer information in an Excel spreadsheet or a Word document, both of which are exportable to almost any program for follow-up mailings promoting future sales. If you choose to have an online management service to track buyer information for you, make sure that you can download the information to your computer (in case you and the online service part company someday).

Generating customised reports

Sales reports, ledgers, and tax information are all important reports for your business. Online services and software supply different versions of these reports.

PayPal allows you to download your sales data into a format compatible with QuickBooks, a highly respected and popular bookkeeping program. You can also choose to download your data in Excel spreadsheet format (the downloads also work in Microsoft Works). PayPal reports are full of detailed information about your sales and deposits. Putting this information in a standard accounting software program on a regular basis makes your year-end calculations easier to bear. (In Chapter 16, we detail what else you may need for this task.)

Submitting feedback

If you're running a lot of auctions, leaving feedback can be a chore. One solution is to automate the submission of feedback through an online service or software. Timing the automation of this task can, however, be tricky.

Don't leave feedback for an eBay.co.uk transaction until after you hear from the buyer that the purchase is satisfactory. Leaving positive feedback immediately after you receive payment from the buyer is too soon. After you receive an e-mail assuring you that the customer is satisfied, manually leaving feedback by going to the feedback forum (or the item page) can be just as easy – if not easier – as bulk-loading feedback.

Managing Your Business with Online Resources and Software

If you search the Internet for auction management services and software, you come up with loads. Most of these services and products are based in the US but offer services worldwide. For simplicity's sake, we examine just a few of these services in this chapter. After speaking to many sellers, we've found online services that offer *uptime reliability* (uptime is key here; you don't want the server that holds your photos going down or mis-launching your auctions) and software that's continually updated to match eBay.co.uk changes.

Using a site or software to run your auctions takes practice, so try any that appeal to you and that offer free preview trials. As we describe these different applications, we include a link so that you can check them out further. Table 9-1 compares the costs of many auction management and online services.

Table 9-1	Cost Comparisons for Auction Management Services and Software
Site Services or Software	*Cost*
All My Auctions (Rajeware.com)	£22 (paid in US dollars)
ándale (`http://uk.andale.com`)	Price scaled according to usage volumes
Auctionsage.com	£17 for three months (paid in US dollars)
AuctionTamer.com	£2/month (paid in US dollars)
SpoonFeeder.com	£12 – £120 (paid in US dollars)
eBay's Selling Manager	Free
eBay's Selling Manager Pro	£4.99/month
IDSAuction (`www.auction-solutions.co.uk`)	Varies
InkFrog.com	£8/month (paid in US dollars)
Kyozou.com	Varies
Trak Auctions (`http://www.jwcinc.net/`)	Free basic package

Some software and services work on a monthly fee, whereas others work on a one-time purchase fee. For a one-time-purchase software application to truly benefit you, it *must* have the reputation for updating its software each time eBay makes a change in its system. The programs that we discuss in this chapter have been upgraded continually to date.

Most services have a free trial period. Don't spend lots of your precious time inputting your entire inventory, only to discover you don't like the way the service works. Instead, input a few items to give the service a whirl.

Online auction management sites

Auction management Web sites handle almost everything, from inventory management to label printing. Some sellers prefer online (or hosted) management sites because you can access your information from any computer. You may use every feature a site offers, or you may choose a bit from column A and a bit from column B and perform the more personalised tasks manually. Read on to determine what service best suits your needs.

Although quite a few excellent online services for automating sales are available, we have room here to show you only a few. Remember that by using an online service, your information resides on a server out there in cyberspace; if you're a control freak, it may be a bit much to bear. Many services are similar in format, so in the following sections we point out some of the highlights of a few representative systems.

 When selecting a service, look for a logo or text indicating that the service is an eBay Certified Developer, Preferred Solution Provider, or API licensee. These people have first access to eBay's system changes and can implement them immediately. Others may have a day or so lag time to update their software.

Following are some of the popular service providers in the online auction management arena:

> ándale (`uk.andale.com`)
>
> Auctionsage (`auctionsagesoftware.com`)
>
> IDSAuction (`www.auction-solutions.co.uk`)
>
> Inkfrog (`www.inkfrog.com`)
>
> Kyozou (`www.kyozou.com`)

ándale offers a suit of services for online auctioneers and targets eBayers more than anyone else, as can be seen in Figure 9-6. The company supplies hit counters for eBay.co.uk auctions, but there's a whole lot more to the company's product range, which includes:

- ✔ **Counters:** Tell you how much traffic your auctions are getting. Allow you to make more informed decisions about when to list items and for how much.

- ✔ **Listing programmes:** Give a more professional look to eBay.co.uk auctions and let you re-list items without having to re-write all the info.

✔ **Image hosting:** Stores images and allows you to reuse them. ándale claims its photos enjoy 99.98% uptime.

✔ **Gallery services:** Give your auctions better cross-promotion by installing a prominent link to your gallery page featuring all your listed items.

Figure 9-6:
ándale's
Web site
homepage

IDS Auction Information Data Systems (www.auction-solutions.co.uk) (See Figure 9-7) is an old head in the auction management business (relatively speaking of course). The company has its home in Norfolk and since its launch in 2000 has grown steadily.

It prides itself on its bespoke and friendly service and even suggests that if you can find any improvements needed with the service, they'll design it for you for free! Customer service is definitely a strong point for these guys and they claim that each customer gets a personal service.

In general, however, IDS offers:

✔ Search and filter facilities, which allow you to retrieve information quickly from current and archived auctions.

✔ Financial analysis.

✔ Printouts of invoices and statements can be set to your specifications.

✔ Auto catalogue creation, which can be set-up to include business logos and graphics.

✔ The ability to share information between multiple sites.

✔ A reporting module: Powerful reporting tools allow you to retrieve and analyse data as you need it.

✔ A user-friendly Windows-style help file.

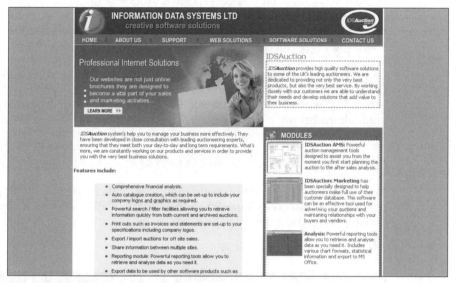

Figure 9-7:
IDS's
Web site
homepage.

eBay.co.uk's Selling Manager

When you subscribe to Selling Manager, the All Selling links in My eBay views are replaced by Selling Manager links. Selling Manager displays a summary of your current transactions. Many sellers (even some PowerSellers) rely on Selling Manager to handle their eBay management chores.

From Selling Manager, you can:

✔ **View listing status:** You can see which sales activities you've completed and what you still have to do.

✔ **Send custom e-mail and post feedback:** Customise your e-mail templates and set up stored feedback comments to help you run through the post-sales process quickly.

✔ **Re-list in bulk:** Re-list multiple sold and unsold listings at once.

✔ **Maintain sales records:** See individual sales records for every transaction, including a history of the transaction status.

✔ **Print invoices:** Print invoices directly from sales records.

✔ **Download sales history:** Export your sales records to keep files on your computer.

✔ **Keep track of NPB and FVF:** File non-paying bidder alerts and final value fee requests.

Auction management software – Turbo Lister

Turbo Lister is simple and easy to use. This software has a built-in WYSIWYG (what you see is what you get) HTML editor, which makes preparing listings offline easy. When you're ready, just click a button and your items are all listed at once. For a fee, you can also stagger listings and schedule them for a later date.

Using Turbo Lister is as simple and straightforward as posting a listing using the Sell Your Item page on the eBay.co.uk site. One of Turbo Lister's benefits is that it allows you to prepare auctions while offline and group them for launching all at once to eBay. Using the program is a two-step process. First, you download the application from eBay.co.uk at

```
pages.ebay.co.uk/turbo_lister/download.html
```

Next, install Turbo Lister on your computer. You can then list auctions on the easy-to-use form (see Figure 9-8) and send them all to eBay in a group. You can also keep the listings in the program for re-listing in the future. What could be simpler?

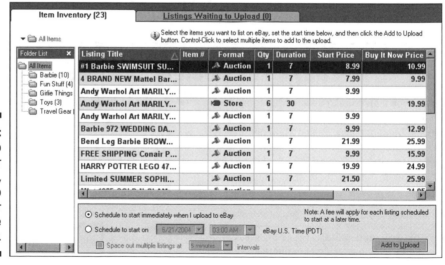

Figure 9-8: The Turbo Lister program, ready to go on your home computer.

Chapter 10

Money and Sense: Budgeting and Marketing Your Auctions

In This Chapter

▶ Marketing your listings by choosing the right category

▶ Using promotional options to your advantage

▶ Paying eBay.co.uk: The low-down on basic fees

*Y*our entire online business is just that: A business. In every business, decisions are made regarding how much money to spend on each division of the company. Because you're the head of your company, you must make these decisions. Even if you're running auctions on a part-time basis, you still have to consider budget concerns. The one area in which you don't have to set aside money is shipping and fulfilment; in the eBay.co.uk model, the buyer pays your shipping and handling costs. (See Chapter 14 for more on shipping.)

When you list an item for sale on eBay, you need to consider what the item will sell for, in what category to list it, and whether to add any eBay listing options. Establish a minimum percentage that you assign as your profit so that you can determine how much to spend on your advertising budget. If your item has a considerable amount of competition in its category, you may want to add some of the options eBay offers to make people notice it and want to buy it. The cost of these options (or advertising) needs to fit into your established advertising budget for the particular item.

In this chapter, we give you a preview of the various options eBay offers its users, highlighting the cost of these options along the way. We also detail the basic eBay.co.uk fees. When you finish reading this chapter, you'll be well on your way to establishing a working budget and have a handle on marketing your items.

Listing Your Items

With tens of thousands of categories, finding the right place for your item can be daunting. (For more on eBay.co.uk categories, see Chapter 2.) You need to apply some marketing techniques when deciding where to place your auctions. Thinking about your budget is also necessary; you can list an item in two separate categories, but you have to pay double for that. Does your budget allow for paying twice?

To find where other sellers have listed items that are similar to yours, perform a completed item search for your item in the Advanced Search page. In the Search box, type your item keywords, tick the option to search Completed listings only, and indicate that you want your results sorted by highest prices first. Figure 10-1 illustrates the results of this kind of search.

Figure 10-1:
Results of the category item search, showing the categories in which the item is listed (on the left).

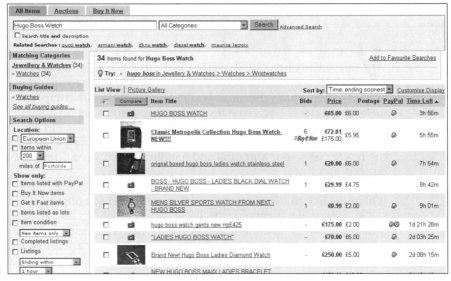

After you have your results, click the completed listings with the highest priced bids. At the top of the auction page, you see the listed category. You may find that your item is listed successfully in more than one category.

Check the active listings; are lots of people selling your item? If you see that you're one of 40 or 50 people selling the item, you need to get creative as to where to list your item. Evaluate the item and its potential buyers. In what categories would someone shopping for your item search?

Suppose you find two perfect categories in which to list your item. eBay.co.uk allows you to list an item in two categories (see Figure 10-2), but is doing so the best marketing decision for your auction? Bear in mind that when you list an item in two categories, you must pay two listing fees. Depending on the time, the season, the availability of your item, and how much you paid for it, you may or may not have the money to budget for listing an item twice.

In addition, many eBay buyers are quite savvy in using the search engine. If buyers search for your item using the search engine rather than by browsing the categories, listing the item in two categories may be a needless expense.

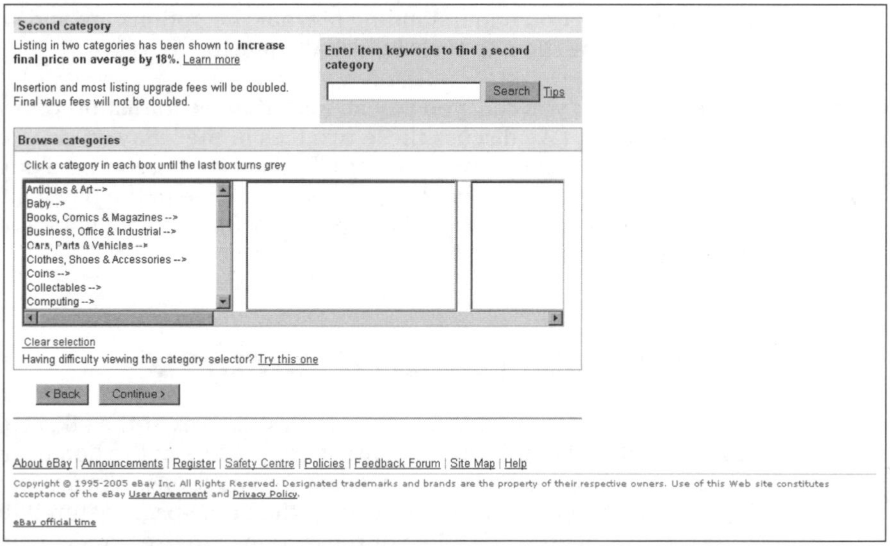

Second category

Listing in two categories has been shown to **increase final price on average by 18%.** Learn more

Insertion and most listing upgrade fees will be doubled. Final value fees will not be doubled.

Enter item keywords to find a second category

[Search | Tips]

Browse categories

Click a category in each box until the last box turns grey

Antiques & Art -->
Baby -->
Books, Comics & Magazines -->
Business, Office & Industrial -->
Cars, Parts & Vehicles -->
Clothes, Shoes & Accessories -->
Coins -->
Collectables -->
Computing -->

Clear selection

Having difficulty viewing the category selector? Try this one

[< Back]   [Continue >]

About eBay | Announcements | Register | Safety Centre | Policies | Feedback Forum | Site Map | Help

Copyright © 1995-2005 eBay Inc. All Rights Reserved. Designated trademarks and brands are the property of their respective owners. Use of this Web site constitutes acceptance of the eBay User Agreement and Privacy Policy.

eBay official time

Figure 10-2:
List your item in two categories in the Sell Your Item form.

You can change your category mid-auction, starting it in one category and ending it in another, as long as your item has not received a bid. And at the end of an auction in which your item doesn't sell, you can use the re-listing feature to run the auction again in another category.

eBay.co.uk's Optional Listing Features

When you come to the point in listing your item that brings you to eBay.co.uk's optional listing features, you see the headline, 'Get more bids with these optional features!' Increasing your bids sounds pretty good, doesn't it? But getting carried away by these options is easy and can lead to spending all your expected profits before you earn them.

In the eBay University Advanced Selling class, instructors quote auction success rates for the features, but in the real life of your business, success varies from auction to auction and category to category. If you take the boldface option and then your auction appears in a category full of boldface auction titles, the bold just doesn't have the punch you paid for. Your auction would stand out more without the bold option. The same logic applies to highlighting. Certain categories are loaded with sellers that go overboard in the use of this feature – all the auction titles appear in a big lavender blur.

Weigh the pros and cons in terms of how these optional listing features affect your eBay business. Does spending a little extra money enhance your item enough to justify the cost? Can you make up the extra money in auction profits? You need a good understanding of what the options are and when and how you can use them to their fullest advantage.

In every auction you run, you pay an insertion fee for listing your auction and a final value fee. (We discuss these two fees in the 'eBay.co.uk's Cut of the Action' section, later in this chapter.) If you accept credit card payments, or use a service such as PayPal, you also pay a fee to the payment service. Estimate your expenses from these basics before you consider spending money for advertising.

Home-page featured auctions

A user who goes to www.eBay.co.uk first arrives at the eBay.co.uk home page. A Featured Items area appears in the middle of the home page; below this area are links to six home-page featured auctions. When you click the All featured items link (see Figure 10-3), the home-page featured items page appears (see Figure 10-4). Most of these items are fixed-price listings that are valued at more than £1,000.

The home-page featured auction option sets you back £49.95 for a single item – but for big-ticket items, you have the perfect location to draw an audience that may easily earn back this sum. People who are new to eBay come in through the front page and the six auctions featured on the home page rotate randomly throughout the day. No guarantee exists that your item will be featured as one of the six home page links – but it will appear in the home page Featured category linked from the home page.

Keep in mind, however, how much you're paying for this option. Unless your auction will bring you more than a few hundred pounds, this feature probably isn't worth the additional cost.

Figure 10-3:
The <u>All featured items</u> link on the eBay.co.uk home page.

Figure 10-4:
The home-page featured items page.

Featured Plus

When you choose the Featured Plus option, your auction is listed at the top of the page when a shopper searches for keywords or browses category listings. Although your auction doesn't appear on the eBay.co.uk home page (see the preceding section), it does appear at the top of your selected *category* home page (see Figure 10-5).

Figure 10-5:
A category page showing the premier position for Featured Plus auctions.

You get extra exposure for just £9.95, but considering your auction budget is still necessary. How much do you expect your item to sell for? Will the £9.95 expense benefit your auction enough to justify the expenditure? Be sure that your item will bring you more than a few hundred pounds before choosing this option.

Subtitle

You may use 55 characters for your item's title. Title search is the de facto search on eBay.co.uk. From the statistics we've seen of our own auctions, 90 per cent of searches were made for title only, versus title and description. But how can you make your item stand out when it shows up with hundreds of other items that look the same? Use the subtitle option!

When your item has something special about it or could use some extra description, the subtitle option allows you more space to give vital informa-tion to the browsing shopper. Take a look at the examples in Figure 10-6.

Figure 10-6:
eBay.co.uk
seller
expressbuy
101 makes
good use of
the subtitle
option by
adding
pertinent
additional
information.

Highlight option

Highlighting makes anything stand out on a white page of text. This tech-nique works just as well on eBay.co.uk as it does on paper. Unfortunately, as with anything in life, less is more. If you choose to list your auction in a cate-gory where all the sellers decide to use the highlight option, the only listings that stand out are the ones *without* highlighting.

The highlight feature sets you back just £2.50. Does your budget allow for that extra expense? To give your auction title a punch for a smaller amount of money, consider the bold option, described later in this section.

Listing Designer

eBay.co.uk comes up with options to fill the needs (or wants in this case) of users. Sellers enjoy putting colourful graphics around their descriptions. The Listing Designer option also helps you design your description, placing pictures in different places on the page. But if you have a good description (creatively done with HTML colour and emphasis) plus a good picture (inserted with the HTML code we gave you), your item will draw bids just the same as if you spent 7p extra (per listing) for the Listing Designer option.

If you want your descriptions surrounded by graphics, make sure they aren't too intensive. Otherwise, the pages load too slowly for dial-up users. Also, you can develop your own template or buy one from savvy eBay graphics gurus (see Chapter 9).

Use a graphics template to 'brand' your listings on eBay.co.uk, giving them a uniform look. If you want to use a template, decide on one and make it your trademark.

Boldface option

The boldface option is probably the most used option in the eBay.co.uk stable. An auction title in boldface type stands out in a crowd, unless . . . yes, that's right, unless it appears in a category loaded with boldface auction titles. If the 75p that eBay.co.uk charges for this benefit is in your auction budget, odds are it will get you many more views than if you don't use it. Boldface is an exceptional buy; we suggest going for it whenever you can.

To recap your title option costs, see the 'Insertion (listing) fees' section later in this chapter.

View counter

Counters have become a popular free option in the online world. Placed on your auction by an outside service at your request, the numeric view counter ticks up each time someone loads your page from eBay.co.uk. The view counter can add up to numbers that impress bidders (convincing them they're viewing a hot deal) or impress other sellers to run out and sell the identical item at eBay.

A counter is a terrific tool for marketing your auctions – sometimes. If you have an auction with no bids and a counter that reads a high number, newbie bidders may be dissuaded from taking a flyer and bidding on your auction. Newbies' thinking might be, if that many people looked at this auction and didn't bid, something must be wrong with the item. As a result, these bidders tend to doubt their own instincts as to what is and isn't a good deal. In reality, however, what may be going on is that savvy bidders are just watching your auction, waiting to bid at the last minute. This argument has a flipside, of course, because people will also be put off if your auction has a low number of hits. Unfortunately, there are no hard and fast rules here.

A *private counter* shields the numbers from the eyes of casual viewers. The figures are available to only you through a password-protected login page.

Various private counters exist. Some of the most helpful private counters are smart counters that offer a breakdown of visitors hour-by-hour. This type of counter is available from several online vendors (see Figure 10-7). eBay.co.uk offers you a free counter, but it's not a smart counter.

Figure 10-7:
Andale's pro
counter.
Find out
more at
uk.
andale.
com/
corp/
index.
jsp.

The gallery

eBay.co.uk bills the gallery as its 'miniature picture showcase', and indeed it is. By adding a gallery photo, a thumbnail image (96 x 96 pixels) of your item appears next to your listing when the user browses the category view or search results, which can reap you many benefits. When someone runs an auction search, eBay defaults to showing all items, and that includes a gallery preview, as shown in Figure 10-8.

☐	📷	WOOD BOX - MUSICAL by tallent of OLD BOND STREET.		£2.00 £2.50	🔔	1d 12h 33m
☐	📷	CLOCKWORK MUSICAL BOX MOVEMENT/ MECHANISM (LOVE STORY)	-	£0.99 £1.00	🔔	1d 14h 56m
☐		PLASTIC DOLL--MONEY and MUSIC BOX.-10inch high	-	£2.00 £3.00	🔔🔔	1d 21h 43m
☐	📷	Musical sleeping Baby in need of TLC	-	£0.99 --	🔔	2d 09m
☐		ROYAL DOULTON BUNNYKINS MUSIC BOX SILVERPLATE *BNIB*	-	£29.99 £4.50		2d 02h 06m
☐		MUSICAL ORNAMENT- VICTORIAN TREASURES Crystals & Pearls	≡Buy It Now	£1.99 £1.00	🔔🔔	2d 02h 44m
☐		GRAND PIANO MUSIC BOX	-	£9.99 £4.00	🔔🔔	2d 03h 02m
☐		SCHMID TEDDY BEAR CHEERLEADER MUSICAL FIGURINE	-	£5.99 £4.00	🔔🔔	2d 03h 59m
☐	📷	MUSICAL ORNAMENT- VICTORIAN TREASURES with Crystals	≡Buy It Now	£1.99 £1.00	🔔🔔	2d 03h 59m
☐	📷	MUSIC BOX	-	£3.99 £1.25	🔔🔔	2d 04h 19m
☐	📷	MUSIC BOX	-	£3.99 £1.25	🔔🔔	2d 04h 20m
☐		1930s MUSICAL MAHOGANY TEA CADDY VGC NR	1	£10.00 £4.00	🔔🔔	2d 04h 41m

Figure 10-8:
Note how the gallery photos draw your attention.

If you don't use the gallery image, but still have a picture in your description, your listing features only a lowly camera icon when searched. Choosing this 15p option may be a worthwhile expenditure. If your item will sell for less than £20, however, the extra charge may not be worth it.

Nothing draws the eye better than the gallery photo next to a listing in a search with hundreds of results. Which auction would you check out: the auction with the tiny camera icon, or the one with the crisp clear gallery picture tempting you to open the listing? Pictures are the key to all quality advertising. Don't miss an opportunity to add this extra little 'billboard' to your listings.

Don't get carried away with the idea that a large percentage of bidders are going to view their search results in the picture gallery option, which results in pages featuring only gallery photos and titles. Those bidders who know what they're doing – and who are searching for a deal – don't dismiss auctions without gallery photos. Bidders with dial-up connections may not have the patience to wade through pages of images.

eBay.co.uk also offers to feature your gallery photo on the top of gallery-only pages for £15.95. These photos run two across the top of the page, as shown in Figure 10-9, rather than the five across for the regular gallery pictures. These featured gallery pictures are also larger (140 x 140 pixels) than the regular gallery pictures.

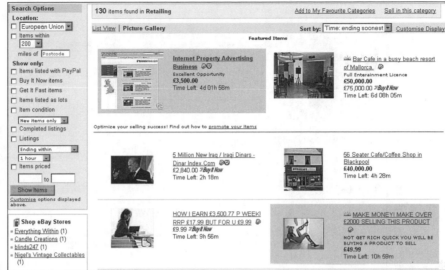

Figure 10-9:
The
eBay.co.uk
picture
gallery page
with a
featured
photo.

If you use the gallery option, crop your photo tight to the subject. That way your item will stand out as much as possible. For more help with your images, see Chapter 11.

Buy It Now

The Buy It Now feature, shown in Figure 10-10, has a few significant benefits. If you have a target price for the item you're listing, make that your Buy It Now price. You can also use this option during frenzied holiday shopping times or with very hot items. Try posting a slightly higher than normal price and perhaps you'll get a sale.

The Buy It Now feature disappears when someone bids on the item or, if you place a reserve on the auction, when a bidder meets your reserve price. You can't use Buy It Now with a Dutch auction.

To use this feature, you must have a feedback rating of at least 10.

Buy It Now costs vary according to the value of your item. The feature costs 5p for items worth £4.99 and under, but 25p for items over £30. If your item will sell for a low price, remember our golden rule: Before paying for a feature, ask yourself whether your listing budget can accommodate it.

CARBON REAR EXHAUST BOX 3" EXIT - UNIVERSAL FITMENT | Item number: 8020345420

You are signed in | Watch this item in My eBay | Email to a friend

≈*Buy It Now* price: £49.99

Buy It Now >

Time left: **42 mins 21 secs**
10-day listing, Ends 17-Jan-06 10:33:21 GMT

Start time: 07-Jan-06 10:33:21 GMT

Quantity: 5 available

History: Purchases

Item location: KINGSTON , SURREY
United Kingdom

Featured Category Auction Listing

Post to: United Kingdom

Postage costs: £8.99 -- Other Courier

Postage, payment details and return policy

Seller information

mwautomotive2 (45 ☆)

Feedback Score: 45
Positive Feedback: 100%
Member since 07-Dec-05 in United Kingdom
Registered as a business seller

Read feedback comments
Add to Favourite Sellers
Ask seller a question
View seller's other items

Standard Purchase Protection Offered.
Find out more

Description | Seller assumes all responsibility for listing this item.

MWAUTOMOTIVE

OUR LISTED STOCK IS IN OUR WAREHOUSE IN KINGSTON LONDON NOT USA, AND NOT 28 DAYS AWAY LIKE MOST OTHER SELLERS - ALSO YOU CAN COLLECT FROM US IN PERSON

Larger Picture

Figure 10-10:
The Buy It
Now
feature.

eBay.co.uk's Cut of the Action

Becoming complacent and blithely ignoring your eBay.co.uk costs as you list items for sale is easy to do. As a person in business for yourself, always take into account outgoing costs as well as incoming profits. The cost of your initial listing is just the beginning of your advertising budget for that item; you have to factor in the cost of all the options and features you use as well. Then, when the item sells, you pay eBay.co.uk a final value fee. (For fees regarding your eBay shop, check out Chapter 5.) In this section, we review the costs for listing an auction and for a fixed-price listing on eBay.

The fees we detail here aren't the end of your fees. If you use a credit card payment service, they also charge you a fee. In Chapter 13, we examine the costs of the most popular credit card payment services.

Insertion (listing) fees

Your insertion fee is based on the highest amount of two things: Your minimum opening bid or your reserve price. If you start your auction at 99p and have no reserve, the listing fee is 15p. But if you start your auction at 99p and set an undisclosed reserve price of £50, your auction costs £1.50 to post. When you place a reserve on your item, you're charged an insertion fee based on the amount of the reserve – plus the reserve auction charge.

The reserve auction charge is automatically refunded if the reserve price is met.

For a summary of eBay.co.uk insertion fees, see Table 10-1. (The fees for eBay Motors are in Chapter 2.)

Table 10-1	eBay.co.uk Listing Fees for Fixed-Price Single Item or Auction
Starting or Reserve Price	*Insertion Fee*
£0.01 – £0.99	£0.15
£1.00 – £4.99	£0.20
£5.00 – £14.99	£0.35
£15.00 – £29.99	£0.75
£30.00 – £99.99	£1.50
£100 and above	£2.00

If your item doesn't sell, you can't get your insertion fee back. This fee is non-refundable. You do have the option of re-listing your unsuccessful auction without being charged a second listing fee, but *only* if your item sells with the second listing. If the item doesn't sell the second time, you *will* be charged again. Writing a better title, starting with a lower opening bid, or adding a snappier description all help in selling the item. Also consider changing the category in which you list the item.

We recap the cost of the various eBay.co.uk listing options in Table 10-2.

Table 10-2	Fees for eBay.co.uk Listing Options
Option	*Listing Fee*
Home page featured	£49.95
Featured Plus	£9.95
Highlight	£2.50
Subtitle	35p
Bold	75p

(continued)

Table 10-2 (continued)

Option	Listing Fee
Listing Designer	7p
Gallery	15p
Gallery featured	£15.95
Buy It Now	5p
List in two categories	Double insertion fee

eBay.co.uk Final Value Fees

eBay.co.uk gets a cut when your auction sells – *the final value fee*. After your auction ends, eBay.co.uk charges the final value fee to your account in a matter of minutes.

An auction in the Properties category is *not* charged a final value fee, Successful auctions in the eBay Motors category, however, are charged a final value fee depending on what your vehicle sells for. (See Chapter 2 for information on fees in both categories.) To help you calculate how much you owe eBay.co.uk for general items, see Table 10-3.

Table 10-3	Final Value Fees
Closing Price	*Final Value Fee*
Item not sold	No Fee
£0.01 – £29.99	5.25% for the amount of the high bid (at the listing close for auction-style listings) up to £29.99
£30.00 – £599.99	5.25% of the initial £29.99 (£1.57), plus 3.25% of the remaining closing value balance
Over £600.00	5.25% of the initial £29.99 (£1.57), plus 3.25% of the initial £30.00 – £599.99 (£18.53), plus 1.75% of the remaining closing value balance

To save yourself brain ache, use an eBay.co.uk fee calculator to check your fees before you set prices. See Chapter 9 for software that does the calculations for you.

Chapter 11

Jazzing Up Your Auctions

· ·

· ·

*R*ule number 1: A good photograph and a concisely written description are the goal for all your auctions. If you're trying to fetch the highest possible bid for an item, keep your auction listings simple and professional: No dancing clowns (unless you're selling clowns), no overdone graphics, and no difficult-to-read typefaces. Less is more.

In this chapter, you find out how to write eye-catching descriptions and improve the visual elements of your auction listings.

Writing Winning Text

When you write descriptions for your auctions, describe your items clearly and completely. Mention everything about the object, including flaws or damage. When you're honest up front, you'll have a happy bidder. Remember to include your terms of sale and specify what type of payments and credit cards you accept. Include your shipping charges, too. Following is a checklist of things to mention:

- ✔ Size, style, colour (garment measurements are also valuable because sizes aren't always universal)

- ✔ Condition (new, new with tags, used, gently used, well-worn)

- ✔ Manufacturer's name

> ✔ Year of manufacture (if important)
>
> ✔ Fabric or material (if important)
>
> ✔ Any damage to the item
>
> ✔ Special features
>
> ✔ That you've stored it in a clean, dry place (if you have)

After you list all the facts, get excited and add a little flowery text in your description. Think infomercial! Think Shopping Channel! The descriptions used by these media make things sound so good that you absolutely *must* have whatever item they're selling. You can use the same technique, if you take the time. In Chapter 12, we give you some more pointers on writing the best auction descriptions possible.

Setting Up Your eBay.co.uk Photo Studio

Taking pictures? No problem! You have a digital camera, and you know how to use it. Just snap away and upload that picture, right? Sorry, but no. A good way and a bad way exist to take photos for eBay.co.uk and, believe it or not, the professional way isn't necessarily the most expensive way.

We recommend that you set up a mini photo studio for taking your eBay auction pictures. That way, you don't have to clean off your kitchen counter every time you want to take pictures.

If you must use the kitchen counter or a desktop, use an inexpensive photo stage, which you can find on – where else – eBay.co.uk.

You need several basic things in your photo studio; the extras you may require are based on the type of merchandise you're selling. An eBay *generalist*, someone who will sell almost anything online – like us! – should have quite a few extras for taking quality photos. Check out a portion of a home photo studio in Figure 11-1.

What you find in this section may be more than you thought you'd need to take good pictures. But your photographs can help sell your merchandise, so take this part of your business seriously. Of course, if you sell only one type of item, you don't need such a varied selection of stuff, just the basic photo set-up. Spend only as much on photographic equipment as is prudent at the time – you can add to it as you go along. Also, check www.coolebaytools.com for more ideas.

eBay Seller's Photo Lighting Kit

Tired of your auctions having fuzzy pictures? The answer is to use this professional photo light kit, designed for online images. It consists of two 10" reflectors with zinc die-cast stand adapters. Each reflector has an integrated ceramic socket for bulbs as high as 250 watts, with wood handling knobs. Two 6 foot all metal adjustable stands complete the kit. The kit comes with a short image tutorial by the author of "eBay for Dummies".

Bid with confidence and win this set at close to wholesale price as it is selling with NO RESERVE! Winning bidder to pay shipping & handling of $9, and must submit payment within a week of winning the auction. Credit cards are accepted through Billpoint and PayPal. Good luck!

GOOD LUCK, HAPPY BIDDING!

Click below to...
View my other auctions – Win more than one and $AVE on shipping!

Figure 11-1:
An eBay photo set-up, featuring here in an eBay.co.uk auction.

Digital camera

Digital cameras are mysterious things. You may read about *mega pixels* (a million pixels) and think that more is supposed to be better, but that doesn't apply to eBay.co.uk applications or to Web images. Mega pixels measure the image resolution that the camera is capable of recording. For online use, all you need from a camera is 640 x 480 pixels (or at most 800 x 600) because computer monitors are incapable of taking advantage of more pixels. If you use a higher resolution picture, all you do is produce a pixel-bloated picture that takes a looooong time to load online.

You don't need a million pixels, but you do need the following:

- **Quality lens:** If you wear glasses we're sure you can tell the difference between a good lens and a cheap one. Really cheap cameras have plastic lenses, and the quality of the resulting pictures is accordingly lousy. Your camera is your work horse, so buy one from a company known for making quality products.

- **Removable media:** Taking the camera to your computer and using cables and extra software to download pictures to your hard drive is annoying. Removable media eliminates this annoyance. The most popular are Smart Media cards (black wafer-thin cards), Compact Flash cards (in a plastic shell), and Sony Media Sticks; all are no larger than a matchbook. Insert these cards into your computer, if your computer has ports for them, or you can get an adapter that connects to your computer through a USB or parallel port. You can get either device on eBay.co.uk for about £20.

Some cameras (specifically the Sony Mavica FD series) use a regular 3½-inch floppy disc as a convenient storage method. These cameras are hugely popular with eBay sellers for just that reason.

✔ **Tripod and tripod mount:** Have you ever had a camera hanging around your neck while you're trying to repackage some eBay merchandise that you've just photographed? Or perhaps you've set down the camera for a minute and then can't find it? Avoid this hassle by using a tripod to hold your camera. Tripods also help you avoid blurry pictures from shaking hands. To use a tripod, you need a *tripod mount*, the little screw hole that you see in the bottom of some cameras. In the following section, we give you some tips on finding the right tripod.

✔ **Macro setting capability or threading for a lens adapter:** If you need to photograph coins, jewellery, or small detailed items, these tools will come in handy. A camera's macro setting enables you to get in really close to items while keeping them in focus. A threaded lens mount enables you to add different types of lenses to the camera for super macro focus or other uses.

✔ **Autofocus and zoom:** These options just make life easier when you want to take pictures. The ability to zoom in and keep things in focus should be standard features.

We bet you can find a camera that fits your needs right now on eBay.co.uk for less than £100. Remember that many digital camera users buy the newest camera available and sell their older, low-megapixel cameras on eBay for a pittance. Many professional camera shops also sell used equipment.

Other studio equipment

Certain endeavours seem to be open pits that you throw money into. You can avoid having your eBay.co.uk photo studio become one of these pits – if you follow our advice.

Tripod

A tripod is an extendable aluminium stand that holds your camera. Look for one that has a quick release so that if you want to take the camera off the tripod for a close-up, you don't have to unscrew it from the base and then screw it back on for the next picture.

The legs of the tripod should extend to your desired height, should lock in place with clamp-type locks, and should have a crank-style geared centre column so that you can raise your camera up and down for different shots. Most tripods also have a panning head for shooting from different angles. You can purchase a tripod from a camera shop or on eBay.co.uk for as little as £15.

Power supplies

Digital cameras can blast through batteries faster than chocolate through a five year old. A reliable power supply is a must and you can accomplish this in a couple of ways:

- **Rechargeable batteries:** Many specialists on eBay.co.uk sell rechargeable batteries and chargers. Pick up quality Ni-MH (nickel metal hydride) batteries because this kind, unlike Ni-Cad (nickel cadmium) batteries, has no memory effect. That means you don't have to totally discharge them.

- **CR-V3 lithium ion batteries:** This is a new kind of battery that takes the place of two standard AA batteries. Lithium batteries are the longest lasting and lightest batteries available, but they're also expensive. Then some smart guy figured out a way to put two batteries into one unit, thus considerably cutting the price. This new battery can average 650 photos before you have to change it. The CR-V3 is available also in a rechargeable form, thereby extending the life even further (and reducing your battery budget significantly).

If your eBay.co.uk photo studio includes a camera on a tripod (and it should), you can use a good, old-fashioned AC adapter (you know, the one that plugs into the wall).

Lighting

Trying to take good pictures of your merchandise can be frustrating. If you don't have enough light and use the camera's flash, the image may appear washed out. If you take the item outside, the sun may cast a shadow.

We've seen some eBay.co.uk sellers use a flash and instruct their children to shine a torch on the item as they photograph it from different angles – all the while hoping that the colour isn't wiped out. The autofocus feature on most digital cameras doesn't work well in low light.

After consulting specialists in the photo business to solve the digital camera lighting problem, we put together an inexpensive studio lighting set for online auction photography. Check out `www.coolebaytools.com` for information on how to obtain this package (refer also to Figure 11-1 to see the lighting set in use in a home photo studio).

Professional studio lights can be expensive, but you may be able to find a set for around £80. (You need at least two lights, one for either side of the item, to eliminate shadows.) Search eBay.co.uk for used studio lighting; we're sure you can find good deals.

Cloud Dome

If you're going to attempt to photograph a lot of jewellery, collectable coins, or other metallic items, you'll become frustrated at the quality of your pictures. Metallic objects seem to pick up random colour from any kind of light you shine on them for picture taking. Gold jewellery photographs with a silver tone and silver looks gold-ish!

After conferring with lots of eBay.co.uk photo gurus, we were told the secret of getting crisp, clear, close-up pictures: use a Cloud Dome. This device stabilises your camera (just as if you were using a tripod) and filters out all unwanted colour tones, resulting in image colours that actually look like your item.

The Cloud Dome is a large plastic bowl that you mount your camera on. You take pictures through the dome. The translucent white plastic diffuses the light so that your item is lit evenly from all sides, eliminating glare and bad shadows. Check out the manufacturer's Web site at `www.clouddome.co.uk` to see some amazing before and after pictures.

The Cloud Dome also manages to get the best images from gems – you can actually capture the light in the facets! Pearls, too, will show their lustre. Several eBay.co.uk members sell the Cloud Dome; we highly recommend it!

Props

To take good photos, you need some props. Although you may think it strange that a line item in your accounting program reads 'Props', they do qualify as a business expense. (Okay, you can put it under photography expense; *props* just sounds so Hollywood!)

How often have you seen some clothing on eBay.co.uk from a quality manufacturer, but you just couldn't bring yourself to bid more than £5 because it looked like it had been dragged behind a car and then hung on a hanger before it was photographed? Can you see how the fabric hangs on a body? Of course not. Take a look at Figure 11-2; that dress looks simply fantastic, darling!

Diane Von Furstenberg BRAND NEW with tags!
100% Silk Jersey dress
Fits Size 6 or 8
This lovely silk number is THE sexiest dress! It's by hot designer Diane Von Furstenberg (who is featured in the new issue of Vogue). It's a fabulous silk jersey spaghetti strap dress, with a sexy cowl neckline. The original price of the dress is $220, and it can be yours for the highest bid. Draping beautifully on the body, it's got a sexy below the knee length and a very flattering cut.
Bid with confidence and bid whatever you feel this great dress is worth to you as it is selling with NO RESERVE! Winning bidder to pay shipping & handling of $5.25, and must submit payment within a week of winning the auction. Credit cards are accepted through Billpoint and PayPal.

GOOD LUCK, HAPPY BIDDING!

Click below to...
View my other auctions - Win more than one and $AVE on shipping!

Figure 11-2: Midge, the mannequin, modelling one of our eBay.co.uk successes.

Mannequin

If you're selling clothing, photograph it on a mannequin. If you don't want to dive right in and buy a mannequin, at least get a body form to wear the outfit. Just search eBay.co.uk for *mannequin* to find hundreds of hollow forms selling for less than £20. If you sell children's clothing, get a child's mannequin form as well; and the same goes for men's clothes. Alternatively, find a friend to model the clothes. No excuse justifies hanger-displayed merchandise in your auctions.

Our mannequin has a great body and everything she wears sells at a profit. Many shops upgrade their mannequins every few years or so. If you know people who work at a clothes shop, ask when they plan to sell their old mannequins; you may be able to pick one up at a reasonable price.

Steamer

Clothing is fairly crumpled when it comes out of a shipping box. An item may also get crumpled lying around, waiting for you to photograph it and sell it on eBay.co.uk. If the clothing isn't new but is clean, run it through your dryer with Dryel (a home dry-cleaning product from the US) to take out any musty smells. Old, musty-smelling clothes can certainly sour a potentially happy customer. You can find Dryel on eBay.co.uk – surprise, surprise!

The clothes you want to sell may be crumpled, but ironing is a bind (and may damage the fabric), so do what retail professionals do: Use steamers to take the wrinkles out of freshly unpacked clothing. Get the type of steamer that you use while the article of clothing is hanging up, so you can just run the steamer up and down and get the wrinkles out. The gold standard of steamers is the Jiffy Steamer: It holds a large bottle of water (distilled only), rolls on the floor, and steams from a hose wand. Some models of Jiffy Steamer sell on eBay.co.uk for under £75. Until you're ready to make an investment that big, at least get a small handheld version that removes wrinkles; search eBay for *(garment,clothes) steamer* to find some deals.

Display stands, risers, and more

Jewellery does not photograph well on most people's hands and actually looks a lot better when you display it on a stand (see Figure 11-3) or a velvet pad. If you're selling a necklace, display it on a necklace stand, not on a person. We bought our display stands from a manufacturer but had to wait several months to receive them. Apparently, this type of quality display stand is made to order, so we recommend searching for them on eBay.co.uk (you'll get them sooner).

Risers can be almost anything that you use to prop up your item to make it more attractive in a picture. Put riser pieces that aren't attractive under the cloth that you use as a background. (You can find risers on eBay.co.uk.)

Figure 11-3:
An eBay.co.uk listing featuring a professional jewellery display.

Ralph Lauren Signed Silver 16' Necklace

This stunning, brand new designer necklace is just the right length, 16" – and adjustable for smaller necks. Signed on reverse of stirrup goldtone plate *(see photo below)*, also signed on the silver toggle. Your chance to get this retail $48 necklace for a fraction of the cost! The perfect gift for you or a friend.

Bid with confidence and bid whatever you feel this item is worth to you, as it is selling with *NO RESERVE*! I pack all my items carefully. Winning bidder to pay shipping & handling of $3, and must submit payment within a week of winning the auction. I will accept credit cards through BillPoint and PayPal - Good Luck, Happy Bidding!

You wouldn't believe what the back of some professional photo set-ups look like. Photographers and photo stylists think resourcefully when it comes to making the merchandise look good – from the front of the picture, anyway! We've seen the most creative things used to prop up items for photography:

- **Bottles of mercury:** Mercury is a heavy liquid metal. A photographer we once worked with used little bottles of this stuff to prop up small boxes and other items in a picture. But mercury is a poison, so we suggest you do the same with small bottles (prescription bottles work well) filled with sand.

- **Beeswax and clay:** To set up photos for catalogues, we've seen photographers prop up fine jewellery and collectable porcelain with beeswax (the kind you can get from the orthodontist works great) or clay. Beeswax is a neutral colour and doesn't usually show up in the photo. However, you must dispose of beeswax often because it picks up dirt from your hands and fuzz from fabric.

- **Museum Gel and Quake Hold:** These two products are invaluable when you want to hold a small object at an unnatural angle for a photograph. (These products are like beeswax and clay, but cleaner.) Museums use these putty-like products to securely keep breakables in one place – even during an earthquake!

- **un-du:** un-du is a clear liquid that removes sticky residue from almost anything. If your item has sticker residue on it, the mess is bound to show up in the picture. Squirt on a little un-du and use its patented scraper to remove the goo and bring back the shine. Although this is sold in the US, you can get hold of un-du (and QuakeHold) through sellers on ebay.com – expect to pay more for shipping!

- **Metal clamps and duct tape:** These multipurpose items are used in many photo shoots in some of the strangest places. Your mannequin may be a few sizes too small for the dress you want to photograph. How do you fix that problem? Don't pad the mannequin; simply fold over the dress in the back and clamp the excess material with a metal clamp, or use a small piece of duct tape to hold the fabric taut.

Keep a collection of risers and propping materials in your photo area so they're always close at hand.

Backgrounds for your images

Backgrounds come in many shapes and sizes. You can use paper, fabric, or one of the portable photo stages for smallish items.

In professional photo-talk, *seamless* is a large roll of 3-foot (and wider) paper that comes in various colours and is suspended and draped behind the model and over the floor. (Ever wonder why you never see the floor and wall come together in professional photos?) Photographers also drape the seamless over tabletop shots. Some people use fabrics such as muslin instead of seamless.

We keep satin and velvet on hand. (Clean black velvet with sticky tape before you use it in a picture – lint appears huge in photos.) Use neutral fabrics (such as white, light grey, natural, and black) for photographing your merchandise so that the colour of the fabric doesn't clash with or distract from your items.

The Cloud Dome people have also invented a great photo stage, which is portable (easy to store), non-breakable, simple to clean, and inexpensive. This stage is sold on eBay.co.uk and is pictured in Figure 11-4.

Figure 11-4:
Cloud Dome's photo stage (bottle not included).

Taking Good Pictures

If you have a small home photo studio set-up (see the preceding section) with a quality camera, a tripod, props, and lights, you're well on your way to taking some quality shots for your auctions. A few things to remember:

- ✔ **Zoom in on your item:** Don't leave a load of extraneous background in your pictures. Crop extra background in your photo-editing program (see the 'Image-Editing Software' section, a bit later in this chapter) before you upload the images to your image-hosting service.

- ✔ **Watch out for distracting backgrounds:** If you don't have a studio table-top, or if the item is something that won't fit on a table, try to make the background of the photo as simple as possible. If you're shooting the picture outside, shoot away from chairs, tables, hoses – you get the idea. If you're shooting in your home, move the laundry basket out of the picture.

One of our favourite eBay pictures featured a piece of fine silver taken by the husband of the woman selling the piece on eBay.co.uk. Silver and reflective items are hard to photograph because they pick up everything in the room in their reflection. In her description, the woman explained that the man reflected in the silver coffeepot was her husband and not part of the final deal. She handled that very well!

✔ **Be sure the items are clean:** Cellophane on boxes can get scruffy looking, clothing can get linty, and all merchandise can get dirt smudges. Not only do your items photograph better if they're clean, they sell better, too.

Clean plastic or cellophane with WD-40 (no kidding); this product takes off any sticker residue and icky smudges. un-du is the best adhesive remover for paper, cardboard, clothing, and more, plus it comes with a handy plastic scraper. Also keep an art rubber around to clean off small dirt smudges on paper items. Any cleaning solution can help your items, but use these chemicals with care so that you don't destroy the item while cleaning it.

✔ **Check the camera's focus:** Just because a camera has an autofocus feature doesn't mean that pictures automatically come out crisp and clear. Low light, high moisture, and other things can contribute to a blurred image. Double-check the picture before you use it.

Using a Scanner

Scanners have come a long way in the past few years. This once expensive item can now be purchased new for a little more than £50. If you sell books, autographs, stamps, or documents, a scanner may be all you need to shoot your images for eBay.co.uk.

When shopping for a scanner, don't pay too much attention to the resolution. As with digital cameras, images for the Internet (JPEGs) needn't be any higher than 72 ppi (pixels per inch). Any quality scanner can get that resolution these days. Quality makes a difference in the manufacture of the scanner, so stick with brand names.

Use a *flatbed* scanner, on which you lay out your items and scan away. You can use an HP OfficeJet, which is not only a scanner but also a printer and reducing/enlarging colour copier – most even come with a fax! These nifty flatbed units are available brand new on eBay.co.uk for around £150.

A few tips on scanning images for eBay.co.uk:

✔ If you're taking traditionally processed photographs and scanning them on a scanner, print them on glossy paper because they scan much better than those with a matt finish.

✔ You can scan 3-D items, such as a doll, on your flatbed scanner and get some respectable-looking images. To eliminate harsh shadows, lay a black or white t-shirt over the doll or her box so that it completely covers the glass. This way you have a clean background and you get good light reflection from the scanner's light.

✔ If an item is too big for your scanner's glass, simply scan the item in pieces, and then reassemble it to a single image in your photo-editing program (see the following section).

✔ Boxed items are a natural for a flatbed scanner. Just set them on top of the glass, and scan away. You can crop the shadowed background with your photo-editing software (see the following section).

Image-Editing Software

Lose the idea that the software that comes with your scanner is good enough. That software may be just fine for some uses, but the kind of control that you need is only available in *real* image-editing software, not a mere e-mail picture generator.

We've always been happy using Photoshop. However, this program is large, expensive, and a bit of an overkill for eBay.co.uk images. Recently we started using Paint Shop Pro by Jasc software (now part of Corel), a robust professional program at a fraction of the price of Photoshop. Paint Shop Pro is also one of the easiest-to-learn programs on the market. We've seen new packages of Paint Shop Pro 8.1 sell for as low as £13.99 (if you're a good shopper, we know you *can* find these deals). Hint: Look for sellers putting *Paint Shop* as one word (*Paintshop*) in the title.

Paint Shop Pro offers features that enable you to make a good picture out of a bad one. This program also has a brilliant export-to-Web feature that compresses the images so that they hold their quality while becoming smaller. Images compressed in this fashion download a lot faster for dial-up customers. You can also touch up your family photos in this easy-to-use program.

Don't forget that you are working with images not only for eBay items but also for your Web site. (Check out Chapter 8 for more about putting together a Web site.) The Corel Web site (www.corel.co.uk/servlet/Satellite?pagename=Corel3Uk/Downloads/Trials) offers free trial downloads.

A Home for Your Images

You need a professional and safe place to store your pictures for eBay.co.uk. If your images don't appear when someone clicks your auction, or if your images take too long to load, a user may click off your auction and go to the next one. If you have more than one option, test each with a few pictures because you want the most reliable one.

If you use auction management software, you may not need an FTP program to upload your images. Most complete management programs integrate their own FTP program as part of the package and may also include image storage space on their server. Check out Chapter 9 for more about auction management software packages.

Always put your eBay.co.uk images in a separate directory – not in an active part of your Web site. You may think that using your business Web site is a good place to store your images, but it isn't. If you want to keep track of your site statistics, such as the number of visitors, hits, and the like, hosting your own images will ruin the data. A call for one of your eBay images counts as a hit on your site, and you never get accurate Web site stats.

Free ISP space

Most ISPs (Internet Service Providers) give you at least 5MB of storage space for your personal home page. Although not appropriate for your final business site, this 5MB space is a perfect place to host your pictures. Everyone has an ISP, and all ISPs give you space. You may have to use an FTP program to upload to your Web space, or your ISP may supply its own uploader. Go to the home pages for your ISP (the member area), and check out what it offers. Visit Chapter 8 for more information on ISP space.

Auction management sites

If you're using one of the auction management Web sites that we discuss in Chapter 9, you're covered for most of your back office tasks. These Web sites supply enough Web space to hold all your eBay.co.uk images. They also have a convenient one-click upload from your hard drive.

If you find that you truly have no place to host your images, take a look at some of the less expensive auction management sites. As of writing, you can get image hosting *and* other auction utilities for around £10 a month at

- ✔ www.auctionpix.co.uk
- ✔ www.tele-pro.co.uk/ssl/submit_image.asp
- ✔ inkfrog.com
- ✔ manageauctions.com

eBay.co.uk Picture Services

You can also use eBay.co.uk Picture Services to host your photos for eBay, but the quality of your photos is better if you host them directly from a site.

Really clear pictures on Picture Services are few and far between. Picture Services reformats your photo to fit in a layout 400 pixels wide by 300 pixels tall and then compresses the file for quick viewing. This process can destroy the quality of your carefully photographed images if you haven't saved them in a compatible size. You're running a business, so be businesslike and use the method that presents your photos in their best light.

To get the free top-of-page image that you see on many auctions, you must use eBay Picture Services. We suggest that you use eBay Picture Services for your primary image and also use secondary images of your items hosted elsewhere. If one of the picture servers goes down, at least your listing will have pictures. The first picture is free; all you have to do is click the box on the Sell Your Item page's Picture Services area, next to Add picture. This picture will also be the default picture for use as your all-important gallery image. (See Chapter 10 for more on using the gallery.)

eBay.co.uk offers two versions of Picture Services. The basic version (see Figure 11-5) allows you to upload eBay-ready images as they appear on your computer.

If you want to rotate or crop the picture, you need the enhanced picture service. Click the <u>Upgrade</u> link, and a screen similar to Figure 11-6 appears.

Figure 11-5:
The basic
Picture
Services
photo-
hosting
page.

> **Add pictures & Gallery**
> Use these tips to add a great photo to your listing.
>
> | eBay Enhanced Picture Services | eBay Basic Picture Services | Your Web hosting |
>
> Upgrade to eBay Enhanced Picture Services at no additional cost. It's faster, lets you upload pictures of any size, and enables you to preview, crop and rotate your pictures.
>
> **Picture 1 (Free)**
> [   ] Browse...
> To add pictures to your listing, click Browse.
> **Picture 2 (£0.12)**
> [   ] Browse...
> **Picture 3 (£0.12)**
> [   ] Browse...
> **Picture 4 (£0.12)**
> [   ] Browse...
> **Picture 5 (£0.12)**
> [   ] Browse...
> **Picture 6 (£0.12)**
> [   ] Browse...
>
> Add up to 6 more pictures
>
> Having problems adding pictures? Try these troubleshooting tips.
> **Gallery options**
> Applies to first picture
> ☐ Gallery (£0.15) [Requires a picture, add a picture now]
>   Add a small version of your first picture to Search and Listings. See example
>
> ☐ Gallery Featured (£15.95) [Requires a picture, add a picture now]

To upload your pictures using the enhanced version, follow these steps:

1. **Click the Add Picture button, which appears in the picture frame.**

   A browsing window appears.

2. **Locate the directory that holds your eBay images on your computer.**

3. **Click the image in the browsing window.**

   The image name appears in the filename box.

4. **Click the Open box.**

   The selected image appears in the picture frame.

5. **To rotate the image, click the circular arrow (at the upper left of the main image box).**

6. **To crop the image:**

   a. **Click the crop box in the right corner of the larger image.**

      Two squares appear at opposite corners of your main image.

   b. **Click the frame on the outside of your image, and move the bar until the offensive area is cropped out.**

      You can crop like this from the sides, top, and bottom of the picture.

Sometimes Picture Services shrinks your image to a too-small size, but you can't do much about it. Just be sure to reload the image each time you re-list the item; otherwise, the gallery image may just get smaller and smaller. eBay continues to improve Picture Services, so don't give up on it. Use Picture Services for the free image, and be sure to upload secondary images from an outside site.

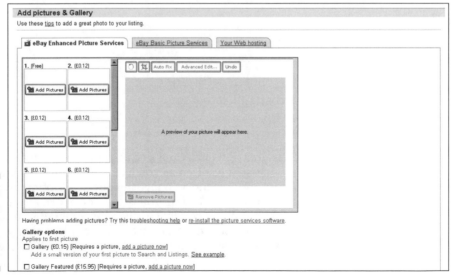

Figure 11-6: eBay.co.uk's Enhanced Picture Services.

HTML Made Easy

Our small grasp of HTML gets us only so far. We usually use a program such as CuteHTML to produce code for our Web site or eBay.co.uk listings. Luckily, you don't have to know a lot of code to produce eBay auctions.

The Sell Your Item form has an excellent, basic HTML generator that has a toolbar similar to the one in a word processor. As you can see in Figure 11-7, you can use the toolbar to change the size, font, or colour of the text. You can also insert coding by switching to the 'Enter your own HTML' view of the description to include your own hosted images in the listing description. (Check out Chapter 9 for some sample coding to use in your own listings.)

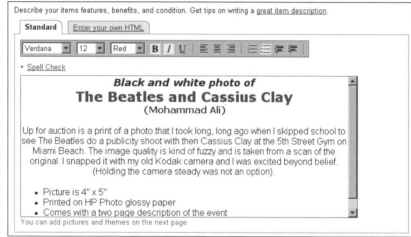

Figure 11-7: eBay.co.uk's HTML code generator.

For a quick and easy HTML fix, go to

```
www.coolebaytools.com
```

Then go to the Tolls area and click <u>Cool free ad tool</u>. You get a quick HTML generator; feel free to use it as often as you like. You incur no charge. You can select border colours and include an image in your description area – nothing fancy, mind you, just nice clean HTML. You type your information as indicated and select colours. When you finish, click the View Ad button. On the next page, you see HTML code for your auction description that you can cut and paste into the auction description area of the Sell Your Item page.

Chapter 12

Providing Excellent Customer Service

'The customer is always right' may be an old adage, but if you want your business to thrive on eBay, you need to take a leaf out of this book.

While not *always* right, the customer is your primary concern – and you must treat them thus. Businesses become successful by providing fantastic customer service and selling quality products. You are no different. The image that you project through your e-mails and ads shows bidders whether you are a good guy or a bad guy. Your e-mails should be polite and professional. Your ads shouldn't make prospective buyers feel like you're hustling them, sneaking in hidden fees, or being pushy with unnecessary bidding.

You don't have to have the most beautiful auctions to succeed on eBay. You need products that sell, and you must take the time to build good customer relations! In this chapter, we cover some ways – from writing effective auction descriptions to sending cordial e-mails – to let your customers know that they're number one in your book.

Providing a Homely Touch

eBay is a person-to-person marketplace. Although many sellers are businesses (like you), the perception is that sellers on eBay are individuals (as opposed to businesses) earning a living. The home-grown personal approach goes a long way to making you a successful eBay seller. One of the reasons many buyers come to eBay is that they want to support the individuals who had the get-up-and-go to start their own small businesses on the site.

After you write a catchy title for your auction (check out Chapter 10 for advice on how to do this), prospective buyers click your listing and scroll down to your description. Do they have to wade through pointless verbiage, losing interest along the way? Or do you get right down to business and state the facts about your item?

Here are a few things to remember when writing your auction description:

- **Write a factual description.** Do you carefully describe the item, stating every fact you know about it? Are you clear in your description and careful not to use any jargon? Does it answer all glaring questions a potential buyer may ask? If not, do some revising.

- **Include some friendly banter.** You want to make the customer feel comfortable shopping with you. Don't be afraid to let your personality show!

- **Update your 'My eBay' page.** Let people know a little about you and who they're dealing with. When customers have to decide between two sellers offering the same item and all else is equal, they typically place their bid with the seller who makes them feel secure.

- **Limit the number of auction rules (or terms of sale).** Some sellers include a list of rules that's longer than the item's description. Nothing turns off a prospective buyer like paragraph after paragraph of rules and regulations. If you really *must* put in a litany of rules, do not use capital letters and apply the following bit of HTML to make the size of the text smaller: `<font size=-1>`

- **Choose a reasonable typeface size.** Many users are still looking at eBay on an 800×600 display. If you design your auctions at 1024×768, your typefaces may be too large for the average user. Forcing users to scroll and scroll to find the details only frustrates them.

- **Quote the shipping charge.** Many bidders pass up auctions that don't disclose the delivery costs. Make use of eBay's shipping calculator to give your customers an idea of the shipping costs. If many others are selling the same item you're selling, quoting reasonable shipping costs will help you reel in buyers.

  Overcharge on shipping is just wrong. eBay buyers expect that you pad up to a pound for packing and shipping costs, but adding more than that can make you look like you're trying to squeeze every last penny out of your bidder . . . not a good feeling when you're on the receiving end!

- **Keep photos a practical size.** A large proportion of users still use a dial-up Internet connection, and if they have to wait for your large pictures to load, they may go elsewhere for the item. If your listing doesn't fully open within a few seconds, the person may back out and go on to another listing.

Telling your story

Being honest and forthright encourages customers to consider your offerings on eBay. Also, if you go the extra mile and give some bonus information, the customer may feel more at ease.

An excellent example comes from a PowerSeller, John Rickmon of e.vehicles. He always throws in a few special touches to draw in the customer. As you may gather by his user ID, John sells vehicles on eBay – and does very well out of it!

John posts his business philosophy at the end of his auctions; here's part of it:

My dealership is entirely focused on the sales of vehicles via the eBay format. I make all purchasing and sales decisions and am 100% responsible for the content of my auctions, including all text and photography.

I personally answer every e-mail and conduct all business regarding the sale of this vehicle.

I buy and list approximately 10–15 units per month; I look at hundreds of vehicles each week that do not cut the mustard.

This is my living. *I do this full time. I do not have a showroom. eBay has been my dealership for years, and all operations are focused towards bringing you the best vehicle possible at the best price you will find. I am committed to this format and take your vehicle purchase very seriously. You are dealing with a secure seller.*

Would you by a used car from this man? We think so!

Communicating with Your Customers

Perhaps English wasn't your favourite subject at school, but when it comes to being a professional, incorporating good grammar, proper spelling, and punctuation in your communications portrays you as a pro. Before writing this book, even we hooked up with some grammar and punctuation sites to brush up on our writing skills. (Okay, we also have brilliant editors covering up our transgressions . . .)

Throughout the rest of this section, we provide some examples of effective e-mails. Study these examples and also check out a few books on business letter writing (for example, *Writing Business Letters For Dummies*, by Sheryl Lindsell-Roberts and published by Wiley). Don't forget good manners either. You don't want to be too formal, but you do want to be personable and polite.

The initial inquiry

The first written communication you have with a prospective buyer is called an *inquiry e-mail*. A bidder can ask you a question about your item by clicking the <u>Ask the seller a question</u> link on the auction or sale page, which automatically generates an e-mail addressed to you. Often these questions are brief.

On average, about 20 per cent of inquiries to sellers don't get a response. We refuse to do business with someone who can't be bothered to respond to a simple question. Often responses are terse, brusquely written notes. Many people choose not to use punctuation or capitalisation in their e-mails – not very professional! Sellers who want our money must take the time to write a short, considerate reply that includes a greeting and a thank you for writing.

Respond quickly, clearly, and politely – including in the text a discreet sales pitch. Remind the soon-to-be bidder that you can combine several wins to save on shipping costs. Use this opportunity to point out other auctions you have that may also interest the writer – they'll be impressed by your customer service.

The letter can be brief and straightforward; for example, the following note was written in response to a question regarding the condition of an aluminium Christmas tree in a recent auction:

Hello,

Yes, the aluminium Christmas tree in my auction is in excellent condition. The 58 branches are full and lush and will look great for the holidays. Please write again if you have any more questions or concerns.

Don't forget to check my other auctions for a colour wheel and a revolving tree turner. They would look great with this tree, and I can combine them for shipping.

Thank you for writing,

Marsha
`www.coolebaytools.com`

Isn't that response nice? The note addresses the question in a respectful and personable manner. Writing an answer like this doesn't take long, and it could make the difference between a sale and a no-sale.

Also, inserting your Web site or eBay store address in your e-mail signature is a great way to get new customers to view your other merchandise (see above).

The winner's notification letter

Have you ever received a bulk-generated standard winner's confirmation letter? The seller hasn't bothered to fill in half the blanks, and you're verging on insulted by the 'can't be bothered' message? Receiving a note like this after you request that the seller combine purchases (and the letter pays no attention to your request) is especially annoying. A personal approach goes a long way with customers as is shown in the message below, sent by Marsha.

We're not saying you shouldn't automate your eBay business. We're merely suggesting – strongly recommending – that you take the time to personalise even your canned e-mail responses. If you decide to send automated responses, choose a program that allows you to combine multiple wins in one letter and to apply the correct shipping costs the first time.

Here's the tried and true winner's notice that Marsha sends out:

Congratulations!

Yours was the winning bid on eBay item #122342911 for the Emilio Pucci book! You got a great deal! I am looking forward to a pleasant transaction and positive feedback for both of us.

Please include a copy of this e-mail with your name and shipping address along with your payment:

Winning Bid Amount $14.95

Shipping and Handling $2.50

TOTAL Amount Due $17.45

You may pay by money order, with a personal check, or with a credit card through PayPal. If you are not set up with them, just e-mail me and I'll send you a PayPal invoice.

A money order or online payment assures immediate shipping upon receipt of payment! If you pay by check, I will ship your item after a 14-day clearing period; be sure to include the item name and your e-mail address with payment. Please send your payment to the address shown below:

Marsha Collier
1234 Anywhere Street
Los Angeles, CA 91352

Your payment is expected on or before Saturday, April 2, 2006. I look forward to receiving it. I will ship on receipt of payment in full, via priority mail with delivery confirmation.

Thank you for your Winning Bid! I am delighted to be dealing with you and know you will enjoy your purchase.

Marsha_c
Marsha Collier
`www.coolebaytools.com`

At the end of a winner's notice letter, offer your winner some special discounts or other offers from your Web site. Include a few items this particular winner may be interested in (based on the current win) and include a link to your site. Also include the reminder that you can combine postage and that you look forward to a response.

The payment reminder

Writing a payment reminder can get sticky. You don't want to aggravate the buyer, but time is money and you could be better off reposting your item. When writing a payment reminder, you need to be firm but pleasant. Real things can happen in people's lives. Family members become unwell, and people just plain forget. Perhaps your payment fell between the seats of the winner's car on the way to the post office. When you honestly forget to send a payment, nothing is more humiliating than someone haranguing you through e-mail. So remember that people do make mistakes, and check the winner's feedback before you send the letter. If you can garner from the feedback that this winner has a habit of not following through on bids, you can definitely be a bit firmer in your wording. Always set a clear deadline for receiving payment, as the following letter shows:

Hello

You won an auction of mine on eBay last week for the Emilio Pucci e book. Your payment was due yesterday, and it still has not arrived. Perhaps sending payment has slipped your mind considering your busy schedule. I know it can easily happen.

Please e-mail back within 48 hours and let me know whether you want to go through with our transaction. I'd like to put the item back up for sale if you don't want it.

Thank you for your bid,

Marsha Collier

Leaving feedback for buyers

After you leave feedback, you can't take it back and you can't repost to correct an erroneous evaluation of another user. We know that leaving feedback after you receive payment is easier, but waiting to see how the transaction evolves afterwards is prudent – especially if the package gets lost in the post or the item is damaged, turning a previously kind and sweet buyer into a screaming nutcase. You should evaluate a buyer based on more than whether the person pays for an item. (Buyers are supposed to do that – it's a contract, remember?) When leaving feedback for buyers, consider the following:

✔ Did they return your communications quickly?

✔ Did they pay in a timely manner?

✔ If a problem occurred with the item or in shipping, did they handle it in a decent manner or did they try to make your life a living hell?

Remember that sellers are judged on communication, shipping time, the quality of packaging, and friendliness. As a seller, you have the duty of leaving quality feedback to set guidelines that all sellers use to rate buyers.

How firm you choose to get with a non-paying bidder is up to you. We've dealt with a few non-paying bidders on eBay, but we've left only two negative feedbacks. Some people who tend to overbid are indeed violating the contract to buy, but legitimate reasons may explain why someone hasn't followed through on an auction. You must decide how forceful you want to be and how far you want to stretch your karma (what goes around comes around). Assess each case individually, and don't be hasty in leaving negative feedback until you know the whole story.

The payment received and shipping notice

We know that you probably aren't going to send out a payment-received letter for every transaction, but wouldn't it be nice if you did? Staying in constant communication with your buyers makes them feel more secure with you and with buying on eBay. You want buyers to come back, don't you?

When you receive payment and are ready to ship, sending a short note like the following helps to instil loyalty in your customer:

Hi there (insert name of winner)

Your payment was received, and your item will ship tomorrow. Please e-mail me when it arrives so that I can hear how pleased you are with your purchase.

When the transaction is over, I hope you will leave positive feedback for me because building a good reputation on eBay is very important. I'd really appreciate it, and I'll be glad to do the same for you.

Thank you for bidding & winning,

Marsha_c
Marsha Collier
www.coolebaytools.com

If you haven't heard from the buyer within a week, send another note.

The 'Your item is on its way' e-mail

We always send out the automatic e-mail from DHL or Parcel Force announcing the shipment tracking number. You can also send out an e-mail from PayPal by inserting the tracking number into the PayPal payment record. These e-mails aren't very personalised, so we follow up with another, more personal note:

Subject: Your book is on the way!

*Hi (*insert buyer's name*)*

You will be receiving another e-mail with the package's delivery confirmation number and information on the mode of shipment.

Thank you for buying my item. If there is any question when the package arrives, PLEASE e-mail me immediately. Your satisfaction is my goal, and I'm sure any problem can be easily taken care of. Please let me know when the package arrives so that we can exchange some very positive feedback!

Marsha Collier
www.coolebaytools.com

Good customer service gets you many repeat customers and loads of positive feedback. Good communication can head off problems before they start. If your customers receive running communication from you throughout your transactions, they're more likely to discuss a glitch than make a knee-jerk reaction and leave negative feedback.

Chapter 13

Money Matters

● ●

In This Chapter

▶ Finding the payment method that suits your needs

▶ Discovering the ins and outs of payment services

▶ Exploring merchant accounts

● ●

The hours you spend selecting your items, photographing them, touching up the pictures, and writing brilliant auction copy all come down to one thing: getting paid. Initially, you may be happy to take any form of payment, but as you become more experienced and collect for more auctions, you can decide which payment methods you prefer and which are more heartache than they're worth.

Receiving and processing payments takes time and patience. The more payment methods that you accept, the more information you have to keep track of. Throughout this chapter, we detail the various payment options (including how to handle payment from international buyers) and how each affects your business.

Big Deals Only: Banker's Draft

Banker's drafts commonly come into play with big transactions – like when you put down a deposit on a house – so they may not be the most convenient way to pay, but they are secure and give peace of mind.

A banker's draft is an 'instant cheque' that the payee's bank makes out – so you know he or she has the funds available to pay for the item, unlike a normal cheque that has to clear.

A bank charges for drawing up a banker's draft, as does PayPal. Unlike PayPal, however, the bank charges the buyer, not the seller. The bank fees are very steep, so give people more than just this option to pay.

Sign on the Line: Cheque and Postal Order

Another useful addition to your payment offering, *cheques* give both parties in the transaction peace of mind. Cheques can be cancelled and traced to an address if things go wrong on either side of the arrangement – although the payee may incur a fee for cancelling payment.

For the buyer, cheques also give proof of payment and are covered by eBay.co.uk's Buyer Protection Programme. Cheques are particularly good for big payments and can be offered alongside Paypal or debit card options to give your customers some flexibility.

Like cheques, *postal orders* are traceable to an address, but they can also be easily bought and sold at your local post office and are available regardless of whether you have a bank account.

Accepting cash payments

We're sure you've received cash from some of your winners. We don't like cash. If the buyer doesn't send the exact amount due, you have to call the buyer, who may claim that the correct amount should be there. Post can be stolen. All of a sudden, *you* must have lost the difference – and you have no recourse with cash.

Postal inspectors are constantly battling this problem, but you won't know your post is being stolen until you've missed enough letters – usually bills and outgoing cheques. Explaining to a buyer that the money never arrived is difficult. The thief has the cash while your reputation may be shot. You can e-mail, phone, and talk and discuss, but the bottom line is that you haven't received your money and the buyer insists you have it.

Hold This for Me: Escrow Service

Escrow.com (eBay's official escrow service, which works for both US and UK customers) can make a buyer feel more comfortable proceeding with transactions of higher value purchases. By using escrow, buyers gain peace of mind because they know the transaction will be completed securely and easily.

You or your buyer must register to use the Escrow.com service. When you want to offer escrow as a payment option in one of your auctions, be sure to indicate as much on the Sell Your Item form so that it appears on the auction page. After the auction, the seller should initiate the escrow by going to www.escrow.com. To proceed with escrow, the buyer must send payment to Escrow.com (see Figure 13-1). Escrow.com accepts all credit cards, banker's drafts, wire transfers, and personal or business cheques. A cheque is subject to a 10-day delay.

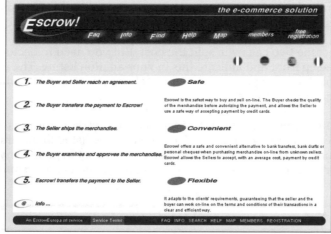

Figure 13-1: Starting an escrow with Escrow. com.

After the buyer makes the payment, Escrow.com asks the seller to ship the item to the buyer. When the buyer receives the merchandise, the inspection period begins promptly at 12:01 a.m. the next weekday and continues for a time previously set by the buyer and seller.

The buyer notifies Escrow.com that the merchandise is approved, and then Escrow.com releases payment to the seller. If the buyer doesn't feel that the merchandise is what he or she ordered, the buyer must return the item to the seller in its original condition, adhering to the Escrow.com shipping requirements. The buyer must also log on to the Web site to input return shipping information.

Helping your buyers buy safely

To give your customers a bit more confidence when they buy from you, why not apply for an accreditation from SafeBuy? The SafeBuy Assurance Scheme is operated by the Software Research Ltd, and is endorsed by TrustUK, the people that set up Which? Displaying the seal gives customers assurance that you are genuine and safe to deal with.

To be eligible for the SafeBuy seal, you must pass a rigorous test to ensure that you're a solid seller: You adhere to the Sale of Goods Act and the Data Protection Act, you won't use spam for marketing purposes, you don't exploit people, and so on.

An annual subscription to the SafeBuy Assurance Scheme costs £69, which seems like a lot, but it may make a big difference if you're selling lots of stock on eBay.co.uk.

In the event of a return, the seller has the same inspection period to ensure that the item was returned in its original condition. After condition is confirmed, Escrow.com will refund the buyer (less the escrow fee and, if agreed on ahead of time, the shipping fee). Either the buyer or the seller can pay the escrow fee; the two can even split the cost. But you need to decide who will pay the fee up front and indicate this in your auction listing. The buyer is responsible for paying the escrow fee for all returns, no matter who had initially agreed to pay the fees.

Table 13-1 includes a listing of the escrow fees. (Credit cards are not accepted for payments of more than $7,500.00.) The fees are listed in dollars because Escrow.com is a US service, but you can find the cost in pounds by doing an online currency conversion – www.xe.com has a good conversion tool.

Table 13-1	Escrow.com Escrow Fees		
Transaction Amount	*Cheque or Money Order*	*Credit Card*	*Wire Transfer*
Up to $1500.00	$22.00 + 0.5%	$22.00 + 3.0%	$37.00 + 0.5%
$1500.01 – $7,500.00	2%	4.5%	$15.00 + 2.0%
$7,500.01 – $20,000.00	1.75%	n/a	$15.00 + 1.75%
Over $20,0000.01	1.5%	n/a	$15.00 + 1.5%

Sadly, scams involving escrow services are beginning to crop up on the Internet. Unscrupulous sellers set up fake escrow sites, sell a load of high value items on eBay to unsuspecting buyers, and then direct the buyers to the faux escrow Web site to set up their escrow. The buyers send their money (thinking the transaction is safe). After the fraudulent seller collects a stack of money, they shut down the Web site and abscond with it! Some buyers are reluctant to use escrow to pay for expensive items. Check out this link to the eBay.co.uk help page for more information

```
pages.ebay.co.uk/help/community/escrow.html
```

1 Take Plastic: Credit Cards

As people become more comfortable with using credit cards on the Internet, so they become more popular for eBay.co.uk payments. Plus, major credit card payment services insure eBay payments to registered users, making credit cards safe for the buyer and easy for you. Credit card transactions are instantaneous; you don't have to wait for a piece of paper to travel cross-country.

For all this instantaneous money transfer, however, you pay a price. Whether you have your own *merchant account* (a credit card acceptance account in the name of your business) or take credit cards through a payment service (more on this just below), you pay a fee. Your fees can range from 2 per cent to 7 per cent, depending on how you plan to accept cards and which ones you accept.

A downside of accepting credit cards for your online sales exists. To protect yourself, please be sure to check the feedback – both feedback they've received and feedback they've left – of all bidders before accepting any form of credit card payment for a big-ticket item. Some buyers are chronic complainers and are rarely pleased with their purchases. A buyer may not be satisfied with your item after it ships and can simply call their credit card company and get credit for the payment; you'll be charged back (your account will be debited) the amount of the sale. (See the 'Forget the buyer: Seller beware!' sidebar in this chapter.)

Credit card payment services

Person-to-person payment systems, such as eBay.co.uk's PayPal, allow buyers to authorise payments from their credit card or current accounts directly to the seller. These services make money by charging percentages and fees for each transaction. The transaction occurs electronically through an automated clearinghouse. The payment service releases to the seller only the buyer's shipping information; all personal credit card information is kept private. A person-to-person payment service transaction speeds up the time it takes the buyer to get merchandise because sellers are free to ship as soon as the service lets them know that the buyer has made payment and the payment has been processed.

From the seller's point of view, person-to-person payment service transaction fees are lower than the 2.5 to 3.5 per cent (per transaction) that traditional credit card companies charge for merchant accounts (get the details in the 'Your very own merchant account' section, later in this chapter). Even traditional retailers may switch their online business to these services to save money. In this section, we discuss the top payment services and how each works.

Forget the buyer: Seller beware!

When buyers dispute a sale, they can simply call PayPal or their credit card company and refuse to pay for the item. You lose the sale and possibly won't be able to retrieve your merchandise. A payment service or merchant account will then *chargeback* your account without contacting you and without negotiating. Technically, the buyer has made the purchase from the payment service – not from you – and the payment service won't defend you. We've heard of chargebacks occurring as long as six months after the transaction, although eBay.co.uk says they can occur no later than 60 days after they sent you the first bill on which the transaction or error appeared. No one is forcing the buyer to ship the merchandise back to you. Just like eBay Fraud Protection (see Chapter 3), the credit card companies skew the rules to defend the consumer. As the seller, you have to fend for yourself. See Chapter 4 on how to report fraudulent buyers. You usually have no way to verify that the shipping address is the one the credit card bills to. So, to add to your problems, the card may actually be stolen.

PayPal confirms through AVS (Address Verification Service) that the buyer's credit card billing address matches the shipping address and gives you the option to not accept payments from buyers whose addresses don't match. PayPal offers seller protection against spurious chargebacks under the following circumstances:

- Fraudulent card use
- False claims of non-delivery

See the section on PayPal for more details on how to be covered by seller protection.

If the issuing bank resolves a chargeback in the buyer's favour, PayPal charges you a fee if you're found to be at fault, but will waive the fee if you meet all the requirements of the PayPal Seller Protection policy.

Major credit card companies are now trying to curb online fraud for their merchant accounts. Visa has the new Verified by Visa acceptance, which takes buyers to a Visa screen (through software installed on the merchant's server) and verifies their identity through a Visa-only password. MasterCard uses SET (Secure Electronic Transactions), a similar encrypted transaction verification scheme. These systems are expected to substantially reduce fraud and chargebacks.

Before you decide which credit card payment service to use, get out your calculator and check their Web sites for current rates. Calculate your own estimates; don't rely on a site's advertised samples. We've found that the charts on the Web tend to leave out certain minor fees. We've also found that comparison charts quoting the competition's prices tend to include optional fees. Beware — and do your own maths.

When you pay the fee to your payment service, realise that the total amount of your transaction – including shipping fees and handling charges – incurs a fee. The payment service charges a percentage based on the total amount running through its system.

An Easy Way to Pay: PayPal

According to eBay.co.uk, nine in ten sellers offer PayPal as a payment option for customers, and you can see why – it provides a secure, tried, and tested way of sending and receiving money for items. eBay also own the company that runs this service – a fair endorsement, we think you'll agree.

Using PayPal is quicker than a cheque or postal order, the system is integrated into eBay, no set up or monthly fees exist, and you can get help round the clock by calling 08707 307 191. On the minus side, PayPal creams off a small amount of money from your auction when you receive payment.

Other PayPal benefits that eBay.co.uk cites include:

- ✓ Sellers don't see buyers' credit card details (they're encrypted through PayPal's system), which limits the risk of unauthorised use.
- ✓ PayPal's Buyer Protection Programme covers items up to £500 if they are lost, stolen or damaged.
- ✓ PayPal can track payments and knows to whom they are sent.
- ✓ Payment is deposited directly into the seller's account.

PayPal (see Figure 13-2) allows buyers to safely click and pay with a credit card or e-cheque directly from eBay after they win an auction or make a purchase. PayPal is conveniently integrated into all eBay transactions. If your auction uses the Buy It Now feature or is a fixed-price listing, buyers can pay for their purchases immediately with PayPal payments.

Figure 13-2:
The
PayPal.com
home page.

To accept credit card payments, you must have a premier or business level account. Buyers may join when they win their first auction and want to pay with PayPal, or they can go to www.PayPal.com and sign up. The situation is slightly different for the seller. You need to set up your PayPal account *before* you choose to accept it in your auctions or sales.

Here are more than a few particulars about PayPal accounts:

✔ Auction payments are deposited into your PayPal account. Choose one of several ways to get your money:

• Have the money transferred directly into your registered current account.

• Keep the money in your PayPal account for making payments to other sellers.

✔ You get your own profile page when you sign up to PayPal (see Figure 13-3) – you can edit account details and general information about what cards you use, view eBay.co.uk auction accounts, and even check your time zone.

✔ As a seller with a premier or business account, you can choose to accept or deny a payment without a confirmed address. A confirmed address means that the ship to address indicated by the buyer is the same as the billing address on the credit card the buyer chose to register with PayPal. On the accept or deny page, information about the buyer is shown, including verification status, account creation date, and participation number.

Figure 13-3:
The PayPal
Member
profile page.

 ✔ PayPal sometimes fines sellers for chargebacks – the fine is calculated in euros but is about £7.50, – or it can retain the value of the chargeback from your PayPal account.

Look at Table 13-2 for more information about PayPal fees.

Table 13-2	PayPal Fees	
Action/Activity	*Personal Account*	*Premier/Business Account*
Open an account	Free	Free
Send money	Free	Free
Withdraw funds	Free for £50.00 or more, £0.25 for £49.99 or less to bank accounts in the UK	
Add funds	Free	Free
Receive funds	Free	1.9% + £0.20 to 3.4% + £0.20
Multiple currency transactions	Exchange rate includes a 2.5% fee	Exchange rate includes a 2.5% fee

A brilliant feature of PayPal is the ability to download your sales and deposit history to your computer. Although PayPal also offers files that integrate with QuickBooks (more on QuickBooks in Chapter 16), the standard downloads are feature-rich. Rather than importing just sales figures, you see each and every detail of your transaction – dates, names, addresses, phone numbers, amounts, and more. Even fees and taxes are broken down separately, making bookkeeping a breeze. The download imports into Microsoft Works and Excel. Downloading your history can help you calculate income taxes and VAT, reconcile your accounts, predict sales trends, calculate total revenues, and perform other financial reporting tasks. Downloaded sales and deposit histories also give you an excellent customer database.

The deposits download gives you detailed information for all the deposits that you receive: payments, PayPal transaction and deposit fees, refunds, rebates, and any adjustments made to your account.

Follow these steps to download your sales and deposit histories:

1. **On your PayPal Main Overview page, click the History tab.**

2. **Click the <u>Download My History</u> link, on the right side of the page.**

3. **Enter the time span and the file format for the information that you want to view.**

4. **Click the Download History button.**

   The information appears on the screen. Or, if the servers are busy, you'll receive an e-mail (usually in a minute or two) when the reports are ready.

5. **Save the file in a directory that you can conveniently access for bookkeeping.**

You can just double-click the file to open it in Excel or Works. You now have all the information you could possibly need to apply to your bookkeeping program.

Registering with PayPal

If you aren't registered with PayPal yet, use the convenient <u>Selling</u> link on the All Selling page, which you reach from your My eBay page. To get more information, just click the <u>PayPal related</u> link to arrive at the PayPal Seller Overview page (see Figure 13-4), and then click the Sign Up button to begin registration. The registration form in Figure 13-5 appears. Type in what country you're from, fill in the basic required information, and you're in.

Figure 13-4:
The PayPal
Seller
Overview
page.

Figure 13-5:
The new
seller
registration
page.

The convenience of PayPal integration into the eBay site shines when your item is purchased. Winners just click a Pay Now button that pops up on your auction page immediately after the listing closes. When you list auctions, you pre-set the shipping and handling charges that appear in the shipping box at the bottom of the page. When winners click the Pay Now button, they're taken directly to a payment page set up with your information. The process is as easy as purchasing something through Buy It Now.

When a purchase is made and the payment is deposited in your PayPal account, the system holds the money until you choose how you want to withdraw it.

PayPal accepts payments from 42 countries. For a current list of countries from which PayPal accepts payments, sign on to your PayPal account and go to

```
www.paypal.com/uk/cgi-bin/webscr?cmd=_display-approved-
               signup-countries
```

Because credit card and identity theft is so prevalent on the Internet, PayPal uses the extra security measure provided by Visa and MasterCard called CVV2. Most credit cards have three additional numbers listed on the back, immediately following the regular 16-digit number. Merchants use these numbers for security or verification but aren't allowed to store them, so they're presumably protected from hackers.

Withdraw your funds from the PayPal account on a regular basis; you need that money to operate your business. Don't let this account become a temporary savings account – unless you choose the PayPal interest-bearing account (check out www.PayPal.com for more details).

Your very own merchant account

If your eBay.co.uk business is bringing in more than £10,000 a month, a credit card merchant account may be for you. At that level of sales, discounts kick in and your credit card processing becomes a savings to your business rather than an expense. Before setting up a merchant account, however, look at the costs carefully. Charges buried in the small print make fees hard to calculate and even harder to compare. Even those credit card companies who advertise low fees often don't deliver. Look at the entire picture before you sign a contract.

Your own bank may be the best place to begin looking for a merchant account: They know you, your credit history, and your business reputation and have a stake in the success of your business. Build good credit before pursuing a merchant account because your credit rating is your feedback to the offline world.

If your bank doesn't offer merchant accounts for Internet-based businesses, find a broker to evaluate your credit history and hook you up with a bank that fits your needs and business style. These brokers make their money from your application fee, from a finder's fee from the bank that you finally choose, or both.

After you get a bank, you are connected to a *processor*, or transaction clearinghouse. Your bank merely handles the banking; the clearinghouse is on the other end of your Internet connection when you're processing transactions, checking whether the credit card you're taking is valid and not stolen or already up to the limit.

Table 13-3 highlights various possible costs associated with setting up and maintaining a merchant account.

Table 13-3	Possible Internet Merchant Account Fees
Fee	*Average Amount*
Set-up fee	£10 – £150
Monthly processing fee to bank	2.5% (1.5% – 5%)
Fee per transaction	10p – 30p
Processor's fee per transaction	20p – 40p
Internet discount rate	2% – 4%
Monthly statement fees	£5 – £10
Monthly minimum processing fee	£10 – £20
Gateway processing monthly fee	£10 – £20
Application fees	£25 – £300
Software purchase	£200 – £500
Software lease	£20 per month
Chargeback fee	£10.00

Remember that some merchant accounts will charge you some of these fees and others may have a load of little snipes at your wallet. In the following list, we define some of the fees in Table 13-3:

✓ **Set-up fee:** A one-time cost that you pay to either your bank or to your broker.

✓ **Discount rate:** A percentage of the transaction amount (a discount from your earnings), taken off the top along with the transaction fee before the money is deposited into your account.

✔ **Transaction fee:** A fee per transaction paid to the bank or to your gateway for the network.

✔ **Gateway or processing fee:** Your fee for processing credit cards in real time paid to the Internet gateway.

✔ **Application fee:** A one-time fee that goes to the broker or perhaps to the bank.

✔ **Monthly minimum processing fee:** If your bank's cut of your purchases doesn't add up to this amount, the bank takes it anyway. For example, if your bank charges a minimum monthly fee of £20 and you don't hit £20 in fees because your sales aren't high enough, the bank charges you the difference.

If you're comfortable with all the information in the preceding list and in Table 13-3, and you're looking for a broker, heed our advice and read everything a broker offers carefully. Don't miss any hidden costs.

The VeriSign Payment Services

If you have less than 1000 transactions a month through eBay.co.uk and your Web site, you may want to check out some of the services from VeriSign, a publicly-traded company and the world's largest Internet trust service. A respected world-class company and the leader in its field, VeriSign offers gateway services at a reasonable price.

To participate in VeriSign's gateway services, you must first sign up for a merchant account from your bank, PayPal, or by applying through preferred Merchant Account providers. The VeriSign service picks it up from there. You can integrate the service directly into your Web site. When you send out your winner's congratulatory letter, include a link to the page on your site that links to VeriSign. When your orders are submitted to VeriSign for processing, both you and your customer receive a transaction receipt acknowledgement through e-mail when the transaction has been processed. VeriSign processes your transactions while you're online.

Visit www.verisign.co.uk/index.html for more details.

Chapter 14

Delivering on Your Promise

*W*e think the best part of eBay.co.uk is making the sale and receiving payment. After that part of the transaction comes the depressing and tedious process of fulfilling your orders. Don't feel bad if this is the point that makes you take pause and sigh. Order fulfilment is one of the biggest problems (and yuckiest chores) that faces any mail order or online enterprise. The onerous task of packing and mailing is the bane of almost all businesses.

But as an eBay businessperson, you *must* attend to these tasks, however much you'd rather not. So in Chapter 17, we detail what you need for packing (boxes, bubble wrap, and so on) and some options for purchasing online postage. And in this chapter, we explain just how your items can get to their destinations, exploring your shipping options, costs, and insurance coverage along the way.

Finding the Perfect Shipping Carrier

When considering shipping options, you first need to determine what types of packages you generally send (small packages that weigh less than two pounds or large and bulky packages) and then decide how you want to send your items. Planning your shipping method before you list the item on eBay.co.uk is a good idea.

Shipping the BIG stuff!

In the US, www.freightquote.com negotiates rates with several major freight forwarders. Before attempting to sell a heavy item, you can sign onto this Web site with the weight and dimensions of your shipment, and it gives you a free quote on the spot. The UK version of the service is under construction at the time of writing, but look for www.freightquote.co.uk in the near future.

Deciding on your carrier can be the most important decision in your eBay business. You need to decide which carrier is more convenient for you (close to your home base, provides pick-up service, gives better customer service) and which is the most economical (leverages your bottom line). Most eBay sellers send packages using ground service rather than airmail or overnight, but a shipper who can give you both options may be offering you a good deal because you don't have to deal with more than one vendor.

Settling on one main shipper to meet most of your needs is important because all your records will be on one statement. You may also need a secondary shipper for special types of packages. One shipper can't be everything to every business, so having an account with more than one can be to your advantage. Also, shippers may not sign up new accounts as readily in the middle of a strike or work slowdown.

In this section, we give you the low-down on the two major carriers – Royal Mail and Parcel2go (backed by DHL), as well as a small online service called www.e-parcels.co.uk Parcel2go and e-parcels.co.uk are run specifically for eBay.co.uk users, so you can see who fits your requirements. However, e-parcels.co.uk only delivers packages up to 30kgs; for bigger deliveries, visit its sister site www.deliverebay.co.uk. For a summary of shipping costs from these three carriers, see Table 14-1.

Delivery costs vary according to the size and weight of the parcel, as well as where you're sending it and how quickly you want it to get there. Compare prices – remember that these vary according to the parcel's vital statistics. Table 14-1 offers a general price guide.

Table 14.1	Sample Shipping Costs within the UK		
Delivery Service	*400g*	*600g*	*800g*
DHL Parcel2go 3-Day Delivery	£8.99 + VAT	£8.99 + VAT	£8.99 + VAT
DHL Parcel2go Jiffy Bag*	£6.99 + VAT	£6.99 + VAT	£6.99 + VAT
Royal Mail Second Class	£1.14	£1.75	£2.90

Delivery Service	400g	600g	800g
Royal Mail First Class	£1.40	£2.15	£3.36
e-parcels.co.uk 48-Hour Delivery	£9.75	£9.75	£9.75
e-parcels.co.uk Next Day Delivery	£10.45	£10.45	£10.45

* Size restrictions apply to this service.

Royal Mail

Royal Mail is the most recognised letter deliverer in the UK, and the company also has a pretty nifty (and cost-effective) parcel delivery service. You can pay for your postage online, receive a discount for sorting packets yourself, and even find out someone's postcode through the Royal Mail Web site (see Figure 14-1).

The biggest benefit, however, is that Royal Mail costs a lot less than many of its rivals – as you can see in Table 14-1. However, as parcels get bigger, the cost difference is less obvious, so compare before you send! Check out www.royalmail.com for more info.

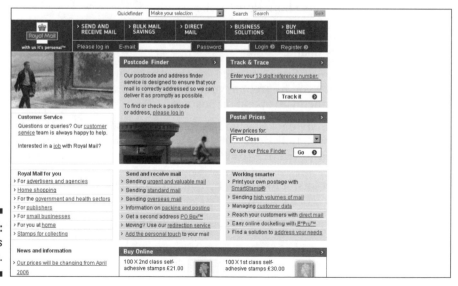

Figure 14-1: Royal Mail's homepage.

The Royal Mail postal prices page (see Figure 14-2) allows you to pick the type of delivery service you require. Do you want insurance? Is the package so urgent that it must be there tomorrow? Do you want recorded delivery for extra peace of mind? Select the shipping options you want, check the costs, and you're on your way.

Figure 14-2: The Royal Mail postage options page.

A few fast facts about Royal Mail services:

- ✔ You can print out your own labels for your packages and track all shipments online.

- ✔ The Smart Stamp service (stamps that you download from the Internet) enables you to prepare your parcel whenever you like and keep track of how much you spend on postage.

- ✔ Send more packages and get bigger discounts. Royal Mail gives you money off bulk deliveries. Go to: `www.royalmail.com/portal/rm/jump2?mediaId=400047&catId=400046` for more info.

You can get lots of hints and tips on improving your postal experience by visiting

```
www.royalmail.com/portal/rm/jump2?catId=400105&mediaId=
400120
```

DHL Parcel2go

Parcel2go is an online shipping specialist with a remit to provide affordable delivery services to small businesses like your eBay.co.uk shop. Parcel2go is backed by DHL – the monster courier service – giving you a bit more peace of mind that your stuff will turn up on time. The company's homepage is shown in Figure 14-3.

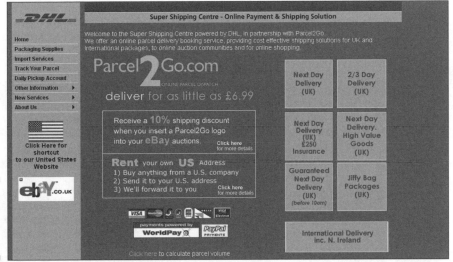

Figure 14-3:
The Parcel2go hub.

Specifically designed with eBay.co.uk in mind, Parcel2go features a small, manageable range of key services. Unlike Royal Mail, which has features coming out of its ears, Parcel2go offers just four options: Next Day Delivery, 2- to 3-day Delivery, Jiffy Bag packages, and International Deliveries. These services are designed to keep costs down, but you can add insurance to next day deliveries.

Prices range from £6.99 for standard Jiffy Bag delivery to £18.99 for high value goods that have to be there tomorrow morning. Remember to add on VAT when ordering.

The service works very simply. You register to the Web site (www.parcel2go. com), fill in your delivery details, pay for delivery, and then the courier comes round and picks up your stuff.

A few fast facts about Parcel2go services:

- ✔ You get a 10 per cent discount if you include a Parcel2go logo in your eBay.co.uk auctions. The service is available only in the UK.
- ✔ You can track your parcels in the UK, Europe, and across the world (see Figure 14-4).
- ✔ You can receive preferential rates if you send more than five parcels a day on average.
- ✔ Parcel2go offers a flat fee for parcels under 25kg and adds on a surcharge for bigger items.
- ✔ Packages are insured up to the value of £100 as standard.

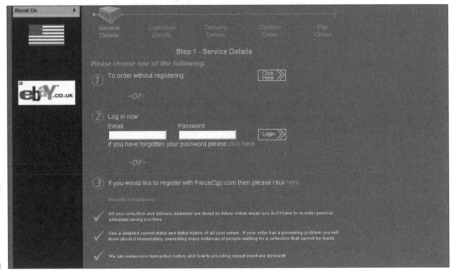

Figure 14-4:
The
Parcel2go
order page.

e-parcels.co.uk (see Figure 14-5) works in much the same way as Parcel2go.com – you select a shipping option and pay a fee, and then e-parcel.co.uk comes round and picks up your item. The fees and options offered by Parcel2go and e-parcels.co.uk vary, of course, so compare them.

e-parcels.co.uk is an online parcel delivery 'broker'. The company works with carriers to provide deals for its customers. Once you book a delivery slot, your parcel is picked up between 10am and 6pm on the day of collection – so the service only works if you're in all day. The company offers a same day delivery service – the cut-off point is 11am.

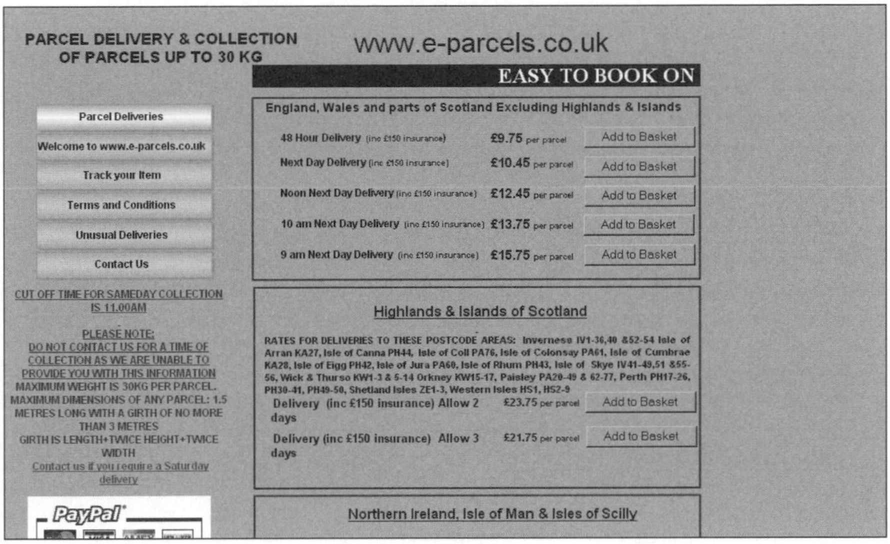

Figure 14-5:
The
e-parcels.
co.uk
homepage.

A few fast facts about e-parcels.co.uk services:

✔ The company's Web site enables you to book collection of your packages, track deliveries, and contact customer services.

✔ The maximum weight and size of parcels you can ship is 30kgs. Maximum dimensions are 1.5 metres in length, and 3 metres girth. Girth here means length + (2 × width) + (2 × height).

✔ www.deliverebay.co.uk, Parcel2go's sister Web site, deals with bigger parcels.

✔ Most of the UK is covered by the same flat rate, but deliveries to Northern Ireland, the Highlands of Scotland, and the Isles of Man and Scilly cost a bit more.

Part IV
Your eBay.co.uk Admin

"We only started our eBay business, webuyoldmasters.co.uk, this morning and the response has been amazing."

In this part . . .

Setting up your eBay.co.uk business as a real business entity involves some unpleasant paperwork, applying for licenses, organising, and record keeping. Even though you should discuss you issues with a professional, we fill in the blanks and get you started on the right track. We also provide a handy checklist of the items you need to run your business online, such as your legal status, book-keeping requirements, and software to automate shipping.

Chapter 15

Going Legit

In This Chapter

▶ Deciding your business format

▶ Covering the legalities

*B*usiness format? 'What's a business format?' you may ask. We hate to be the ones to tell you, but you can't just say, 'I'm in business,' and be in business. When you started selling on eBay.co.uk, maybe you were happy just adding a few pounds to your income. Now that the money is coming in faster, you have a few more details to attend to. Depending on how far you're going to take your business, you have to worry about taxes, bookkeeping, and possible ramifications down the line.

We want to remind you that we're *not* lawyers or accountants. The facts we give you in this chapter are gleaned from what we've learned over the years. When you begin a formal business, involving a lawyer and an accountant is a smart move. At the very least, visit www.startups.co.uk, a great Web site that offers some excellent business startup advice and success stories.

One of the first rules in the eBay.co.uk User Agreement reads '. . . your eBay account (including feedback) and User ID may not be transferred or sold to another party'. This rule means that if you begin your business on eBay.co.uk with another person, you need some kind of agreement up front about who gets the user ID in case of a sale. And if you sell your business, the person with the original ID needs to be involved actively with the new company – as the rules say, your feedback can never be transferred or sold. A new owner has to start a new account on eBay.co.uk with a new name – unless the principal from the old company was contractually involved and was the actual eBay seller.

To our knowledge, no one has tested this rule in court, and we bet you don't want to be the first to face eBay's top-notch lawyers. Know that this is the rule about feedback and User ID and plan for it.

Types of Businesses

Businesses come in several forms, from a sole trader all the way to a multinational corporation. However, a corporation designation isn't as scary as it may sound. Yes, Microsoft, IBM, and eBay are corporations, but so are many individuals running businesses. Each form of business has its plusses and minuses – and costs. We go over some of the fees involved in incorporating later in this chapter. For now, we detail the most common types of businesses, which we encourage you to weigh carefully.

Before embarking on any new business format, consult with a professional in the legal and financial fields.

Sole trader

If you're running your business by yourself part time or full time, you're a *sole trader*. 'A sole trader is the simplest form of business – nothing is easier or cheaper. Most people use this form of business when they're starting out. Many people then graduate to a more formal type of business as things get bigger.

If a husband and wife file a joint tax return, they *can* run a business as a sole trader (but only one of you can be the proprietor). However, if both you and your spouse work equally in the business, running it as a partnership – with a written partnership agreement – is a much better idea. (See the next section, 'Partnership', for more information.) A partnership protects you in case of your partner's death. In a sole proprietorship, the business ends with the death of the proprietor. If the business has been a sole proprietorship in your late spouse's name, you may be left out in the cold.

While being in business adds a few expenses, you can deduct from your taxes many expenses relating to your business. As a sole trader you *can* run the business out of your personal bank account (although we don't advise doing so). The profits of your business are taxed directly as part of your own income tax. As a sole trader, you're at risk for the business liabilities. All outstanding debts are yours, and you could lose personal assets if you default.

Also, you must consider the liability of the products you sell on eBay.co.uk. If you sell foodstuff, vitamins, or neutraceuticals (new age food supplements) that make someone ill, you may be personally liable for any court-awarded damages. If someone is hurt by something you sell, you may also be personally liable as the seller of the product.

Partnership

A business involving two or more people can be a *partnership*. A general partnership can be formed by an oral agreement. Each person in the partnership contributes capital or services and both share in the partnership's profits and losses. The income of a partnership is taxed to both partners, based on the percentage of the business that they own or upon the terms of a written agreement.

Make sure that you can have a good working relationship with your partner: This type of business relationship has broken up many a friendship. Writing up a formal agreement when forming your eBay.co.uk business partnership is an excellent idea. This agreement is useful in solving any disputes that may occur over time.

In your agreement, outline things such as

- ✔ How to divide the profits and losses
- ✔ Compensation to each of you
- ✔ Duties and responsibilities of each partner
- ✔ Restrictions of authority and spending
- ✔ How disputes should be settled
- ✔ What happens if the partnership dissolves
- ✔ What happens to the partnership in case of death or disability

One more important thing to remember: As a partner, you're jointly responsible for the business liabilities and actions of the other person or people in your partnership – as well as your own. Again, this is a personal liability arrangement. You are both personally open to any lawsuits that come your way through the business.

In most cases, one of the partners has to fill in a self-assessment tax form supplied by HM Revenue & Customs.

Limited company

A *limited company* is similar to a partnership, but also has many of the characteristics of a corporation. A limited company differs from a partnership mainly in that the liabilities of the company are not passed on to the owners. Unless you sign a personal guarantee for debt incurred, the owners are responsible only to the total amount they have invested into the company. But all owners *do* have liability for the company's taxes.

You need to put together an operating agreement, similar to the partnership agreement. This agreement also will help establish which members own what percentage of the company for tax purposes.

A limited company has to pay corporation tax on its income and profits. In a limited company, the owners are responsible for working out how much tax the company needs to pay. A self-assessment form can be submitted to HM Revenue & Customs.

Corporation

A *corporation* has a life of its own: Its own name, its own bank account, and its own tax return. A corporation is a legal entity created for the sole purpose of doing business. One of the main problems a sole trader faces when incorporating is realising that he or she can't help themselves to the assets of the business. Yes, a corporation can have only one owner: The shareholder(s). If you can understand that you can't write yourself a cheque from your corporation, unless the cheque is for salary or for reimbursement of legitimate expenses, you may be able to face the responsibility of running your own corporation.

As a corporation, several ways exist to avoid a big tax bill – investing profits back in to the business is one of them. If your business gets so big that tax becomes an issue (congratulations!), you almost certainly need an accountant to deal with your company finances. For a quick guide to tax liabilities, however, see Table 15.1.

Table 15-1	Corporation Tax Considerations	
Corporation Tax Rate	*Level of Profit on Which Rate Is Charged*	*2005/06 Rates & Allowances*
Starting rate	On profits of £0 – £10,000	0% (Note: from 1 April 2004, a minimum rate of 19% is charged when profits are distributed to non-company shareholders. The zero rate remains if profits are re-invested in the business.)
Marginal starting rate relief	On profits of £10,001 – £50,000	19% less relief. The relief is £50,000 minus the amount of profits multiplied by 19/400.

Corporation Tax Rate	Level of Profit on Which Rate Is Charged	2005/06 Rates & Allowances
Small companies' rate	On profits of £50,001 – £300,000	19%
Marginal small companies' relief	On profits of £300,001 – £1,500,000	30% less relief. The relief is £1,500,000 minus the amount of profits multiplied by 11/400.
Main rate	On profits of £1,500,001 and above	30%

Often in small corporations, most of the profits are paid out in tax-deductible salaries and benefits. The most important benefit for a business is that any liabilities belong to the corporation. Your personal assets remain your own, because they have no part in the corporation.

Taking Care of Regulatory Details

Here are some important words to make your life easier in the long run: Don't ignore regulatory details. Doing so may make life easier at the outset, but if your business is successful, one day your casual attitude will catch up with you. Ignorance is no excuse. To do business, you must comply with all the rules and regulations that are set up for your protection and benefit. We've included some major regulations in this section, but for a complete list go to www.businesslink.gov.uk – the government's business support service.

Health & Safety

You are legally obliged to create a safe environment when you create your eBay.co.uk office, especially if you have employees. The Health & Safety Executive says you must minimise occupational risk by giving regular breaks, providing training, and establishing safe work stations without the risk of tripping or slipping.

Privacy laws

The Privacy and Electronic Communications Directive regulates the use of unsolicited e-mails (spam), text messages, and cookies (which store details about people coming to your Web site), so you can't spam people or send out marketing material without people's say-so.

Product descriptions

eBay.co.uk has its own rules about product descriptions. You must describe your items accurately and not add on any little fictitious details to help them sell ('this pair of shoes belonged to John Lennon', for example). This regulation is mirrored in UK law covering product descriptions.

Online contracts

Since 2002, all contracts written online are binding – that means bidding on eBay.co.uk, too. So if you offer something for sale and your offer is accepted, then you're legally obliged to come up with the goods – literally.

Chapter 16

Practising Safe and Smart Record-Keeping

· ·

· ·

*B*ookkeeping can be the most boring and time-consuming part of your job. You may feel that you just need to add your product costs, add your gross sales, and hey presto, you know where your business is. Sorry, not true. Did you add that roll of parcel tape you picked up at the supermarket today? Although it cost only 99p, that item is a business expense. How about the mileage driving back and forth from car boot sales and flea markets? The costs of those trips are expenses, too. We suspect that you're also not counting quite a few other 'small' items just like these in your expense column.

Once you actually get into the task, you may enjoy posting your expenses and sales. Doing so gives you the opportunity to know exactly where your business is at any given moment. Using an easy software program increases the likelihood of your enjoying the bookkeeping process. In this chapter, we give you the low-down on the basics of bookkeeping, emphasise the importance of keeping records in case HM Revenue and Customs (HMRC) come calling, and explain why using QuickBooks is the smart software choice. This chapter is *required* reading.

Keeping the Books: Basics That Get You Started

Although posting bookkeeping can be boring, clicking a button to generate your tax information is a lot easier than manually going over pages of sales information on a pad of paper. We like to use a software program to speed the process up, particularly QuickBooks (more about that in the later section 'QuickBooks: Making Bookkeeping Simple').

You *could* use plain ol' paper and a pencil to keep your books; if doing so works for you, great. But even though bookkeeping by hand may work for you now, it definitely won't in the future. Entering all your information into a software program now – while your books may still be fairly simple to handle – can save you a lot of time and frustration in the future, when your eBay.co.uk business has grown beyond your wildest dreams and no amount of paper can keep it all straight and organised. We discuss alternative methods of bookkeeping in the 'Bookkeeping Software' section. For now, we focus on the basics of bookkeeping.

To effectively manage your business, you must keep track of *all* your expenses – down to the last roll of tape. You need to keep track of your inventory, how much you paid for the items, how much you paid in shipping, and how much you profited from your sales. If you use a van or the family car to pick up or deliver merchandise to the post office, keep track of this mileage as well. When you're running a business, you should account for every penny that goes in and out.

Bookkeeping has irrefutable standards that are set by the Accounting Standards Board. Assets, liabilities, owner's equity, income, and expenses are standard terms used in all forms of accounting to define profit, loss, and the fiscal health of your business.

Every time you process a transaction, two things happen: One account is credited while another receives a debit. To get more familiar with these terms (and those in the following list), see the definitions in the chart of accounts later in this chapter (in Table 16-1) and in Appendix A (a mini glossary we've included for your convenience). Depending on the type of account, the account's balance either increases or decreases. One account that increases while another decreases is called *double-entry accounting*:

- ✔ When you post an expense, the debit *increases* your expenses and *decreases* your bank account.
- ✔ When you purchase furniture or other assets, it *increases* your asset account and *decreases* your bank account.
- ✔ When you make a sale and make the deposit, it *increases* your bank account and *decreases* your accounts receivable.
- ✔ When you purchase inventory, it *increases* your inventory and *decreases* your bank account.
- ✔ When a portion of a sale includes VAT, it *decreases* your sales, and *increases* your sales tax account.

Manually performing double-entry accounting can be a bit taxing (no pun intended). A software program automatically adjusts the accounts when you input a transaction.

As a business owner, even if you're a sole trader (see Chapter 15 for information on business types), you should keep your business books separate from your personal expenses. (We recommend using a program such as Quicken to keep track of your *personal* expenses for tax time.) By isolating the business records from the personal records, you can get a snapshot of what areas of your sales are doing well and which ones aren't carrying their weight. But that isn't the only reason keeping accurate records is smart; there's HM Revenue and Customs to think about, too. In the next section, we explain Her Majesty's interest in your books.

Records Her Majesty May Want to See

To help you get started with your business, the Department of Trade and Industry maintains a small business Web site (shown in Figure 16-1) at the following address:

```
www.businesslink.gov.uk
```

In this section, we highlight what information you need to keep and how long you should keep it (just in case you're chosen for an audit).

Hiring a professional to do your year-end taxes

When we say that you must hire a professional to prepare your taxes, we mean an accredited chartered accountant – they're a valuable addition to your business arsenal. Although the people at your local 'We Do Your Taxes in a Hurry Shop' may be well meaning and pleasant, they may have completed only a short course in the current tax laws. Doing so does not make these people tax professionals. When business taxes are at stake, a professional with whom you have a standing relationship is the best choice. If you don't know a professional accountant, ask around or contact your local Chamber of Commerce or a respectable organisation like the Institute of Chartered Accountants (www.icaew.co.uk/) or the Association of Chartered Certified Accountants (www.acca global.com/).

Posting bookkeeping can be boring. At the end of the year when a professional is doing your taxes, however, you'll be a lot happier – and your tax preparation will cost you less – if you've posted your information cleanly and in the proper order. For this reason, using QuickBooks (see the 'QuickBooks: Making Bookkeeping Simple' section) is essential to running your business.

Figure 16-1:
DTI home
page for
small
businesses.

Supporting information

Aside from needing to know how your business is going (which is really important), the main reason to keep clear and concise records is because the taxman may come knocking one day. You never know when the Revenue will choose *your* number and want to examine *your* records. In the following list, we highlight some of the important pieces of *supporting information* (things that support your expenses on your end-of-year tax return):

- ✔ **Receipts:** Save every receipt that you get. If you're on a buying trip and have coffee at a motorway service station, save the receipt – that drink is a deduction from your profits. Everything related to your business may be deductible, so save airport parking receipts, cab receipts, receipts for a pen that you picked up on your way to a meeting, *everything*. If you don't have a receipt, you can't prove the write-off.

- ✔ **Merchandise invoices:** Saving all merchandise invoices is as important as saving all your receipts. If you want to prove that you paid £400 and not the £299 retail price for an item that you sold on eBay.co.uk for £500, you'd *better* have an invoice of some kind. The same idea applies to most collectables, in which case a retail price can't be fixed. Save all invoices!

- ✔ **Contractor invoices:** If you use outside contractors – even if you pay the teenager next door to go to the post office and bank for you – get an invoice from them to document exactly what service you paid for and how much you paid. These invoices provide supporting information that can save your bacon, should it ever need saving.

✔ **Business cards:** If you use your car to look at some merchandise, pick up a business card from the vendor. If you travel to a meeting with someone, take a card. Having these business cards can help substantiate your deductible comings and goings.

✔ **A daily calendar:** Every time you leave your house or office on a business-related task, use a Palm Handheld (or a diary if you're feeling low-tech) to make note of it. Keep as much minutia as you can stand. A Palm Desktop can print a monthly calendar. At the end of the year, staple the pages together and include them in your files with your substantiating information.

✔ **Credit card statements:** You're already collecting credit card receipts. If you have your statements, you have monthly proof of expenses. When you get your statement each month, post it into your bookkeeping program and itemise each and every charge, detailing where you spent the money and what for. (QuickBooks has a split feature that accommodates all your categories.) File these statements with your tax return at the end of the year in your year-end envelope (shoe box?).

We know that all this stuff piles up, but you can go to the shop and buy some plastic file storage containers to organise it all. To check for new information and the low-down on what you can and can't do, ask an accountant. Also visit the HMRC Tax Information for Business site, shown in Figure 16-2, at

`www.hmrc.gov.uk/businesses/index.shtml`

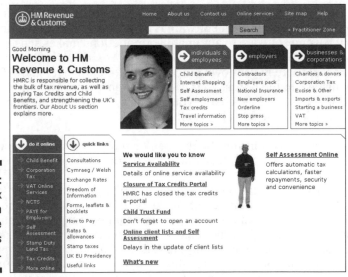

Figure 16-2: Get tax information from the horse's mouth here.

How long should you keep your records?

How long do you have to keep all this supporting information? We hate to tell you, but the period in which you can amend a return or in which HMRC can assess more tax is up to six years, and in extreme circumstances can extend even longer, so you must keep records for at least this long. HMRC states that if keeping records for six or more years causes you serious storage problems, then you may be allowed to get rid of some records a bit earlier. Contact the National Advice Service on 0845 010 9000 for more information if this issue applies to you.

Even though we got this information directly from the HMRC Web site, it may change in the future. You can download a PDF copy of the current recommendations by going to the following address:

```
www.hmrc.gov.uk/helpsheets/e11.pdf
```

If Adobe Acrobat Reader isn't installed on your computer, you can download the software (for free) from the HMRC Web site. Bottom line: Storing your information for as long as you can stand it and staying on top of any changes HMRC may implement doesn't hurt.

Bookkeeping Software

Keeping track of your auctions is hard without software, but keeping track of the money you make without software is even harder (and more time consuming). If using software to automate your auctions makes sense, so does using software to automate your bookkeeping. You can afford to make a mistake here and there in your own office, and no one will ever know. But if you make a mistake in the books, your friendly tax inspector will notice – and be quite miffed. He may even charge you a penalty or two so that you'll remember not to make those mistakes again.

Penalties for mistakes in your books aren't small. A late tax return will cost you a £100 tax penalty, which can be quite an expensive lesson.

Spreadsheet software can be a boon when you're just starting out in business. A program such as Microsoft Works (which comes free on most new computers) or Excel is an excellent way to begin posting your business expenses and profits. The program can be set up to calculate your expenses, profits, and (we hope not too many) losses. Microsoft Works comes with several free financial worksheet templates that you can easily adapt for an eBay.co.uk small business. Also, you can find current Excel templates to get you started at www.microsoft.com/uk/office/prodinfo/default.mspx. Spending any extra money on templates when you're first starting out isn't necessary!

With official bookkeeping software, reconciling a chequebook is a breeze. You merely click off the deposits and cheques when the statement comes in. If you make a mistake when originally inputting the data, the software (comparing your balance and your bank's) lets you know that you've made an error. Efficiency of this kind would've put Bob Cratchit out of a job!

We researched various Web sites to find which software was the best selling and easiest to use. We had many discussions with accountants, and bookkeepers. These professionals consider Intuit's QuickBooks the best accounting software for business, which is why we devote so much of this chapter to it. Some people begin with Quicken and later move to QuickBooks when their business gets big or incorporates. Our theory? Start with the best. This software isn't that much more expensive than others – we've seen new, sealed QuickBooks Pro 2005 software for as low as £100 on eBay.co.uk – and it will see you directly to the big time.

QuickBooks: Making Bookkeeping Simple

QuickBooks offers several versions, from basic to enterprise solutions tailored to different types of businesses. QuickBooks Basic and QuickBooks Pro have a few significant differences. QuickBooks Pro adds job costing and expensing features and the ability to design your own forms. QuickBooks Basic does a very good job too, so check out the comparison at www.quickbooks.co.uk and see which version is best for you. We use (and highly recommend) QuickBooks Pro, so we describe this version in the rest of this section.

QuickBooks 2005 For Dummies by Stephen L. Nelson (Wiley) is amazingly easy to understand. This book answers – in plain English – just about any question you'll have about using the program for your bookkeeping needs. Spend the money and get the book. Any money spent on increasing your knowledge is money well spent (and is a tax write-off).

We update our QuickBooks software yearly, and every year it takes us less time to perform our bookkeeping tasks (because of product improvements). If you find that you don't have time to input your bookkeeping data, consider hiring a bookkeeper. Professional bookkeepers probably already know QuickBooks, and they can print daily reports to keep you apprised of your business condition. Also, at the end of each year, QuickBooks supplies you with all the official reports your accredited chartered accountant needs to do your taxes. (Yes, you really do need a qualified accountant; see the 'Hiring a professional to do your year-end taxes' sidebar elsewhere in this chapter.) You can even send your accountant a backup on a zip disk or a CD-ROM. See how simple bookkeeping can be?

QuickBooks Pro

When you first fire up QuickBooks Pro, you need to answer a few questions to set up your account. Among the few things you need to have ready before you even begin to mess with the software are the following starting figures:

- **Cash balance:** This may be the amount of money deposited from your eBay.co.uk profits. Put these profits into a separate account to use for your business.

- **Accounts receivable balance:** Does anyone owe you money for some auctions? Outstanding payments make up this total.

- **Account liability balance:** Do you owe some money? Are you being invoiced for some merchandise that you haven't paid for? Add up any outstanding liabilities and enter the total when QuickBooks asks you to.

If you're starting your business in the middle of the year, gather any previous profits and expenses that you want to include because you'll have to input this information for a complete annual set of diligently recorded books. This process is going to take a while. But after you've gathered together your finances, even if it takes a little sweat to set it up initially, you'll be thanking us for insisting you get organised. Having properly organised books just makes everything work smoother in the long run.

QuickBooks integrates with PayPal

PayPal can provide your payment history in QuickBooks format. They (PayPal) even offer a settlement and reconciliation system download that breaks up your PayPal transactions into debits and credits – a handy feature! One warning though: Only financial transactions are recorded and organised using this feature. When you use QuickBooks to its fullest, your inventory is in the program. When you purchase merchandise to sell, QuickBooks sets up the inventory – and deducts from it each time you input an invoice or a sales receipt. This way your inventory receipts follow recognised standards. *eBay Timesaving Techniques For Dummies* by Marsha Collier (Wiley), shows you the procedures for posting your weekly (or daily) sales in QuickBooks by using sales receipts.

QuickBooks EasyStep Interview

After you've organised your finances, you can proceed with the QuickBooks EasyStep Interview, which is shown in Figure 16-3. The EasyStep Interview is designed to give those with accounting-phobia and those using a bookkeeping program for the first time a comfort level. If you mess things up, you can always use the back arrow and change what you've input. If you need help, simply click the Help button and the program answers many of your questions. If things go hideously wrong, you can always delete the file from the QuickBooks directory and start again.

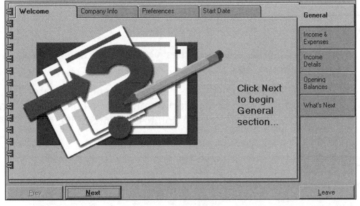

Figure 16-3:
The
QuickBooks
Pro
EasyStep
Interview
start page.

For the whirlwind tour through the QuickBooks EasyStep Interview, just follow these steps (which are only a general guideline):

1. **Start QuickBooks, and choose the Create a New Company option.**

   You're now at the EasyStep Interview.

2. **On the first page of the interactive portion of the interview, type your company name (this becomes the filename in your computer) and the legal name of your company.**

3. **Continue to follow the steps, answering other questions about your business, such as the address and the type of tax form you use.**

4. **When QuickBooks asks what type of business you want to use, choose Retail: General.**

   QuickBooks doesn't offer an online sales business choice, so Retail: General is the closest to what you need (see Figure 16-4). With the chart of accounts that we feature in the following section, you can make the appropriate changes to your accounts to adapt to your eBay business.

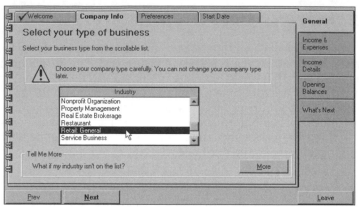

Figure 16-4:
Selecting
your
company
type.

5. **When QuickBooks asks whether you want to use its chosen chart of accounts, choose Yes.**

   See Figure 16-5. You can always change the accounts later. If you want to spend the time, you can also input your entire custom chart of accounts manually (but we *really, really* don't recommend it).

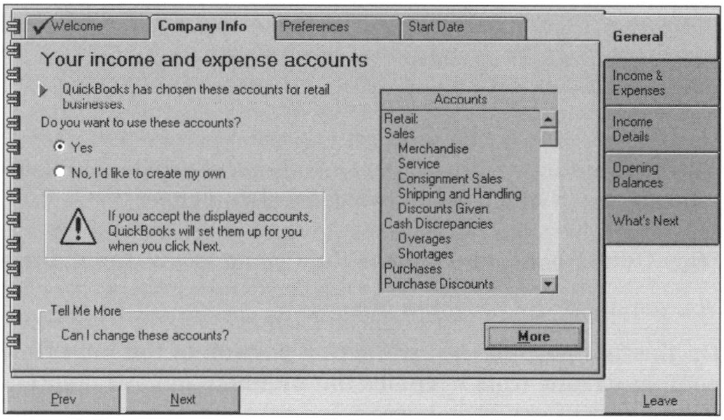

Figure 16-5:
Accepting
the
QuickBooks
chart of
accounts.

6. **Answer some more general questions, which we're sure you can handle with the aid of the incredibly intuitive QuickBooks help area.**

7. **When the preferences pages appear, select the 'Enter the bills first and then enter the payments later' option.**

   That way, if you input your bills as they come in, you can get an exact idea of how much money you owe at any time by just starting the program.

8. **Decide whether you want to use QuickBooks to process your payroll.**

   Even if you're the only employee, using QuickBooks payroll information makes things much easier when it comes to filling out your payroll deposits. QuickBooks automatically fills in forms for your tax processing and prints the appropriate form ready for your signature and mailing.

9. **Answer a few more questions, including whether you want to use the cash basis or accrual basis of accounting.**

   The *accrual* basis posts sales the minute you write an invoice or post a sales receipt, and posts your expenses as soon as you post the bills into the computer. Accrual basis accounting gives you a clearer picture of where your company is financially than cash basis accounting does. The *cash* basis is when you record bills by writing cheques – expenses are posted only when you write the cheques. Doing business on a cash basis may be simpler, but the only way you'll know how much money you owe is by looking at the pile of bills on your desk.

   If you're new to bookkeeping, you may want to go through the interview step-by-step with a tutor at your side. For more details, check out *QuickBooks 2005 For Dummies* (Wiley) – this book can teach you almost everything you need to know about QuickBooks.

10. **If you're comfortable, just click Leave and input the balance of your required information directly into the program without using the interview.**

QuickBooks chart of accounts

After you finish the EasyStep Interview and successfully set yourself up in QuickBooks, the program presents a chart of accounts. Think of the *chart of accounts* as an organisation system, such as file folders. The chart of accounts keeps all related data in the proper area. When you write a cheque to pay a bill, it deducts the amount from your current account, reduces your accounts payable, and perhaps increases your asset or expense accounts.

You have a choice of giving each account a number. These numbers, a kind of bookkeeping shorthand, are standardised throughout bookkeeping; believe it or not, everybody in the industry seems to know what number goes with what item. To keep the process simple, we like to use titles as well as numbers.

To customise your chart of accounts, follow these steps:

1. **Choose Edit⇨Preferences.**
2. **Click the Accounting icon (on the left).**

3. **Click the Company preferences tab and indicate that you'd like to use account numbers.**

   An editable chart of accounts appears, as shown in Figure 16-6. Because QuickBooks doesn't assign account numbers as a default, you need to edit the chart to create them.

Figure 16-6: Your chart of accounts now has numbers generated by QuickBooks.

4. **Go through your QuickBooks chart of accounts and add any missing categories.**

   You may not need all these categories, and you can always add more later. Table 16-1 presents a chart of accounts written by an accountant for an eBay.co.uk business. Figure 16-7 shows a customised chart of accounts.

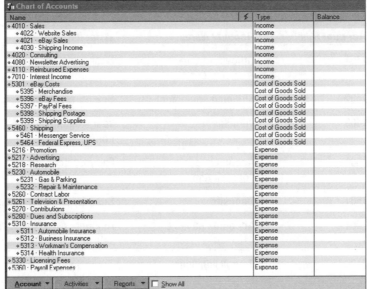

Figure 16-7: Customised chart of accounts for an eBay.co.uk business.

Table 16-1	eBay.co.uk Business Chart of Accounts	
Account Number	*Account Name*	*What It Represents*
1001	Checking	All revenue deposited here and all cheques drawn upon this account
1002	Money market account	Company savings account
1100	Accounts receivable	For customers to whom you extend credit
1201	Merchandise inventory	Charge to cost of sales as used, or take periodic inventories and adjust at that time
1202	Shipping supplies	Boxes, tape, labels, and so forth; charge these to cost as used, or take an inventory at the end of the period and adjust to cost of sales

(continued)

Table 16-1 *(continued)*

Account Number	Account Name	What It Represents
1401	Office furniture & equipment	Desk, computer, telephone
1402	Shipping equipment	Scales, tape dispensers
1403	Vehicles	Your vehicle, if owned by the company
1501	Accumulated depreciation	For your accountant's use
1601	Deposits	Security deposits on leases
2001	Accounts payable	Amounts owed for the stuff you sell, or charged expenses
2100	Payroll liabilities	Taxes deducted from employees' cheques and taxes paid by company on employee earnings
2501	Equipment loans	Money borrowed to buy a computer or other equipment
2502	Car loans	When you get that hot new van for visiting your consignment clients
3000	Owner's capital	Your opening balance
3902	Owner's draw	Your withdrawals for the current year
4001	Merchandise sales	Revenue from sales of your products
4002	Shipping and handling	Paid by the customer
4009	Returns	Total amount of returned merchandise
4101	Interest income	From your investments
4201	Other income	Income not otherwise classified
5001	Merchandise purchases	All the merchandise you buy for eBay.co.uk; you'll probably use sub-accounts for individual items

Account Number	Account Name	What It Represents
5002	Freight in	Freight and shipping charges you pay for your inventory, not for shipments to customers
5003	Shipping	Shipping to your customers: Royal Mail, e-parcels.co.uk, DHL, and so on
5004	Shipping supplies	Boxes, labels, tape, bubble wrap
6110	Car expense	When you use your car for work
6111	Petrol and oil	Filling up the tank!
6112	Repairs	When your business owns the car
6120	Bank service charges	Monthly service charges charges, and so forth
6140	Contributions	Charity
6142	Data services	Do you have an outside firm processing your payroll?
6143	Internet service provider	What you pay to your Internet provider
6144	Web site hosting fees	Fees paid to your hosting company
6150	Depreciation expense	For your accountant's use
6151	eBay fees	What you pay eBay every month to stay in business based on your sales
6152	Discounts	Fees you're charged for using eBay and accepting credit card payments; deducted from your revenue and reported to you on your eBay statement
6153	Other auction site fees	You may want to set up subcategories for each site where you do business, such as Yahoo! or Amazon.com
6156	PayPal fees	Processing fees paid to PayPal

(continued)

Table 16-1 *(continued)*

Account Number	Account Name	What It Represents
6158	Credit card merchant account fees	If you have a separate merchant account, post those fees here
6160	Dues	If you join an organisation that charges membership fees (relating to your business)
6161	Magazines and periodicals	Books and magazines that help you run and expand your business
6170	Equipment rental	Postage meter, occasional van
6180	Insurance	Policies that cover your merchandise or your office
6185	Liability insurance	Insurance that covers you if someone slips and falls at your place of business (can also be put under Insurance)
6190	Disability insurance	Insurance that will pay you if you become temporarily or permanently disabled and can't perform your work
6191	Health insurance	If provided for yourself, you may be required to provide it to employees
6200	Interest expense	Credit interest and interest on loans
6220	Loan interest	When you borrow from the bank
6240	Miscellaneous	Whatever doesn't go anywhere else
6250	Postage and delivery	Stamps used in your regular business
6260	Printing	Your business cards, correspondence stationery, and so on
6265	Filing fees	Fees paid to file legal documents
6270	Professional fees	Fees paid to consultants
6280	Legal fees	If you have to pay a lawyer

Account Number	*Account Name*	*What It Represents*
6650	Accounting and bookkeeping	Fees paid to a bookkeeper or accountant
6290	Rent	Office, warehouse, and so on
6300	Repairs	Can be the major category for the following subcategories
6310	Building repairs	Repairs to the building where you operate your business
6320	Computer repairs	What you pay the person who sets up your wireless network
6330	Equipment repairs	When the photocopier or phone needs fixing
6340	Telephone	Regular telephone, fax lines
6350	Travel and entertainment	Business-related travel, business meals
6360	Entertainment	When you take eBay's CEO out to dinner to benefit your eBay business
6370	Meals	Meals while travelling for your business
6390	Utilities	Major heading for the following subcategories
6391	Electricity and gas	Electricity and gas
6392	Water	Water
6560	Payroll expenses	Wages paid to others
6770	Supplies	Office supplies
6772	Computer	Computer and supplies
6780	Marketing	Advertising or promotional items you purchase to give away
6790	Office	Miscellaneous office expenses, such as bottled water delivery
6820	Taxes	Major category for the following subcategories
6840	Local	council tax
6850	Property	Property taxes

Chapter 17

Building an eBay.co.uk Back Office

- -

In This Chapter

▶ Organising your stock

▶ Keeping inventory

▶ Exploring shipping materials

▶ Becoming your own post office

- -

The more items you sell, the more confusing things can get. As you build your eBay.co.uk business, the little side table you use for storing eBay merchandise isn't going to work. You must think industrial. Even part-time sellers can benefit by adding a few professional touches to their business areas.

In this chapter, we emphasise the importance of setting up and organising your back office. We cover everything from stacking your stock to keeping inventory to choosing packing materials and online postage services. Organisation is your byword. Dive right in. The sooner you read this chapter, the sooner you can build your eBay back office and get down to business.

The Warehouse: Organising Your Space

Whether you plan to sell large or small items, you need space for storing them. As you make savvy purchases, maintaining an item's mint condition is one of your greatest challenges. Organised storage in itself is an art, so in this section we cover the details of what you need to safeguard your precious stock.

Shelving your profits

Before you stock the shelves, it helps to have some! You also need a place to put the shelves: Your garage, a spare room, or somewhere else. You have a choice between three basic kinds of shelves:

- **Plastic:** If you're just starting out, you can always go to the local DIY shop to buy inexpensive plastic shelves. They're light and cheap – and they'll buckle in time.

- **Wooden:** When you think about cheap wooden furniture, one shop springs to mind: Ikea. It's got loads of different styles with a starting price of less than £1 – you can't argue with that when your starting up on a budget!

- **Steel:** If you want to get your storage right first time, buy steel shelving. The most versatile steel shelving is the wire kind (versus solid-steel shelves), which is lighter and allows air to circulate around your items. Steel wire shelving assembles easily. The shelving comes with levelling feet and 4-inch casters, so should you need to move a shelf unit, you can. Installing casters is up to you. You can combine steel wire shelving units to create a full wall of shelves. Each shelf safely holds as much as 250kgs of merchandise.

  Search eBay.co.uk for **shelving** to find sellers offering this kind of indus-trial shelving. The main problem with ordering this product online is that the shipping usually costs more than the shelving.

Box 'em or bag 'em?

Packing your items for storage can be a challenge. Pick up some plastic bags in different sizes. Sandwich bags are perfect for storing smaller items, for example. When items are stored in plastic, they can't pick up any smells or become musty before you sell them. The plastic also protects the items from rubbing against each other and causing possible damage. If you package your merchandise one item to a bag, you can then just lift one off the shelf and put it directly into a shipping box when the auction is over.

Your bags of items have to go into boxes for storage on the shelves. Clear plastic storage boxes are great for bulky items. These big plastic containers are usually 26 inches deep, so before you buy them make sure they'll fit on your shelving comfortably and that you'll have easy access to your items. Using cardboard office-type file storage boxes from an office supply shop is another option. These cardboard boxes are 10 x 12 x 16 inches, which is a nice size for storing medium-size products; they're also the most economical choice. The downside is that you can't see through cardboard boxes, so if your label falls off, you have to take the box off the shelf and open it to check its contents. Smaller see-through plastic boxes with various compartments, such as the kind sold in DIY shops as toolboxes, work great for storing very small items.

When using large plastic bins, tape a pad of Post-it notes on the end of the box so you can quickly identify the contents. You _can_ use regular sticky labels, but changing them leaves large amounts of paper residue over time, and your storage ends up looking sloppy and unprofessional.

Inventory: Keeping Track of What You Have and Where You Keep It

Savvy eBay.co.uk sellers have different methods of handling inventory. They use everything from spiral-bound notebooks to sophisticated software programs. Although computerised inventory tracking can simplify this task, starting with a plain ol' handwritten ledger is fine, too. Choose whichever method works best for you, but keep in mind that as your eBay business grows, a software program that tracks inventory for you may become necessary.

Most of these inventory systems wouldn't work for a company with a warehouse full of stock but will work nicely in an eBay sales environment. Many sellers tape sheets of paper to their boxes to identify them by number, and use that as a reference to a simple Excel spreadsheet for selling purposes. Excel spreadsheets are perfect for keeping track of your auctions as well, but if you're using a management service or software, you don't need both for physical inventory. After you're running a full-time business, however, you have to keep the tax inspectors happy with pounds and pence accounting of your inventory, so keep your inventory records in a standardised program such as QuickBooks (discussed in Chapter 16). In Chapter 8, we detail a variety of auction management software and Web sites, many of which include physical inventory tracking features.

You may also want to use Excel spreadsheets for your downloaded PayPal statements, to hold information waiting to transfer to your bookkeeping program.

Plan in advance where you want to put everything. Organise your items by theme, type, or size. If you organise before planning, you may end up with organised chaos.

The Shipping Department: Packin' It Up

In this section, we look at some of the essentials for a complete, smooth-running shipping department, such as cleaning supplies and packing materials. The *handling fee* portion of your shipping charges pays for these kinds of items. Don't run low on these items and pay attention to how you store them – they must be kept in a clean environment.

Packaging clean up

Be sure the items you send out are in tip-top shape. A few everyday chemicals can gild the lily, for example:

- **WD-40:** The decades-old lubricant works very well at getting price stickers off plastic and glass without damaging the product. The plastic on a toy box may begin to look nasty, even when stored in a clean environment. A quick wipe with a paper towel with a dash of WD-40 will make the plastic shine like new. WD-40 also works incredibly well for untangling jewellery chains and shining up metallic objects.

- **Goo Gone (available from US eBay sellers):** Goo Gone works miracles in cleaning up gooey sticker residue from non-porous items.

- **un-du (available from US eBay sellers):** This amazing liquid easily removes stickers from cardboard, plastic, fabrics, and more without causing damage. un-du comes packaged with a patented mini-scraper top that can be used in any of your sticker cleaning projects. If you can't find un-du, check out `www.coolebaytools.com` for places to purchase it. You can also use lighter fluid (which is, of course, considerably more dangerous and may damage your item).

Removing musty odours from apparel items

Clothing can often pick up odours that you just don't notice. We recently bought some designer dresses on eBay.co.uk from a seller who had the typical disclaimer in her description: 'No stains, holes, repairs, or odours. Comes from a smoke-free, pet-free home.' Unfortunately, the minute we opened the box we could smell the musty odour of an item that had been stored for a long time.

To prevent that unpleasant storage odour, keep a packet of Dryel Fabric Care System around.

Dryel is a safe, do-it-yourself dry cleaning product. Just place your better eBay clothing items in the patented Dryel bag with the special sheet and toss it in the dryer as per the instructions on the box. Your garment will come out smelling clean and wrinkle free. For more information, visit Dryel's Web site at `www.dryel.com`. If you find Dryel hard to get hold of, Febreeze works well as a quick fix, and this product is available everywhere!

Packing materials

To ensure that your items arrive at their destinations in one piece, keep the following on hand at all times:

✔ **Bubble wrap:** A clean, puffy product that comes in rolls, bubble wrap is available in several sizes. Depending on your product, you may have to carry two sizes of bubble wrap to properly protect the goods. Bubble wrap can be expensive, but check out vendors at eBay.co.uk; you'll find quite a lot of them (and possibly a deal). See Figure 17-1.

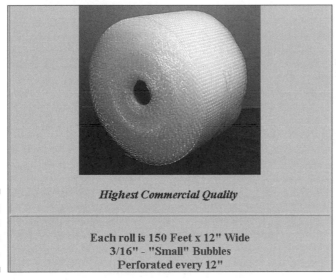

Highest Commercial Quality

Each roll is 150 Feet x 12" Wide
3/16" - "Small" Bubbles
Perforated every 12"

Figure 17-1:
Bubble
wrap in its
pure form.

✔ **Styrofoam packing beads:** Polystyrene beads (or peanuts) protect just about everything you ship. Storing them is the tricky part. One of the most ingenious storage solutions we've seen is putting the beads into big plastic rubbish bags, and then hanging these bags on cup hooks (available at the hardware shop) around the walls in a garage. When packing with peanuts, be sure that you place the item carefully and use enough peanuts to fill the box *completely*; leaving any airspace defeats the point of using the peanuts in the first place.

✔ **Plastic bags:** Buy plastic bags in bulk to save money. Buy various sizes and use them for both shipping and storing. Even large kitchen rubbish bags are good for wrapping up posters and large items; the plastic protects the item from inclement weather by waterproofing it.

✔ **Two or three-inch shipping tape:** You need clear tape to place over address labels to protect them from scrapes and rain. Don't risk a lost package for want of a few inches of tape. See the following section on boxes for more information.

✔ **Padded envelopes:** If you send items that fit nicely into these bubble wrap-lined envelopes, use them (see Figure 17-2). This type of envelope – with paper on the outside and bubble wrap on the inside – is perfect for mailing small items or clothing using first class mail. Jiffy bags are available in quantity (an economical choice) and don't take up much storage space. Table 17-1 shows you the industry-standard sizes of jiffy bags and their suggested uses.

Bubblefast's Mailers are lightweight yet hold up under the toughest mailing conditions. Air cushioning offers maximum protection.

Features	Benefits
High-quality bubble cushioning	Outperforms other shippers in burst, puncture and cushioning tests
Lightweight air cushioning	Controls shipping costs
Slip lining and low-resistance bubble	Makes product insertion and removal quick and simple
Clean and water resistant	Ideal for sensative product shipping

Figure 17-2:
Jiffy bags
for sale on
eBay.co.uk.

Table 17-1	Standard Bag Sizes
Measurements	*Suggested Items*
4" x 8"	Collector trading cards, jewellery, computer disks
5" x 10"	Postcards, paper ephemera
6" x 10"	Dolls' clothes, CDs, DVDs, Xbox or PS2 games
7¼" x 12"	Cardboard sleeve VHS tapes, jewel-cased CDs, and DVDs
8½" x 12"	Clamshell VHS tapes, books

Measurements	Suggested Items
8½" x 14½"	Toys, clothing, stuffed animals
9½" x 14½"	Small books, trade paperbacks
10½" x 16"	Hardcover books, dolls
12½" x 19"	Clothing, soft boxed items
14¼" x 20"	Much larger packaged items, framed items and plaques

Packaging – the heart of the matter

Depending on the size of the item you sell, you can purchase boxes in bulk at reliable sources. Try to purchase from a manufacturer that specialises in B2B (business to business) sales. Some box companies specialise in selling to the occasional box user – knowing the size that you need enables you to bulk buy.

The Post Room: Sendin' It Out

In this section, we give you the low-down on the main Internet postage vendor: Royal Mail.

Printing labels on your printer is convenient until you start sending out a dozen packages at a time, then cutting the paper and taping the label gets a bit too time consuming. Do yourself a favour and get a label printer. Yes, these printers can be expensive, but you can find some great deals on eBay.co.uk. A label printer can save you countless hours.

Royal Mail has an online postage service called SmartStamp that enables you to print postage directly from your computer while online. To register online and download their software, go to the Royal Mail Web site at

```
www.royalmail.com
```

and click the <u>SmartStamp</u> link.

Here are some features of the SmartStamp service:

- ✔ You can print postage directly onto envelopes or labels.
- ✔ You can personalise your mail with a company logo.

✔ No minimum mailing amount is required, so a small time eBayer can benefit as much as a multi-national company.

✔ You can even add your own company strapline or promotional message.

With SmartStamp you pay a monthly or annual subscription plus whatever you shell out in postage costs. At time of writing, Royal Mail offers the service for £4.99 a month or £49.99 a year.

Part V
The Part of Tens

"Everyone laughed when I said I could make a successful business out of my hobby trainspotting – Well, thanks to eBay......."

In this part . . .

Not everyone is a shooting star at eBay.co.uk, but it's a good goal to reach for. For your inspiration, I've included profiles on some interesting people – from all walks of life – who've turned their sales through eBay.co.uk inot a profitable enterprise, some working only part-time. These are not people in big companies. Instead, they're people like us, working hard to expand their business on eBay.co.uk. In the second chapter, I provide information on moving merchandise that you think you might never sell.

Chapter 18

Ten Successful (and Happy) eBay Sellers and Their Stories

In This Chapter

▶ People who make their living selling at eBay . . .

▶ . . . and love it!

*W*e enjoy hearing stories about how much people like eBay. We enjoy it even more when we hear that they're doing something that they get pleasure from while earning a good living. One of the best parts of teaching at eBay University is talking to the hundreds of sellers who attend. We get the opportunity to bounce ideas around with them and find out about the creative ways they spend their time at eBay.

We thought you might like to know more about some of the people at eBay and eBay.co.uk, so we interviewed them; it was so much fun getting to know about each of them. They have different backgrounds and lifestyles – but they all have one thing in common: eBay!

In favour of highlighting some regular folks at eBay, we dispensed with the customary writer thing (you know, finding the largest PowerSellers at eBay to interview). No one's a success overnight, and the people we discuss in this chapter certainly have been plugging away at eBay, increasing their businesses and becoming successful. We dug through some old feedbacks (all the way back to 1997) and contacted sellers to see how they're doing these days.

In this chapter, you'll find a mix of UK and US sellers, who together have decades of eBay experience to share. All have enjoyed success and are loved by their customers. Here are their stories (and their advice).

Rockem Music

Member since December 2002; Feedback 9334; Positive Feedback 100%

Apart from making armfuls of cash, achieving a 100% feedback rating is what every eBay business dreams of; maintaining such an exulted position is worthier still. At time of writing, music e-tail business Rockem Music has achieved just that – no negative feedback. Impressive stuff; especially when you consider how active they are.

Rockem Music is the brainchild of brothers Dave and Rob Hockman, who quit their jobs (one as a drum teacher, the other as a traffic policeman) in 2002 to set up shop on eBay.co.uk supplying musical equipment to UK and international markets.

Rob says they came up against some stiff resistance when starting their business and that distributors were initially sceptical of their credentials as a viable business – despite their combined £20,000 deposit to the contrary! Nowadays, being taken seriously is not a problem, especially with their Platinum PowerSeller status, a feedback rating approaching 8,000, and turnover passing £350,000 in 2005.

The pair credit their success to honesty, fairness and sheer hard work. Dave says a good way to run your business is via eBay's guiding principles – especially the bit about mutual respect.

The guys have just relaunched their non-eBay Web site: `www.rockemmusic.com` (see Figure 18-1) and are developing their own line of drum kits – not bad progress in just three years, eh?

Figure 18-1:
Rockem Music's eBay.co.uk home page.

Abovethemall

Member since April 1998; Feedback 3827; Positive Feedback 99.9%

Aside from being pretty, bright, and talented, Marjie Smith is a heck of an eBay seller. She's not only a PowerSeller, she's the founder of the Disabled Online Users Association (DOUA) – her other full-time job.

She discovered eBay when she was running an e-mail discussion group of women who collected Beanies Babies. Many were looking for connections to complete their collections. Being the head 'nut' (nicknamed that by the group after the Ty Beanie 'Nuts' the Squirrel), it was her job to help them accomplish this goal. The rest, they say, is history.

Marjie runs 50 to 100 auctions a week and keeps her eBay store as stocked as she possibly can. She's an authorized Etienne Aigner representative and has exclusive agreements with several unique gift lines. But she's quick to point out that she'll sell anything! She once found a box of old, beat-up books next to a dumpster outside a thrift shop. She waited till no one was looking and snapped them up and sold them on eBay. That box of books netted her a cool $300 profit.

Just like many of the sellers we profile here, Marjie spends as many as 70 hours a week on her eBay enterprises. Her biggest sale came from a woman who used Buy It Now to purchase more than $1000 worth of lovely Etienne Aigner accessories from her eBay store in one day.

eBay has really changed her life. 'Being a successful eBay seller has truly given me my wings. I am independent, self-sufficient, and financially stable. I know I won't get laid off, downsized, or put out to pasture before I'm ready. I'm my own boss, work my own hours, set my own limits, and can readily achieve them thanks to the platform that eBay provides to all sellers. When they say it's a level playing field, believe it.'

Aside from an eBay store, Marjie sells from her Web site www.abovethe mall.com (see Figure 18-2) and runs the site for DOUA, www.doua.info.

Marjie's words for new sellers on eBay? Remember back to when you were a new buyer. Take all the good from the sellers who've helped you along the way, add your own flavour, and always do right by your customers.

Figure 18-2:
The Above-themall
Web site.

Incentive

Member since September 1997; Feedback 330; Positive Feedback: 99.7%

Patrick Horsman's eBay.co.uk watch business is not the most prolific listed here, in fact he rarely sells more than one item a day, but he illustrates brilliantly how eBay can compliment an existing business. Oh yeah, and he's a great seller too, having received only positive feedback in the last 12 months (that means no neutral as well as negative feedback).

Patrick runs several Web sites dedicated to all things that go tick, and one that offers corporate gift ideas. These are his main businesses, but he assures me that eBay.co.uk remains an integral part of what he does.

As an early starter on the dot-com scene, Patrick spent his first two years selling to eBayers in Canada and the US; apparently his first sale was to a Canadian and came in at C$4,500 – not a bad start!

He believes the secret of his success to date is his honesty, expertise and his focus on describing his products in a way people can understand. Watches have high ticket prices, and quite rightly people are sceptical if they don't have the items in their hands. Patrick says he spends a lot of time simply 'reassuring people'.

It's not all been plain sailing, however. He once lost £1,400 in a convincing escrow scam and nowadays is very careful to check out buyers that sound too good to be true. He says a Web search often reveals more than you'd expect about a buyer and he never sends items to an address that isn't confirmed by eBay or PayPal.

Patrick recommends that sellers "be totally honest in describing the item. Many eBayers hype up what they are selling, only for the purchaser to find they have not bought the item they expected".

Bubblefast

Member since May 1999; Feedback: 16,920; Positive Feedback 100%

Marsha has a good story about Bubblefast: I first met the Bubblefast 'family' when I needed to move my mother's things from Florida to California. When I got the price quote from the moving company for rolls of cushioning, it was so high I nearly fell over! I knew that I could find a better price at eBay – and I did. Bubblefast prices were 50 percent less than the moving company had quoted, and they shipped the wrap directly to my mom's house so that I could meet it there to wrap her valuables.

The Bubblefast business began with Robin and her husband Alan. Their first transaction at eBay took place in early 1999, when Alan bought a Macintosh computer. When it came to finally selling, Alan figured that all eBay sellers would need shipping supplies. At first, they sold just one product, a 150-foot roll of ³⁄₁₆ inches (small size) bubble cushioning. Now they sell more than 65 variations of 8 or 9 products: bubble cushioning, antistatic bubble, bubble bags, bubble-lined mailers, rolled shipping foam, boxes, sealing tape, and stretch film.

Alan passed away in 2001, and Robin and her family carried on the business. On the bright side, Robin remarried and now (with a combined family) they have even more indentured employees. The Le Vine Family – Robin, Mark, Jenny (16), Steven (11), Sara (9), Michelle (20), Grandma Gloria – and family friends Syble and Billy, work closely together, putting in 70 to 80 hours a week.

A seller with many repeat customers (more than 21,000 positives; repeat customers help build businesses!), they decided to branch out and go into consignment selling. They registered on eBay as Trading Assistants and now they're 'up to their eyeballs in new business'. It works out really well for them, because they're already in the shipping supply business. No package is a challenge!

Mark uses Turbo Lister for the Bubblefast auctions. Fashion mavens Jenny and Michelle scrutinise and help write descriptions for consignment listings. Jenny also posts feedback several times a week. Robin still handles order entry and answers the phone and e-mail. Grandma Gloria, her friend Syble, and elf Billy handle the packing and shipping. They ship anywhere from 100 to 200 orders a day – their total shipping bill is $25 to $30K month. The family has customers from around the world – they've shipped to every state in the US and internationally as far as Japan – who buy from their auctions (see Figure 18-3), eBay store, and Web site (www.bubblefast.com). Last year their business grossed $650,000. The profit margin in the Bubblefast products is low, so they have to make it up in volume.

CLICK HERE TO SEE OTHER BUBBLE PRODUCTS			
Big Bubble (1/2")			
Buy 1 roll of 1/2" x 12"	62.5'		$5.50
Buy 2 rolls of 1/2" x 12"	125'	Save Over 5%!	$10.25
Buy 8 rolls of 1/2" x 12"	500'	Save Over 15%!	$37.00
Buy 1 roll of 1/2" x 24"	62.5'	Save Over 5%!	$10.25
Buy 4 rolls of 1/2" x 24"	250'	Save Over 15%!	$37.00
Little Bubble (3/16")			
Buy 1 roll of 3/16" x 12"	150'		$8.95
Buy 2 rolls of 3/16" x 12"	300'	Save About 10%!	$16.25
Buy 8 rolls of 3/16" x 12"	1200'	Save About 10%!	$61.00
Buy 1 roll of 3/16" x 24"	150'	Save About 15%!	$16.25
Like Both? Try our Combo Pack			
Buy 1 roll of 1/2" x 12" and 1 roll of 3/16" x 12"	212.5'	Save 5%!	$13.75
Can't Decide Between Bubble or Foam? Why Not Try Both?			
Buy 1 roll of 3/16" x 12" Bubble and 1 roll of 1/8" x 12" Foam		Save 5%!	$19.45

Figure 18-3: A Bubblefast store link.

eBay has totally changed this family's life. Alan used to say 'Our family is together all the time now; we've learned to pull together for a common goal.' It's still true today with the family business he started.

The Le Vine family's tip for eBay sellers: 'If you want to create a thriving eBay business and are willing to put the time and energy into it, the possibilities are endless. With a minimal investment of money, you have the potential to reach the world! Treat every customer like you want to be treated. After all this time, the customer is still always right.'

iPosters

Member since May 2002; Feedback 16227; Positive Feedback 99.8%

Nick Talley, owner of UK-based print and poster business iPosters, believes the main benefit of eBay is that it opens your business to a huge potential customer base. He likens having an eBay presence to having a shop in every town across the Western world – a world where the little guys compete on the same footing as multi-national companies.

Nick came to eBay.co.uk after 16 years running a same-day courier service, which he eventually gave up on because of the ever-rising tide of bills. He set up his own Web site www.pop-culture.biz (see Figure 18-4) and soon began posting selected items onto eBay.co.uk. To Nick, eBay seemed as good a way as any to make some extra cash.

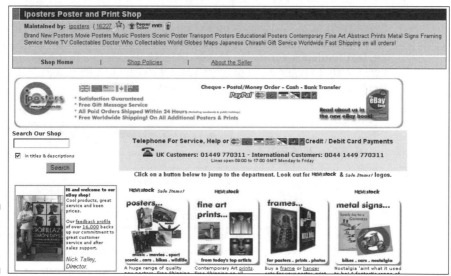

Figure 18-4: iPosters' home page.

Four years and some big profits later, Nick believes the secret of his success is 'good old-fashioned customer service' and some great product lines. He also claims that many eBay sellers come across as unprofessional, a problem that he turned to his advantage with a sharp home page and snappy service.

Nick says eBay's evolving rules and dealing with the taxman are two of the largest potential pitfalls for a business owner. Beat these by updating your accounts constantly and by checking up on eBay regulations on the announcements page.

McMedia DVD

Member since July 2001; Feedback 22190; Positive Feedback 100%

Sean McLane has been selling full-time on eBay.co.uk for less than two years, but he's built up a selling record and reputation that most eBayers would kill for.

He joined eBay.co.uk in 2001 after quitting a successful 12-year career in the retail industry. The eBay shop came about almost by accident when Sean decided to upgrade his film collection to DVD and got rid of hundreds of old VHS videos on eBay.

That got him thinking: why work for other people when you can turn your hobby (films and computers in this case) into a business and become your own boss? With a young family to support and care for, Sean saw working from home on his eBay business as the best solution (see Figure 18-5).

Since then he's gradually stepped up the number and range of products on offer and has focused on getting the customer experience right – hence the perfect feedback score. He reckons McMedia offers a fast and professional service that bigger e-tail players cannot match but also, as a VAT registered business, has credibility that some eBayers lack.

Figure 18-5: McMedia's eBay.co.uk home page

Despite his success, Sean is adamant that eBay is not a get rich quick solution. He puts his own achievements down to patience and dedication. He spent six months sourcing the right suppliers and says nowadays he spends more time 'at work' than he did when he was an employee. The good news is that, despite the long hours he still gets to see much more of his wife and kids.

He has some wise words for budding eBay tycoons: 'Selling on eBay full time works for me. It enables me to live my life the way I want to live it. But this would not suit everyone. It can be a lonely career, with no work colleagues, and a reduced social life. If you are going to do it, then go into it with your eyes open – having done your research and understanding fully that working for yourself is great, but you sacrifice a few things to do so. You need to be 100% dedicated to it to make it work.'

Melrose_Stamp

Member since March 1998; Feedback 8948; Positive Feedback 100%

A while back, one of us (Marsha) needed a rubber stamp or two for her business and didn't have time to go out to a printing store and place an order. She thought surely someone on eBay sells custom rubber stamps! She was right. That's when Marsha met Jeff Stannard of Melrose Stamp Company. He specialises in self-inking custom rubber stamps and also sells stock design stamps.

Jeff was an assistant in a New York State economic development agency when he started his part-time business on eBay. Being around entrepreneurs gave him the inspiration he needed to quit his job and take his part-time sales to the next level.

He's had his eBay store since 2001 (see Figure 18-6) and works the business himself with no employees. His biggest sale came from a Chamber of Commerce in South Carolina. They ordered 65 custom stamps to use for a promotional day, where various merchants stamp a customer's card indicating the customer visited the store during the promotional day.

eBay has certainly changed his life. No longer a nine-to-fiver, Jeff works more than 60 hours a week. All his life he wanted to run his own business. 'My business model would fail if it were locally based only. With eBay, I'm living my dream and selling my products globally. It's a life of independence, free from the corporate rat race!'

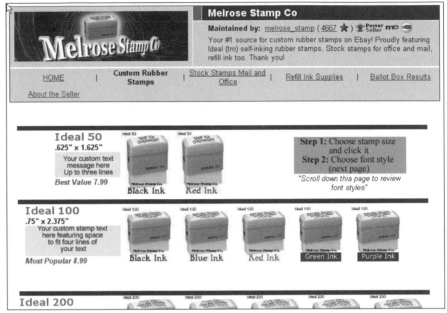

Figure 18-6:
Just one category from Melrose_ Stamp's eBay store.

Jeff's advice to new eBay sellers? 'Invest time to create a business plan. A business plan will help you identify your strengths and weaknesses, threats and opportunities. Build into the plan a set of financial projections as well; this will help you to clearly identify investment and working capital needs. Treat your eBay operation as a real, sustainable business and you will go far!'

Noblespirit

Member since September 1998, Feedback 15,270; Positive Feedback 99.1%

Joe Cortese is a funny and creative guy, but we always wondered where his user ID came from. Joe was very close to his father, who passed away in 1995. His user ID at eBay was conceived as a tribute to his Dad, a 'noble spirit', Joe says 'through this name he is with me every day and guides me still'.

Now that we've got you all misty-eyed, let us tell you how Joe got started on eBay. Joe's business was (and still is) centred around purchasing large estates and selling the contents to various dealers around the world. In 1997, on a train trip to Florida, he chatted with a fellow passenger who collected World War II memorabilia. The gentleman had a side business, selling pieces from his collection (and others) on eBay – something that Joe had never heard of.

About a year later, Joe decided to give this eBay thing a whirl. A local auctioneer was helping sell off some of the contents of Joe's house, including a Civil War vest pocket bible with dated notations about battles. The auctioneer told Joe that it was worth only about $15 (about £9). Doubting the proposed value, Joe decided to sell the bible on eBay. When it sold for $375.00 (about £213), he was hooked.

Joe is now the largest eBay seller of collectables on eBay – specialising in coins and stamps. He acquires merchandise and also takes collections on consignment. All his auctions are run with no reserve price (see Figure 18-7). 'Selling at no reserve is the most exciting aspect but it requires fortitude, consistency, and diversity. We might sell a Barbie doll one day and a $10,000 Ming Dynasty vase the next,' quips Joe.

Joe even found time to develop with a programmer his own proprietary software, Meridian, to automate his auction business. You can read more about that on his Web site, `www.noblespirit.com`.

Joe's tip for new sellers mirrors our thoughts exactly: 'Sell what you know, sell what you love. Those are the things you will sell best. Don't view eBay as a blanket golden opportunity to start a business unless you are prepared to make the same investment that you would be making to start that business in the real world.'

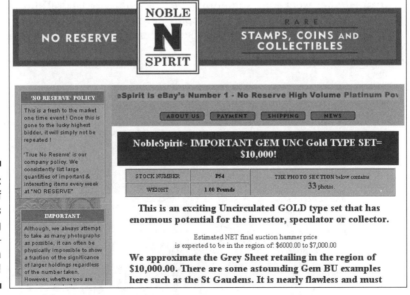

Figure 18-7: One of Noblespirit's fascinating auctions – without a reserve!

PreservationPublishing

Member since April 1998; Feedback 1,200; Positive Feedback: 99.9%

Jillian Cline is not only a part-time seller on eBay, she trains dogs, writes books, and sells original dog products (books, cards, t-shirts, and other specialty items) through her own dealer network at dog shows throughout the country and through ads in magazines. eBay is a natural extension of her business.

She's also a collector and veteran eBay shopper. Her first transaction was buying a small bronze bulldog that was signed on the collar. She purchased it for half of what she had previously paid in an antique store for similar items. She now haunts eBay regularly for small bronze and metal bulldogs. She also purchased a framed, signed, and numbered Blue Dog lithograph by Louisiana artist George Rodrigue. She paid $1,800 on eBay and had it appraised recently for $8,000!

Her own eBay store is open 24/7, even though running her business can be difficult. Her husband is often transferred, forcing her to move. It would be impossible for her to have a traditional job, but eBay allows her to conduct business wherever they go.

She can run auctions (as in Figure 18-8) any time she likes. She used to have to spend her weekends schlepping her merchandise to dog shows and setting up a booth. With eBay she can display her pet products online and handle orders as they come in. Jillian also sells from her Web site, www.preservation publishing.com.

Figure 18-8:
A Preservation Publishing auction.

Elegant Vintage Pit Bull blank Greeting cards
This lot consists of 2 beautiful, top quality 5"x7" (finished size) cards are blank inside, so you can compose your personal messages - with matching envelopes. They're also ideal to frame and hang in your home as reminders of days gone by. *They make great gifts too!*

Buyer to pay shipping & handling via First Class Mail of $1.75 (Add up to five additional packs for a low Priority Mail shipping rate of $4. Winner must submit payment within a week of winning the item.

Jillian says: 'Don't give up! Keep listing different items in auctions to draw people to your eBay store. Use cross-promotions and take advantage of eBay's occasional listing sale days. On those days test new products – and lots of them!'

Vinyl Tap

Member since May 2000; Feedback 8230; Positive Feedback 99.9%

With one of the best names we've come across on eBay.co.uk, Vinyl Tap is always going to attract attention. It's a mail order business with 20 years experience and several employees – not your average eBay punter. We've been in contact with Andrea Beevers, Vinyl Tap's eBay Co-ordinator (her title gives you some idea of the company's approach to eBay).

Vinyl Tap started small, listing hard-to-find records here and there, but gradually the business snowballed and in no time at all they became PowerSellers with customers in several countries. (See Figure 18-9.)

According to Andrea, the secret of Vinyl Tap's success lies in its first rate customer service, which continues after the sale. It's pretty rare, for example, to see a full money-back guarantee being offered by an eBay seller. She also believes that good communication is of the utmost importance.

Figure 18-9:
Vinyl Tap's home page on eBay.co.uk

Discussing eBay's drawbacks, Andrea cites the unpredictability of customers – you can get 50 orders one day and five the next, she says. But the pros far outweigh the cons, especially now that millions of people around the world understand what eBay is all about. 'That's a pretty big market for any business,' she laughs.

Chapter 19

Ten Strategies to Sell Your Stuff Successfully

*O*kay, so we've given you an entire book on how to sell well, but this chapter has the key pointers that you should take as gospel if you're going to be a success on eBay.co.uk. Dan has quizzed some of the UK's most successful eBay sellers to find out the secrets of their success, most of which, as it turns out, are really simple – but hugely effective.

Take Great Pictures

To be a great eBay.co.uk seller, you've got to have great pictures. eBay sellers I've spoken to can't emphasise enough how important it is to get clear shots of what you're selling. After all, you can wax on forever about how good your item is, but if looks dodgy, then people ain't gonna bid on it!

If you're serious (and you should be), think carefully about where you take your pictures. Good light is a must, and you can get this by investing in some basic lighting equipment or simply by using a room that enjoys good natural light.

What's going on behind your item is also important. In terms of background, less is more. Ideally you want nothing at all, a white screen background is good for focusing attention on your item. A good rule of thumb is that if more is going on in the background than in the foreground, you may want to rearrange your set-up.

You don't need an all-singing, all-dancing, 20-mega-pixel camera to get good shots – but it does have to be digital. If in doubt, ask around a few of your local photography shops which camera is best for posting online, then buy it on eBay. See Figure 19-1 for an example of a good snap.

Chapter 11 offers advice on taking great digital pictures for online auctions. Keep the following checklist in mind as well to get the best out of your photography:

- Make sure there's lots of light.
- Remove anything attention-grabbing from the background.
- Position the item so that people can see it clearly.
- Take several photos and use the best ones.
- Don't use a camera phone; they make things look smudged.

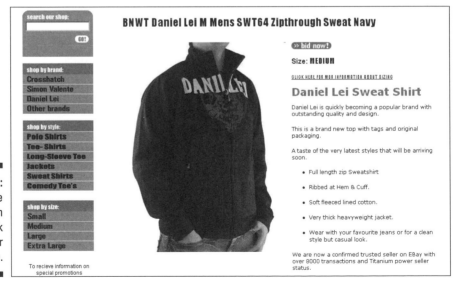

Figure 19-1:
A nice picture from eBay.co.uk PowerSeller CodeNine.

Assessing Your Market – Will It Sell?

When it comes to researching your market on eBay.co.uk, normal business rules apply. If you don't put in some legwork before you set up your shop, you'll suffer in the long run. It's no good deciding to sell watches, for example, if there are already 100 full-time professional watch retailers pumping out high quality Rolexes, Casios and Swatches on the cheap.

Just like any business, you have to make sure that there is a sufficient gap in your market and also that there's enough demand for what you want to sell. If not, then you may find yourself with a ton of unsold merchandise.

The best way to conduct research is to check out who's already buying and selling your product lines on eBay.co.uk. A simple keyword search should suffice, along with a search of completed auctions so you can get a feel for your items' sale value.

Ask yourself the following questions: who's selling the same product as you? How much for? How often are they doing it? At what time during the day and what day of the week are items most likely to get snapped up for a high price?

By gaining a complete picture of your market before you start selling, you'll effectively hit the ground running. Trust us, it'll make you a better seller. See Chapter 7 for more tips on researching your market.

Assessing Yourself (Can You Do It?)

Being inspired to set up an eBay.co.uk business is one thing, but committing to the business is quite another. When you see successful sellers making money it's tempting to copy them, but they are committed and you should be too.

Being an eBay.co.uk PowerSeller is a high-pressure job. It is demanding on your time and energy –when you're not listing items and sending out parcels, you're answering queries and maintaining your Web site. Be prepared to put in the hours; if you're not happy with this commitment, then stop now!

Setting Perfect Pricing

Price your items too high and you'll scare people away, but price them too low and people may doubt the quality of what you're selling. Pricing – like auction length – is an exact science in a variable eBay environment. You have to get it right, especially if you want to include a 'Buy it Now' price (see Chapter 10 for more info on this).

Once again, the key to getting your price right is doing some research. Take a look at what price your item has gone for in the past, who bought it and when the auction ended. Use this info to set your own price, as well as your auction length and on what day it starts. See what I mean about exact science?

Describing Your Items

Another way of adding value to your auctions lies in how you describe the stuff you're selling. Of course, saying that an item is 'old and shabby' isn't going to earn it much interest from buyers, but over-egging it could have the same negative effect.

Don't say it's the best thing since sliced bread unless it actually is. Be positive and enthusiastic in your descriptions, by all means, but you must be realistic too.

Overstating the worth of your item may win you a few extra pounds initially, but you'll soon get a bad reputation and that small gain will be cancelled out by the cost of returns and negative feedback.

When it comes to expensive auctions, like cars, furniture or holidays, the lengthier the description the better. People simply won't go for a description like, "car, very fast". They want to know about service history, mileage, add-ons and so on; few will risk bidding on something they know little about.

Figure 19-2 is a good example of what you should include.

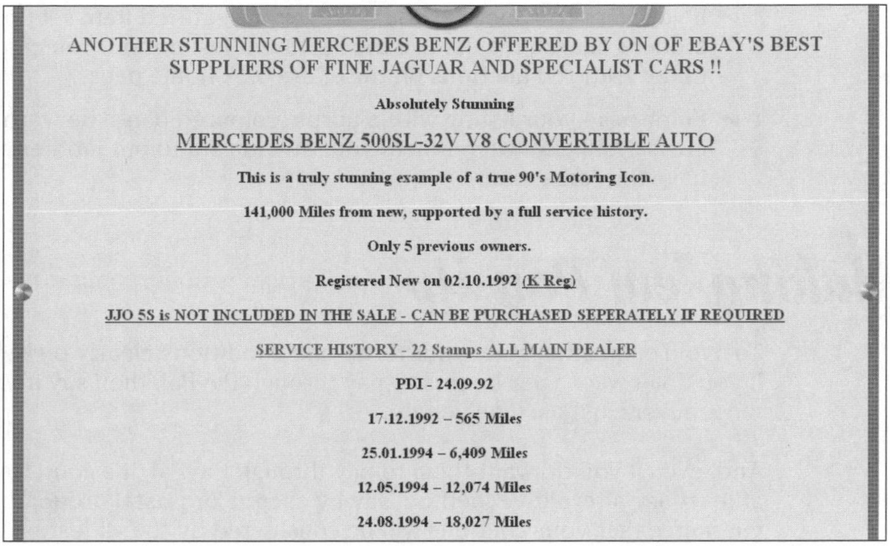

Figure 19-2:
The
beginning
section of
an auction
for a sparkly
Mercedes
Benz.

ANOTHER STUNNING MERCEDES BENZ OFFERED BY ON OF EBAY'S BEST
SUPPLIERS OF FINE JAGUAR AND SPECIALIST CARS !!

Absolutely Stunning

MERCEDES BENZ 500SL-32V V8 CONVERTIBLE AUTO

This is a truly stunning example of a true 90's Motoring Icon.

141,000 Miles from new, supported by a full service history.

Only 5 previous owners.

Registered New on 02.10.1992 (K Reg)

JJO 5S is NOT INCLUDED IN THE SALE - CAN BE PURCHASED SEPERATELY IF REQUIRED

SERVICE HISTORY - 22 Stamps ALL MAIN DEALER

PDI - 24.09.92

17.12.1992 – 565 Miles

25.01.1994 – 6,409 Miles

12.05.1994 – 12,074 Miles

24.08.1994 – 18,027 Miles

Anything to Add?

Simply write out your auction without any pictures, bold face or emphasis, and you probably won't get the right money. On a Web site where millions of items are sold every year, it's a good idea to make yours stand out.

We talked about pictures earlier in this chapter, but it's worth restating their importance. While the phrase 'no picture, no sale' is not quite true, you can bet that plenty of potential buyers will skip over your auction unless it has a picture to draw their eye.

A good rule of thumb is the more valuable your auction, the more money you should spend on it. If you're selling an expensive piece of antique furniture, then people are likely to want plenty of evidence that it is what you say it is.

Depending on your item (and what your rivals are doing) you might want to add a few further frills:

✔ Listing it in bold face for 70p. Items in bold are eye-catching – as long as they're not surrounded by other bold typeface auctions.

✔ If you want to appear in your category's Featured Item section and in a bidder's search results use the FeaturedPlus! option. You can find it under featured auctions on the eBay.co.uk home page.

✔ Emphasise your listing with a purple coloured band. Be warned, this costs £1.50 and will not help your auction stand out if other eBayers have the same idea.

Making 'em Pay Up

To avoid confusion, state your terms and conditions clearly on the auction. If you don't want your buyers to pay through PayPal, then say it explicitly – most buyers just assume you do.

And, even if you do want them to pay through PayPal, it's good to give buyers at least one alternative method, say by cheque or postal order. That should guarantee that your auctions will be considered by the widest possible pool of people.

When the auction ends, send the winning bidder a note thanking them for their interest and congratulating them on winning the auction. As an aside you should include an invoice for the full amount owed including postage and packaging.

If there's no response, don't start threatening negative feedback – that'll get you nowhere – be patient and calm. Entice payment rather than demand it, and most people will oblige by sending you the money. Go to Chapter 12 for complete details of the payment process, including what to do if a bidder simply won't pay up.

Packaging Precious Products

If you want repeat business, make sure your customers get their items in one piece (unless, of course, they're buying a set). You don't have to go far on eBay.co.uk to find a seller with negative feedback because their stuff has arrived in bits.

It's pretty straightforward really. If you're posting something that's fragile, then make sure it's not going to break. Polystyrene beads, egg boxes and cotton wool are your friends here – use them!

If you're serious about developing customer loyalty, get some leaflets printed up and pop one in each parcel you send out. Big online retailers use this tactic to remind customers where they bought from and to show off other product lines – there's no reason why you shouldn't do the same.

Keep Communicating

It's the best way to make customers feel relaxed. Imagine paying for an item (especially if it's expensive) and then hearing nothing for a week. You'd start to get nervous, wouldn't you!? It's best to allay these fears with a few well-timed updates informing your customer that you've received payment and the goods are in the post.

Another nice touch is to send a message to your customer a week after posting them your item. You enquire whether they received it all right and if you could have done anything better, then refresh their memories about the rest of the stuff you have for sale.

Sell Everything for £1

If your cupboards are overflowing with stuff you can't sell, it might be time for a clear out. Stick it on eBay.co.uk at a starting bid of £1 with no reserve and see what happens!

Appendix A

Glossary

· ·

About Me page: The free Web page given to every eBay.co.uk user. An excellent promotional tool.

absentee bid: A bid that an auctioneer places on a lot (or lots) – up to a maximum amount that you designate – in your absence. When you want to participate in a live auction but can't attend it physically, you can pre-arrange to have the saleroom place absentee bids for you.

accounts payable: The amount your business owes to vendors, office supply stores, your credit card charges, and the like. This includes any money your business owes.

accounts receivable: The money people owe you, such as the cheques and money orders you're expecting in the post; the money sitting in your PayPal account that you haven't transferred to your checking account.

chartered certified accountant: Someone who has been educated in accounting and has passed the relevant examinations. Accredited chartered accountants are at the top of the accounting professional heap.

announcements pages: eBay.co.uk pages where you get all the latest eBay information. You need to check these pages periodically. If you follow the Announcements link, which is at the bottom of every eBay page, you end up at the Community announcements page at `http://www2.ebay.com/aw/marketing-uk.shtml?ssPageName=f:f:UK`.

as is/where is: An item that comes with no warranty, implied or otherwise, regarding the merchantability of the product.

bid increment: The amount that a bid must advance, based on the auction's high bid.

bid retraction: A cancelled auction bid. Retractions can occur only under extreme circumstances (such as when you type the wrong numerals).

bid shielding: An illegal process wherein two bidders work together to defraud a seller out of high bids by retracting a bid at the last minute and granting a confederate's low bid the win. Not as much of an issue anymore due to eBay's new bid retraction policy; *see also* bid retraction.

bonding: A surety bond can be issued by a third party (usually an insurance company) to guarantee a seller's performance in a transaction.

card not present: Credit card services use this term to describe transactions that typically happen over the Internet or by mail order. The term means that the seller hasn't seen the actual card.

caveat emptor: Latin for *let the buyer beware*. If you see this phrase posted anywhere, proceed cautiously – you're responsible for the outcome of any transaction in which you take part.

chargeback: When someone calls his or her credit card company and refuses to pay for a transaction. The credit card company will credit the card in question while making you pay back the amount.

consignment: When someone hands over merchandise to you, which you then auction on eBay.co.uk. You make a little commission and the other person sells something without the hassle.

corporation: A separate entity set up to do business.

DBA: Doing business as. These letters appear next to the common name of a business entity, sole trader, partnership, or corporation that conducts business under a fictitious name.

DOA: Dead on arrival. The product you purchased doesn't work from the moment you opened the package.

DUNS number: Data Universal Numbering System number. An identification number issued to businesses from a database maintained by the great and powerful Dun and Bradstreet. These numbers are issued to allow your business to register with more than 50 global, industry, and trade associations, including the United Nations, the US Federal Government, the Australian Government, and the European Commission. You can get your number at no cost by logging on to www.dnb.com/US/duns_update/.

entrepreneur: You! An entrepreneur is someone who takes the financial risk to start a business. Even if you're buying and reselling car boot sale items, you're still an entrepreneur.

FTP: File Transfer Protocol. The protocol used to transfer files from one server to another.

hammer fee: A fee that the auction house charges at a live auction. Read the information pack *before* you bid on an item in a live auction. Hammer fees usually add 10–15 per cent to the amount of your bid.

HTF: Hard to find. An abbreviation that commonly appears in eBay.co.uk auction titles to describe items that are, uh, hard to find.

invoice: A bill that outlines the items in a specific transaction; who the item is sold to, and all costs involved.

ISBN: International Standard Book Number. Just like a car's licence plate number, the ISBN identifies a book by a universal number.

keystone: In the bricks-and-mortar retailing world, 100 per cent mark-up. A product sells for keystone if it sells for twice the wholesale price. Products that you can sell at keystone are very nice to find.

mannequin: A representation of the human form made of wood, fibreglass, or plastic. Essential for modelling clothing for your eBay.co.uk apparel sales.

MIB: Mint in box. Okay, the item inside the box is mint, but the box looks like a car drove over it.

MIMB: Mint in mint box. Not only is the item in mint condition, so is the box it comes in.

mint: An item in perfect condition is described as mint. This is truly a subjective opinion, usually based on individual standards.

MSRP: Manufacturers suggested retail price. The price hardly anybody pays.

NARU: Not a registered user. A user of eBay.co.uk or other online community who has been suspended (for any number of reasons).

OOP: Out of print. When a book or CD is being published, it usually has its own lifetime in the manufacturing process – and is OOP when no longer being made.

provenance: The story behind an item, including who owned it and where it came from. If you have an interesting provenance for one of your items, put it in the auction description because it adds considerable value to the item.

QuickBooks: A top-of-the-heap accounting program that helps you to keep your records straight.

register: Similar to a chequebook account listing, QuickBooks keeps registers that go up and down depending on the amount of flow in an account balance.

ROI: Return on investment. A figure expressed as a percentage that stands for your net profit after taxes and your own equity.

sniping: The act (or fine art) of bidding at the very last possible second of an auction.

sole trader: A business owned by only one person; the profits and losses are recorded on that person's personal tax return.

split transaction: A transaction that you must assign to more than one category. If you pay a credit card bill and a portion of the bill went to purchased merchandise, a portion to petrol for business-related outings, and yet another portion to eBay.co.uk fees, you must post each amount to its own category.

tax deduction: An expenditure on your part that represents a normal and necessary expense for your business. Before you get carried away and assume that *every* penny you spend is a write-off (deduction), check with your accountant to outline exactly what is and what isn't.

TOS: Terms of service. eBay.co.uk has a TOS agreement; check it out at `pages.ebay.co.uk/help/newtoebay/about_user_agreement.html`.

wholesale: Products sold to retailers (you!) at a price above the manufacturer's cost, allowing for a mark-up to retail. We hope you buy most of your merchandise at wholesale. Shops such as Costco sell items in bulk at prices marginally over wholesale.

Appendix B

The Hows and Whys of a Home Network

● ●

*W*hat is a network? A *network* is a way to connect computers so that they can communicate with each other – as if they were one giant computer with different terminals. The best part is that a network enables high-speed Internet connection sharing, as well as the sharing of printers and other peripherals. By setting up a computer network, one computer may run bookkeeping, another can run a graphics server, and others may be used as personal PCs for different users. From each networked computer, programs and files on all other networked computers can be accessed.

Today's technologies allow you to perform this same miracle on the *home network*. You can connect as many computers as you like, and run your business from anywhere in your home – you can even hook up your laptop from the bedroom if you don't feel like getting out of bed.

Now for the *whys* of a home network. A network is a convenient way to run a business. All big companies use a network, and so should you. You can print your postage, for example, on one printer from any computer in your home or office. You can extend your DSL line or Internet cable connection so that you can use it anywhere in your home – as well as in your office.

In a network, you can set certain directories in each computer to be *shared*. That way, other computers on the network can access those directories. You can also password-protect certain files and directories to prevent others – your children or your employees – from accessing them.

We devote the rest of this appendix to a quick and dirty discussion of home networks installed on Windows-based PCs. We give you a lesson on what we know works for most people. At this point, we want to remind you that we're not techno-whizzes (just like we're not lawyers or accountants). For more information about home networking, see *Home Networking For Dummies* by Kathy Ivens (Wiley).

What we know about home networks, we've found out the hard way – from the school of hard knocks. A lot of research went into this appendix as well, so humour us and read on.

Variations of a Home Network

You have a choice of four types of home network: Ethernet, powerline, home phoneline, and wireless. See Table B-1 for a quick rundown of some pros and cons of each.

Table B-1	Types of Network Pros and Cons	
Type	**Pros**	**Cons**
Traditional Ethernet*	Fast, cheap, and easy set-up	Computers and printers must be hardwired; cables run everywhere
Home phoneline	Fast; runs over your home phone lines	Old wiring or not enough phone jacks may be a drawback
Powerline	Fast; your home is already pre-wired with outlets	Electrical interference may degrade the signal
Wireless network**	Pretty fast; wireless (no ugly cords to deal with)	Expensive; may not be reliable because of interference from home electrical devices

*Connects computers with high quality cable over a maximum of 328 feet of cabling.

**Several types of wireless are available. See 'Hooking Up with Wireless' later in this chapter.

The home phoneline network is fading in popularity because people don't have enough phone jacks in their house to make it an easy proposition.

The wireless network is currently the hot ticket and highly touted by the geek gurus. However, the wireless signal may experience interference because the network runs with the same 2.4 GHz technology as some home wireless telephones. We have a wireless network as a secondary network, and it works, sort of. Our primary network is a hybrid, combining Ethernet, home phoneline, and wireless.

With broadband over powerline, you get high-speed Internet directly into your home electrical system. Just plug in your powerline boxes (see the section 'Powerline network', later in this appendix) and you're up and running!

All networks need the following two devices:

 ✔ **Router:** A router allows you to share a single Internet IP address among multiple computers. A router does exactly what its name implies; it routes signals and data to the different computers on your network. If you have one computer, the router can act as a firewall or even a network device leading to a print server (a gizmo that attaches to your router and allows you to print directly to a printer without having another computer on).

 ✔ **Modem:** You need a modem for Internet connection. You get one from your cable or phone company and plug it into an outlet with cable (just like your TV) or into a special phone jack if you have DSL. The modem connects to your router with an Ethernet cable.

If you have broadband, you don't even need to have a main computer turned on to access the connection anywhere in your house. If you keep a printer turned on (and have a print server), you can also connect that to your router and print from your laptop in another room – right through the network.

Before touching your network card or opening your computer to install anything, touch a grounded metal object to free yourself of static electricity. Otherwise, a spark could go from your hand to the delicate components on the network card or another card, thereby rendering the card useless. Better yet, go to an electronics shop and purchase a wrist-grounding strap that has a cord with a gator clip, which you clip to a metal part of the computer before touching anything inside for safety.

Powerline network

An ingenious invention, a *powerline network* uses your existing home power-lines to carry your network and your high-speed Internet connection. You access the network by plugging a powerline adapter from your computer into an electrical outlet on the wall. Powerline networks have been around for a while and are in the second round of technological advances.

Hooking up a powerline network is incredibly easy. Most installations work immediately straight out of the box. Figure B-1 shows you the base set-up. Computers in any other rooms need only a powerline bridge adapter with an Ethernet cable to a network card.

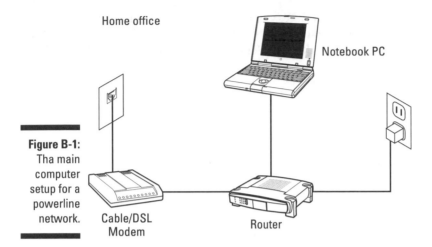

Home office

Notebook PC

Figure B-1:
Tha main
computer
setup for a
powerline
network.

Cable/DSL
Modem

Router

To set up a powerline network, you need the following (in addition to a router and modem):

- **Electrical outlets:** We bet you have more than one in each room of your house.

- **An Ethernet card for each computer:** Many new computers already have an Ethernet card. If your computer doesn't, you can get inexpensive Ethernet cards for around £10.

- **Powerline Ethernet bridge for each computer:** You plug an Ethernet cable from your computer into the powerline Ethernet bridge, and then plug Netgear's Ethernet bridge into a wall outlet.

Hooking up the powerline network goes like this:

1. **The high-speed connection comes in through your DSL or cable line.**

2. **Plug the cable line (or phoneline for DSL) into your modem.**

3. **Connect one 'in' Ethernet cable from your modem to a router.**

4. **Connect one 'out' Ethernet cable from the router to a local computer.**

5. **Connect another 'out' Ethernet cable to the powerline adapter.**

6. **Plug the powerline box into a convenient wall outlet.**

Home phoneline

Wall telephone cabling in the average home contains four wires, and your telephone uses only a portion of two. Plenty more room exists in the cable for your network. Figure B-2 shows you what the typical home phoneline set-up looks like.

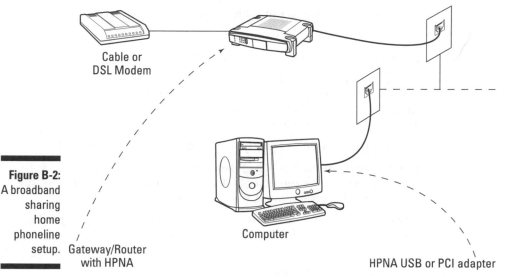

Figure B-2:
A broadband
sharing
home
phoneline
setup.

Cable or
DSL Modem

Gateway/Router
with HPNA

Computer

HPNA USB or PCI adapter

TIP

The phoneline network sends data at a speedy 10MB per second (the same speed as a regular Ethernet network) and can operate with computers or other equipment placed as far as 1,000 feet apart and will work in homes as large as 10,000 square feet. Best of all, you can talk on the same phoneline without causing any interference.

To set up your network to carry files and your high-speed connection throughout your house, you need some extra hardware:

- ✔ **Bridge:** A device that connects your Ethernet (router connection) with your powerline network. You can get a device that combines the router and the bridge.

- ✔ **HPNA network adapter for each computer:** You need an adapter that enables your computer to become one with other computers on the network. These adapters are available also as a USB device, eliminating the need to install a card in your computer.

- ✔ **Phone jacks:** Pretty essential for plugging in the phone wire from the adapter.

To install a home phoneline network, just follow these steps (but follow your manufacturer's instructions if they vary from this information).

If you're installing a USB (universal serial bus) adapter, don't bother trying to open your computer. Just plug in the adapter to an available USB port and proceed to Step 5.

1. **Turn off your computer and disconnect its power cord.**

2. **Open the cover of your computer.**

3. **Install the network card in an available slot.**

   Touch the card only by the metal part on its outside edge. When installing the card, press firmly down on the top of the card with your thumb to properly seat the card in the slot. Fasten the card to the chassis by tightening the screw on the metal edge.

4. **Replace the cover on your PC and reconnect the power cord.**

5. **Connect one end of the (RJ-11) telephone cord that came with your network card to the port labelled *To Wall* on the card, and plug the other end into a convenient wall telephone jack.**

   If you have a telephone that needs to use that wall jack, connect the cord to the port labelled *To Phone*; your phone will work through the network card.

6. **Power up your computer.**

   If you're lucky, your computer will see the new hardware and ask you to install the driver. If you're not lucky, check the instructions (as a last-ditch effort, you can always read the instructions!) for troubleshooting tips.

7. **When asked, insert the CD or the disk that came with the card (containing those tricky drivers) and follow the on-screen instructions.**

   As you go through the instructions, decide on a name for each computer that you want to install on the network.

8. **Set up directories that you want shared on the network.**

   Go to My Computer, select the directories (denoted by folder icons) that you want to share, right-click, and indicate that you want to share these directories with other computers on the network. Do the same with your local printers.

9. **Repeat Steps 1–8 on each computer.**

   As you add a computer, double-check that it can communicate with the other computers that you've already installed on the network by trying to open a shared directory on a remote computer and printing a test page on a remote printer.

10. **If your network is not functioning properly after you complete all recommended steps, call technical support as many times as necessary to get your network up and running.**

When your network connection is flying and working flawlessly, you can add your broadband.

11. **To install the broadband connection, take the Ethernet cable from the modem and connect it to the back of your router. Then connect another Ethernet cable from the router to the phoneline network bridge.**

12. **Connect the phoneline that comes with your bridge from the bridge to a telephone wall jack.**

Hey presto – you should be able to go with your Internet connection on all the computers in your network.

The wall connectors each have an outlet for a telephone cord that you plug into your wall jack. (You can also cheat in one room and connect two computers to one phone jack with a splitter that makes two jacks out of one.)

Hooking up with wireless

Wireless networking – also known as WiFi or, to the more technically inclined, IEEE 802.11 – is the hot new technology for all kinds of networks. Wireless networking is an impressive system when it works, with no cables or connectors to bog you down.

If you're concerned about your next-door neighbour hacking into your computer through your wireless connection – stop worrying. Wireless networks are protected by their own brand of security, called WEP (or Wired Equivalent Privacy). WEP encrypts your wireless transmissions and prevent others from getting into your network. Although super-hackers have cracked it, WEP is still the best possible system at present.

To link your laptop or desktop to a wireless network with WEP encryption, you enter a key code from the wireless access point. Just enter the code into your wireless card software on every computer that uses the network, and you should be able to link up.

You may get confused when you see the different types of wireless available. The following list provides the low-down on the variations:

✔ **802.11a:** This wireless format works really well – fast with good connectivity. Unfortunately, this format is also very expensive. 802.11a is used when you have to connect a large group, such as at a convention centre or in a dormitory. The format delivers data at speeds as high as 54 Mbps (megabits per second). It runs at the 5 GHz band (hence its nickname WiFi5), so it doesn't have any competition for bandwidth with wireless phones or microwave ovens.

✔ **802.11b:** This wireless type is the most common, and is used on the most platforms. It travels over the 2.4 GHz band. The 802.11b version is slower than the 802.11a version, transferring data at only 11 Mbps. However, the 802.11b is a solid, low-cost solution when you have no more than 32 users per access point.

The lower frequency of 2.4 GHz drains less power from laptops and other portable devices, so laptop batteries will last longer. Also, 2.4 GHz signals travel farther and can work through walls and floors more effectively than 5 GHz signals.

✔ **802.11g:** This format is the newest type based on the 2.4 GHz band. The 802.11g speeds data up to a possible 54 Mbps, and is backward compatible with 802.11b service.

Installing your wireless network isn't a gut-wrenching experience either (although it can be if the signal doesn't reach where you want it). You hook up your computer (a laptop works best) to the wireless access point (the gizmo with the antenna that broadcasts your signal throughout your home or office) to perform some set-up tasks such as choosing your channel and setting up your WEP code. (The wireless access point comes with its own instructions.)

After you complete the set-up and turn on your wireless access point, you have a WiFi hotspot in your home or office. Typically, a hotspot provides coverage for about 100 feet in all directions, although walls and floors cut down on the range.

Here are some simplified steps on configuring your network:

1. **Run a cable from your cable connection or a phone cord from your DSL line to your modem.**

2. **Connect one Ethernet cable from your modem to your router.**

3. **Connect one Ethernet cable to your wireless access point.**

Take a look at this network diagram from Netgear in Figure B-3.

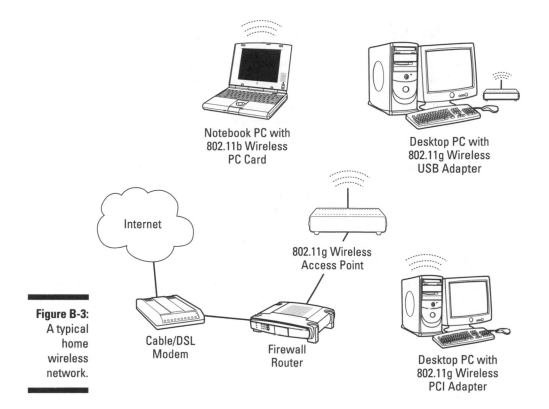

Figure B-3:
A typical
home
wireless
network.

Internet Security and Your Home Network

A dial-up connection exposes your computer to the Internet only when you dial up and get connected. Most broadband Internet connections are always on, which means your computer is always exposed. Shield your computer with a strong firewall and an antivirus program.

Firewall software

When you're connected to the Internet, you're exposed not only to hackers but also to threats such as *Trojan horses*, programs that can get into your computer when you innocently view an infected Web site. Once inside your computer, the Trojan horse, like ET, phones home. From there, an evil-deed-doer, now with a direct line to your computer, may be able to wreak havoc with your precious data.

If you're technically inclined – and even if you're not – visit the Web site for Gibson Research Corporation (www.grc.com). Gibson Research is the brain-child of an early PC pioneer, Steve Gibson, who's renowned as a genius in the world of codes and programming. Steve is *the* expert when it comes to expos-ing the vulnerabilities of systems over the Internet. A few free diagnostic programs on this site will check your computer's vulnerability to Internet threats.

Shields Up and LeakTest are programs that test your computer and terrify you with results that expose the vulnerability of your Internet connection. We learned about ZoneAlarm on Steve's site. This free program has won every major award in the industry as the most secure software firewall. If your main concern is safety, visit www.zonelabs.com for a free download of ZoneAlarm.

Antivirus software

Even if you have a firewall, you still need antivirus software to protect you from the idiots who think sending destructive code through e-mail is fun. The leading programs in this area are Norton AntiVirus and McAfee. One of the problems inherent in buying software is that you may be urged to load much more than you need onto your computer. If all you need is an antivirus soft-ware, purchase only an antivirus software. But don't delay. Buy the software now and update the antivirus files each week so that you're fully protected from the latest viruses.

Index

• *F* •

Notes

FOR DUMMIES®

Do Anything. Just Add Dummies

HOME

UK editions

0-7645-7027-7

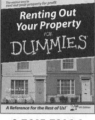

0-7645-7016-1

0-7645-7054-4

PERSONAL FINANCE

0-7645-7023-4

0-470-02860-2

0-7645-7039-0

BUSINESS

0-7645-7018-8

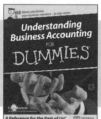

0-7645-7025-0

0-7645-7026-9

Other UK editions now available:

Answering Tough Interview Questions For Dummies
(0-470-01903-4)

Arthritis For Dummies
(0-470-02582-4)

Being The Best Man For Dummies
(0-470-02657-X)

British History For Dummies
(0-7645-7021-8)

Building Confidence For Dummies
(0-4700-1669-8)

Buying a Home On A Budget For Dummies
(0-7645-7035-8)

Cognitive Behavioural Therapy For Dummies
(0-470-01838-0)

Cleaning and Stain Removal For Dummies
(0-7645-7029-3)

CVs For Dummies
(0-7645-7017-X)

Detox For Dummies
(0-470-01908-5)

Diabetes For Dummies
(0-7645-7019-6)

Divorce For Dummies
(0-7645-7030-7)

eBay.co.uk For Dummies
(0-7645-7059-5)

European History For Dummies
(0-7645-7060-9)

Gardening For Dummies
(0-470-01843-7)

Genealogy Online For Dummies
(0-7645-7061-7)

Golf For Dummies
(0-470-01811-9)

Irish History For Dummies
(0-7645-7040-4)

Kakuro For Dummies
(0-470-02822-X)

Marketing For Dummies
(0-7645-7056-0)

Neuro-Linguistic Programming For Dummies
(0-7645-7028-5)

Nutrition For Dummies
(0-7645-7058-7)

Pregnancy For Dummies
(0-7645-7042-0)

Retiring Wealthy For Dummies
(0-470-02632-4)

Rugby Union For Dummies
(0-7645-7020-X)

Small Business Employment Law For Dummies
(0-7645-7052-8)

Su Doku For Dummies
(0-4700-189-25)

Sudoku 2 For Dummies
(0-4700-2651-0)

Sudoku 3 For Dummies
(0-4700-2667-7)

The GL Diet For Dummies
(0-470-02753-3)

Wills, Probate and Inheritance Tax For Dummies
(0-7645-7055-2)

FOR DUMMIES®

A world of resources to help you grow

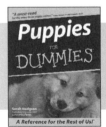

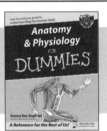

FOR DUMMIES®

The easy way to get more done and have more fun

LANGUAGES

0-7645-5194-9

0-7645-5193-0

0-7645-5196-5

Also available:

Chinese For Dummies
(0-471-78897-X)

Chinese Phrases
For Dummies
(0-7645-8477-4)

French Phrases For Dummies
(0-7645-7202-4)

German For Dummies
(0-7645-5195-7)

Italian Phrases For Dummies
(0-7645-7203-2)

Japanese For Dummies
(0-7645-5429-8)

Latin For Dummies
(0-7645-5431-X)

Spanish Phrases
For Dummies
(0-7645-7204-0)

Spanish Verbs For Dummies
(0-471-76872-3)

Hebrew For Dummies
(0-7645-5489-1)

MUSIC AND FILM

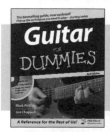

0-7645-9904-6

0-7645-2476-3

0-7645-5105-1

Also available:

Bass Guitar For Dummies
(0-7645-2487-9)

Blues For Dummies
(0-7645-5080-2)

Classical Music For Dummies
(0-7645-5009-8)

Drums For Dummies
(0-7645-5357-7)

Jazz For Dummies
(0-471-76844-8)

Opera For Dummies
(0-7645-5010-1)

Rock Guitar For Dummies
(0-7645-5356-9)

Screenwriting For Dummies
(0-7645-5486-7)

Songwriting For Dummies
(0-7645-5404-2)

Singing For Dummies
(0-7645-2475-5)

HEALTH, SPORTS & FITNESS

0-7645-7851-0

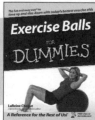

0-7645-5623-4

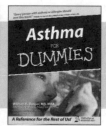

0-7645-4233-8

Also available:

Controlling Cholesterol
For Dummies
(0-7645-5440-9)

Dieting For Dummies
(0-7645-4149-8)

High Blood Pressure
For Dummies
(0-7645-5424-7)

Martial Arts For Dummies
(0-7645-5358-5)

Menopause For Dummies
(0-7645-5458-1)

Power Yoga For Dummies
(0-7645-5342-9)

Weight Training
For Dummies
(0-471-76845-6)

Yoga For Dummies
(0-7645-5117-5)

FOR DUMMIES®

Helping you expand your horizons and achieve your potential

INTERNET

0-7645-8996-2

0-7645-8334-4

0-7645-7327-6

Also available:

eBay.co.uk
For Dummies
(0-7645-7059-5)
Dreamweaver 8
For Dummies
(0-7645-9649-7)
Web Design
For Dummies
(0-471-78117-7)

Everyday Internet
All-in-One Desk Reference
For Dummies
(0-7645-8875-3)
Creating Web Pages
All-in-One Desk Reference
For Dummies
(0-7645-4345-8)

DIGITAL MEDIA

0-7645-9802-3

0-471-74739-4

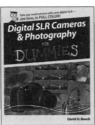

0-7645-9803-1

Also available:

Digital Photos, Movies, &
Music GigaBook
For Dummies
(0-7645-7414-0)
Photoshop CS2
For Dummies
(0-7645-9571-7)
Podcasting
For Dummies
(0-471-74898-6)

Blogging
For Dummies
(0-471-77084-1)
Digital Photography all in
one desk reference
For Dummies
(0-7645-7328-4)
Windows XP Digital Music
For Dummies
(0-7645-7599-6)

COMPUTER BASICS

0-7645-8958-X

0-7645-7555-4

0-7645-7326-8

Also available:

Office XP 9 in 1
Desk Reference
For Dummies
(0-7645-0819-9)
PCs All-in-One Desk
Reference For Dummies
(0-471-77082-5)
Pocket PC For Dummies
(0-7645-1640-X)

Upgrading & Fixing PCs
For Dummies
(0-7645-1665-5)
Windows XP All-in-One Desk
Reference For Dummies
(0-7645-7463-9)
Macs For Dummies
(0-7645-5656-8)

8323_p4